*W*elcome to the 5th dimension. *Y*ou have arrived and are now learning to function in a new reality. *T*his information will help you acclimate to the higher vibrations of the *N*ew *P*lanet *E*arth where your real work is just beginning. *T*he *G*ame you have been playing is complete. *Y*ou have graduated and are now creating *H*ome on your side of the veil. *W*elcome to the *N*ew *P*lanet *E*arth.

*W*elcome *H*ome

*t*he *G*roup

Life on the New Planet Earth is ever changing. Therefore, this book comes with a lifetime upgrade on personal inscriptions. Present this book to Steve or Barbara Rother in person at any time for an update.

Welcome Home

Life on the New Planet Earth

Cover Photo: 'Lanai Sunset in Maui' By Pete Rosendale
847 426 7373 Finelight2002@aol.com

Illustrations by Phyllis Brooks   www.tailiquay.com

Welcome Home

Life on the New Planet Earth

Published by: **Lightworker**

P.O. Box 1496
Poway Ca. 92074-1496 USA
www.Lightworker.com
Publisher@Lightworker.com

Lightworker Books and Tapes can be purchased in retail stores or by telephone. Toll free in the US and Canada at (877) 248 5837
Outside the US and Canada please call 001 858 748 5837

Welcome Home ~ Life on the New Planet Earth
by Steve Rother and the Group
Edited by Sandra Sedgbeer
Copyright © 2002 – Steve Rother
Printed in Canada
First Edition:
First Printing August -2002
Second Printing Dec -2002

ISBN 1928806-09-0 $14.95 us

Dedication

This book is dedicated to the Translation Teams of the Lightworker organization. Through the grace of these wonderful volunteers we are currently presenting information from the Group in 13 languages at the Lightworker web site. Thanks for your help in spreading the Light!

A special thanks to the man who stepped into his passion to help us all spread the Light:

Translation Team Co-Ordinator
Jean Paul 'JP' Dery

The Translation Team at Lightworker

Assistant Team Co-Ordinator   **Uma**

* indicates a Team Leader
+ *Book* indicates that they also help in the translations of the books.

Chun-Ming Chio *	Chinese	Finnbogi Runna Andersen	Icelandic
Conny Lindstrom Andersen *	Danish	Gudmundur Skarphedinsson *	Icelandic
Lykke Rasmussen	Danish	Paula Launonen *	Italian
Grethe Bie Jensen	Danish	Vigdis Nøst *	Norwegian
Inge Kok	Dutch	Flavia Lages	Portuguese
Aart Wouters	Dutch	Gustavo Amorim *	Portuguese
Fokje Ritsma	Dutch	Junia Maria Lopes-Debevc	Portuguese
Ingrid Kramer	Dutch	Maria Godinho	Portuguese
Jessica Francke	Dutch	Maria Lucia Garcia	Portuguese
Liane, Julia De Clerck	Dutch	Simone Maldonado	Portuguese
Maria Pieters	Dutch	Suzana Magalhaes	Portuguese
Monique van Gremberghe	Dutch	Adriana Miniño	Spanish
Nel Scherder +Book	Dutch	Cecilia Sosa Penalba	Spanish
P.C.M. van Nieuwkuyk	Dutch	Doris Millares	Spanish
Pieter J. Hendriksen *	Dutch	Enita Zirnis *	Spanish
Abdelkader Bouderousa	French	Graciela Castex	Spanish
M 'Jaart' Jacquart *	French	Jaime Calderón Vargas	Spanish
Karima Landin Høstbæk	French	Larys Cartaya	Spanish
Thérèse Royer +Book	French	Maria Cristina Ariza	Spanish
Ursule Mayor	French	Maria Valentini	Spanish
Ellen Heidbohmer	German	Miguel Molina	Spanish
Elvira Uschold	German	Virginia Irene Loyola	Spanish
Eva Reinermann +Book	German	Jeanette Ettberger	Swedish
Ines Kallab	German	Sevinc Sultan Yazla	Turkish
Josef Resperger +Book	German	Esen Dincer	Turkish
Norbert Richter * +Book	German	Ferhat Sertac Dogan	Turkish
Wolfgang Eckert +Book	German	Murat Oz *	Turkish
Eleni Loginidou *	Greek	Nagihan Likmur	Turkish
Dan Shakhar	Hebrew	Selin Demircl	Turkish
Klodette Shefer *	Hebrew	Yeliz Abupoolu	Turkish
Tamar Lifshitz	Hebrew		
Smadar Bergman +Book	Hebrew		
Lena Hefetz	Hebrew		

Also see the Dutch Version of Lightworker.com
www.Lichtwerker.com
produced by Ingrid Kramer and Janosh Stoffers

Acknowledgments

This book is truly a 'group' effort. Barbara and I wish to give special thanks for those who make it possible to spread this Light.

Steve Hansen	Gemma Sedgbeer
Phyllis Brooks	Mike Iaquinta
Peter Hyman	James Tipton
Rebecca Hannah	Nancy Mott
Ingrid Kramer	Janosh Stoffers
Shala Mata	Rob Saunders
Ruth Poscai	Ron McCray
Lourdes Resperger	Josef Resperger
Phyllis Tyler	Kathy Wilson
Nel Scherder	Ernst Scherder
Chris Reimer	Carol Holaday
Evan Thomas	Michael Ananda
David Solinger	Lorena Solinger
Nomi Boodanox	Twyla Astbury
Claire Gibb	Isha Lerner
Karl & Julie Zielke	Nancy Vanderwal
Marcia Schanzmeyer	Ilan Wainer
Len & Mary Ellen Delekta	Donna May
Marie DeMaria	Karl & Julie Zeilke
Peg Hampton	Eve Meng

Thanks to a special lady who helps us give the work a touch of class. **Sandie Sedgbeer**

Table of Contents

4. Ana and the Bird _____ 71
The new relationship to our guides

5. Dawn of the New Light_____ 83
Seven Seconds to the New Light

6. Reaching for Higher Truth_____ 95
Higher Truths to Support Higher Vibrations

7. ~Triology~ _____ 105
The Others of E- vibration

8. The Government of Mu _____ 123
New Paradigms of Business and Government

9. Responsibility, the Balance of Power _____ 133
Enhancing Personal Power

10. The Five Traditions of Abundance _____ 141
Stepping into the New Energy

Section III QUESTIONS TO THE GROUP _____155

11. Q & A ON THE FOLLOWING SUBJECTS

SECTION IV WHERE DO WE GO FROM HERE? __295

12. New Realities _____297
A glimpse of Home in a special live presentation.

Introduction

The Chinese have a saying:

"May you live in interesting times."

There is no doubt in my mind that we have achieved that with room to spare. The events now unfolding on Planet Earth are unprecedented. To us it may seem like nothing is moving; that we are stuck in our own lives and progress. In reality things are happening in the blink of an eye. In this reality we walk down a hallway of linear time. The interesting part is that we think we are moving forward but in fact we are walking backward down this hallway. From this position we can only see our past, a little of our present and nothing at all of our future. You have changed more in the last five years than you have in the past five lifetimes. The Group says that I have cashed in all my Karma chips to be here at this precise moment in time. They say there is a reason I wanted to be here now and that my planning was perfect because here I am. The world as we know it is changing. Whether we like it or not we humans are evolving and, like you, I am right in the center of the action. Yes, we certainly do live in interesting times.

About the Group

The Group's message and our work is about human empowerment. It's not always an easy message for us to understand because they are not sensational nor will they tell us which way to turn or what we "should" do. They say we have a tendency to give away our power. This is why they rarely talk about themselves, who they are or where they come from. They want us to know that this is not about them. . .

it's about us.

The most the Group has ever revealed about their own origins is contained in the Beacons of Light message entitled "The Family of Michael," which is available on the Lightworker web site. Their sole intention is to re-mind you what you came here to do and to help you to do it.

In this Book

The work of the Group is available on the web site: www.Lightworker.com. The monthly messages referred to are the Beacons of Light ~ Re-minders from Home. With the exception of Ana and the Bird and The Two Misdirections of Atlantis, this book contains entirely new material that has not been published elsewhere. Some of the chapters in this book are from live channels presented during our seminars. Others have been channeled expressly for this book.

This book is divided into four sections:

1. Current Events.   Where we are, how we got here and where we are heading.

2. The New Planet Earth.   Describes the new attributes of living in the 5th dimension on the New Planet Earth.

3. Questions to the Group.   Questions to and Answers from the Group on a wide range of topics taken from live channels.

4. Where do we go from Here?   Points to re-member when creating a New Reality

The Group's purpose is to prepare us for what lies ahead. In book one, Re-member , they provided us with the foundation. This book takes us to the next stage of our evolution and opens the doorway to discovering our full powers of creation.

At each of our seminars we include a live question and answer session with the Group. For many people these are the highlights of our seminars. Since many of the questions raised at these sessions relate to what is happening in the world at this very moment we have included a selection of the most enlightening and relevant Q & A's here.

According to the Group, the events taking place right now have greater implications than we suspect. As startling and unexpected as some of these have been, they merely mark the beginning. The evolution of mankind has begun. The ball is rolling forward and now there is no turning back. . . are you ready?

Double Decker Bus

The Group has talked often about the great changes that we are now experiencing, and they have given us many insights into what lies ahead. However, they always make it very clear that they do not foretell the future. . . since we have yet to write it. They use the analogy of a double decker bus to explain their perspective. We are all drivers of our own bus. Imagine the Group as passengers on the upper deck who have an unobstructed view of the road ahead. They can help us by alerting us to potential hazards and unexpected twists and turns but they cannot predict how we will react or the directions we will take.

Nothing is predestined. Everything is a possibility

They say there is only one "rule" that we have placed on the Gameboard. . . and that is the rule of Free Choice.

It is therefore important to the Group that you understand that whatever they say here should not be taken as a hard and fast prediction. It is simply the view as it exists from the top of the bus. You always have the power to change your life.

Phyllis Brooks

Section I

Current Events

Altering Cosmic Events to a Higher Outcome

Chapter I

Welcome to the

New Planet Earth

Stepping into the 5th dimension.

Cosmic Events

Do you re-member the doom and gloom prophecies around the year 2000? Have you noticed that we are all still here? The Group says that these prophecies were real at the time they were made. Through our advances as a collective of humanity we altered the outcome. There are other events that were set into motion that shall continue to unfold. The only difference is, their outcome will not be as originally planned.

As we crossed into the new millennium, the Group said the year 2000 would be the year of crystal intent. Whatever we did, thought or intended at that time would set the energy for the next twelve years to come. In turn, those twelve years would set the energy for the next millennium. Now we find ourselves in the years of action.

On April 2nd 2001 a burst of raw "Light energy" was emitted from our Sun as a solar flare. NASA classified this as an X20 – the largest in recorded history. On April 15th another solar flare measuring X16 occurred. Had either of these bursts of energy been pointed directly toward our Earth they would most likely have knocked out many of the power grids and much of our electrical infrastructure. As it was, they still caused worldwide disruption in communications. At the same time, a lot of unexplained "gremlins" disrupted computer and internet services.

In an earlier channel the Group mentioned that the Sun's polarity had been reversed, setting up the conditions for the vortexes on the Sun to erupt as solar flares. Now, here is the interesting part: This reversal of the Sun's polarity was the trigger that was originally intended to set into motion the reversal of the Earth's magnetic poles. According to the Group, this reversal has already happened five times in the Earth's history. The polar shift that was originally scheduled to happen within the next few years was to be the sixth and FINAL reversal.

In short this was meant to be the beginning of the end. Instead, they set into motion a different series of events that are just now unfolding. The energy filtering on to the Earth as a direct result of these solar events, is the Crystal Energy of the New Earth

The Group says that the sun is due to reverse its polarity once again in the year 2012. The recent solar flares signal the beginning of an eleven-year period that will be like none that has gone before. The choices we make during this eleven-year period will determine the final outcome of the New Game. They advise us to choose our thoughts even more wisely now as our powers of creation are greatly enhanced. Even as you are reading this book the everyday decisions you are making are contributing to the creation of the New Planet Earth. This is the call to Light. This is the true work of Lightworkers in all walks of life. This is the moment when your Light can make the biggest difference.

With recent terrorists events we find ourselves right in the middle of a grand cosmic event. According to the Group we are now standing at the crossroads. The prophecies of Armageddon are indeed being played out but we do have a choice as to how we will experience them. We have already changed the script to the extent that we have softened the impact of the anticipated apocalypse. The Group says to watch the 'Red Dragon' (China). If the 'Red Dragon' lies dormant, this will signify that humanity has moved past the marker that could have triggered the last great war. If the 'Red Dragon' becomes involved, what was predicted as Armageddon could become a reality. What the Group wants us to understand is that we are the creators, the architects of our reality. It is entirely up to us where we go from here.

The Crystal Energy of the New Earth is a blending and balancing of the male/female energies that will take us to our next level of existence. The people that will resist this new balanced energy the most will be those the Group refers to as the

'Old Guard' (male dominated and often extremist groups such as the Taliban).

On August 25th 2001 there was another solar flare that tipped the scales on our planet. Although it was only an X5 the vortex of energy was angled more directly toward the Earth. This had the effect of drastically raising the new energy. To most of us this energy felt wonderful. However, this threatened the 'Old Guard' so much that it sparked a reaction a few days later on September 11th.

And that's not all. In addition to affecting our electrical systems, the Crystal Energy entering through the solar flares can drastically affect our emotional systems. Most Lightworkers are "energy empaths." This makes them overly sensitive to energy fields around them. To these sensitive people the new energy is not infiltrating but rather bombarding us. All of this makes for a very confusing time for Lightworkers on our Planet.

Even though most people do not understand the implications of the cosmic script that is now being enacted, many intuitively know that something momentous is going on. The planet is no longer going to tip on its side as we have already re-written that script. At the same time, however, we are seeing many other cosmic events unfolding. This is the reason for the sense of cautious expectation that so many people are now beginning to feel. Exciting? A bit scary? You bet! Welcome to the New Energy. Our powers are now greatly enhanced. Funny thing about increased power, it also comes with increased responsibility. . . as many world leaders are now beginning to discover.

As in all things we have choice. We now have choice about how this new energy and this new power will affect us. Choose wisely your point of perception and the camera angle from which you view these events. Time and again the Group has said that many of us cashed in all of our "Karma Chips" to be here at this pivotal time. Some of you even rushed back without resting between incarnations just to take your place in the front row. Expect the best and hold hands with those around you. Together we will create a miracle!

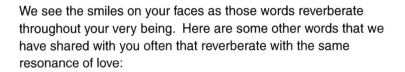

Greetings from Home

We see the smiles on your faces as those words reverberate throughout your very being. Here are some other words that we have shared with you often that reverberate with the same resonance of love:

Welcome Home

Welcome to the 5th dimension. You have arrived here to accomplish the intentional creation of Home on your side of the veil. Your world and your Game are changing. You are now beginning to hold your powers of creation once again. This time you are intent on carrying that power while still remaining firmly within your Bubbles of Biology.

The 5th dimension holds possibilities of which you are not yet aware. The purpose of this book is to make you aware of them. We tell you that you have arrived in a new world. A primary attribute of this dimension is that the time lag of creation is drastically shortened. Here, when you have a thought, it will manifest much faster. Most people who are now stepping into the 5th dimension are unaware that they have arrived. Since their thoughts and expectations are still of a 3rd dimensional reality, what they see is a 3rd dimensional representation, which is actually a reduced version of the magnificent creation that exists here. In other words, you are walking around in the indescribable beauty of the 5th dimension, yet, because you are viewing it through the same old 3rd dimensional glasses you do not see what is really in front of you.

It will take time for most of you to understand that things are different here. Those of you who acclimate first to the higher potentials will help the others along. That is why you came here. The 5th dimension is a resting place for the new humanity and the location where you have already begun your creation of the New Planet Earth.

Please understand that here in the 5th dimension things are different. One of the first things we ask you to begin releasing, **even as you read this book,** is the concept of right and wrong. It is time for the concept of cause and effect to take its rightful place. Understand, however, that it is not yet time for all of the attributes of the 3rd dimension to be replaced. We will speak more of this later. For now, we merely ask that you refrain from judging all 3rd dimensional attributes as bad, since 'judgment' is itself a 3-D attribute. Allow yourselves room to grow, knowing that this transition will take time, that as you acclimate you will incorporate more of these higher truths into your being.

We are so very proud of you for your accomplishments. The work you have done could have been accomplished in no other manner. You look to us and see that our vibration is of a much higher frequency than your own. You look to us for guidance and wisdom. We tell you that it is we who are deeply honored to be in the presence of the masters of the Gameboard.

The Old Game ~ The New Energy

The Game as you originally devised it was to see if you could claim and hold your true power while still on the Gameboard. To that end you agreed to wear the veils that have kept you from seeing who you are. You do not even re-member that you are heirs to the throne of forever. In fact, you are the sparks of God that are changing all that is.

Until recently, dreamtime was your primary access to your memories of Home. Now that your vibration is rising and the veil is thinning you are re-membering Home in your waking state.

This is why many of you have been experiencing a greater longing for Home. Some of you are experiencing these memories of Home as vivid dreams. Others are experiencing them as a profound sadness and yearning, like that of a child who has been sent far away from Home. At the same time, you are feeling anxious and restless, as if you know there is something important that you need to be doing but you cannot re-member what it is. However you experience these memories, be advised that the energy is rising and the Game is changing. Can you feel the anticipation in the air? Have no doubt; this is the most exciting time in the history of the Universe.

Even as we speak, you are creating the New Planet Earth.

History from a Higher Perspective

Since this is such a pivotal moment in your history, we shall take this moment to recap the events that have led to the creation of the New Planet Earth.

As we have already spoken, the Game began in this fashion: Think of what you call God as a circle of moving energy. In this form the God energy can see everything with the exception of one thing: It cannot see itself. In order to view itself it needed to take finite form – i.e., create a beginning and an end. This was accomplished by twisting the circle in on itself, crossing over to form a figure eight. Interestingly, this is what you have called the infinity sign. As the energy continues to flow in this new configuration it has to cross itself. Much like a grinding wheel, the friction created at this magical point causes sparks to fly off in different directions. Because those brightly lit sparks have a limited life they are the finite expression of the infinite energy.

Those sparks are your souls.

As sparks you have created many Games. In some of those Games you retained some recollection of your source and your original power. When you created the Game you are now playing, you wanted to make it more challenging. For the first time ever you decided to play under the veil of *complete* forgetfulness. This kept you from seeing who you are and allowed the results of the experiment to remain untainted. As if that were not enough, you complicated things even further by insisting that in all matters you would always retain free choice. In fact you were to be the *only* planet of free choice.

Up to this point the Game, as you designed it, has effectively kept you from seeing the full extent of your own power. And you wonder why you are so confused? Of course you have felt trapped and restricted – that is exactly how you intended it to be. As the finite expression of the infinite creator it was important that you experience the restraints of finite space. Now that, too, is beginning to change.

The Lesson: To Carry the Power of God

Re-member, the entire purpose of the Game is to be able to study the nature of God. When you took finite form you gave yourself a beginning and an end and left the circle of God. The circle of God is the first dimension. As you passed through the second dimension you gained the properties of polarity. Then you entered the 3rd dimension where you have been playing the Game for quite some time.

Being finite in nature it was necessary to specify an end point to the Game. You even scripted many possible endings. You humans are so imaginative!

For the longest time it appeared that you had set your goals entirely out of reach. Since you disallowed predetermination you left the field wide open for *any* event to proceed. And that is exactly what happened. Certain events that occurred at the beginning took the Game much further into darkness than you had originally intended. As a result of these unforeseen events the veils became even thicker, causing you to fall into the dream from which you are only now beginning to awaken.

The Cosmic Joke

From our perspective in this first dimension of Unity, it was fascinating to watch as you walked around unable even to see the power that you carry. Imagine the frustration we experienced as we watched you creating everything in your reality, unaware that *you* were the ones responsible for everything that was happening around you. The interesting part was watching you in your self-created field of polarity, creating belief systems to support your illusions of polarity.

Your perception was that everything was finite. You therefore created paradigms and beliefs that you needed to explain and justify your own perceptions. A good example is your belief in lack. Lack cannot exist in infinity, which is why it does not exist on this side of the veil. What you have yet to recognize is that lack is just a reflection of your belief that your soul is as finite as your body. Lack is just a reflection of your belief in restriction, which stems from being constrained in finite form. Therefore it is natural for you to believe that there is a restriction on abundance. This restriction is of your own creation; it is all in your own mind. We have a lot more to share with you on this subject, as you will discover when we reveal the Five Traditions of Abundance.

For now, we will tell you something quite astonishing; the cosmic joke is that you are not just a spark of God, you are God. This means that you have exactly the same powers of creation. Watching you wander around thinking that you have no control when in reality you create everything brings us great humor. Knowing this, you can see how we are so amused when you ask questions like "Why do bad things happen to good people?" Even more humorous is when you ask "Why do good things happen to bad people?" You humans are such fun to watch! You take your Game so seriously.

The Earth Connection

You will recall that we have spoken previously of your connection to the Earth. You will re-member that we said that at the beginning of the Game you did not inhabit dense physical bodies, but rather, you occupied bodies of pure light. At that time the Earth was vibrating at a much higher rate, and consequently its temperature was extremely high. As the Earth cooled and gained density your relationship to Her began to weaken. It was as if the two of you were evolving at different rates and thus were pulling apart.

This was the point at which you decided to take on a denser form yourself. You accomplished this by ingesting elements of the Earth such as leaves and sprouts. As your Lightbody began to adjust you then started consuming nuts and fruits. It was not long before you were eating very dense foods, not only from the plant level but also from the animal level of vibration. Today you still 'ground' yourselves in this same manner. This explains why the Keeper is so fond of chocolate. This was the beginning of what you know today as biology, which is your spirit inhabiting a combination of plant and animal life. At the time you thought this evolution from Lightbody to dense body was taking forever. From the larger perspective it took place in the blink of an eye.

Does this sound familiar? Can you see the parallel? The events that we have just described are a mirror image of what you are experiencing now. In other words, the events are now in reverse.

Earth Makes a Decision to Ascend

As you devised the Game, the period that you call the industrial revolution was set to mark the beginning of the end of the Game. However, at the very last moments in the Game you began to stir and awaken. As you are now beginning to discover with your own sciences, the Earth is a living, sentient being. We are now going to show you how strong the connections are between you and the Earth.

You are aware that your bodies have several levels of which your physical body is the densest. In the same way the Earth has several levels, which we call overtone levels. Just a few of these overtone levels are the mineral kingdom, the plant kingdom, the animal kingdom, and – are you ready for this? - human beings. There are many other overtone levels of which you are not even aware. But that will change very soon.

About 60 years ago you began to awaken from the dream. At this point the Earth Herself made a decision to begin moving to a higher vibrational level. To accomplish this She needed to raise her temperature. Without any conscious forethought, you did your part in assisting Her in this process. This has led to what you know today as Global Warming. You see this as harmful and devastating to your environment. But we tell you this was in perfect order as without it the Earth would not have been able to move forward. This is just one illustration that demonstrates why your relationship to the Earth is inseparable. Please understand that it is therefore vital to your own continued existence that you learn to create together with the Earth.

You have already moved to a higher vibrational level. What went before was perfect but you must now discontinue your actions of lower vibrational living and focus your creative abilities on working together with the Earth.

The Earth is now raising Her temperature again and as she does your relationship to Her will once more need adjustment in order to keep your full energy connection. This adjustment has already begun. Your human biology is now changing, and the hidden strands of DNA are reconnecting. Changes are taking place within your own physical and ethereal bodies. Your own range of perception is widening and, yes, the veil that you designed so well is thinning. You are drawing closer to Home every moment.

The Aspen Grove

Even your true energy connection has been kept from you in order to facilitate the game and though they are thinning, the veils you wear are still firmly in place. Your connection and your true power have been with you since the beginning. You are now seeing small glimpses of Light through these veils. To keep your energetic connection to the Earth and all things as you shift dimensional levels, we offer you this simple explanation. It is a favorite of the Keeper.

There is a grove of Aspen trees in Utah. It has been noted as the largest living organism on the Earth. Below the ground where you cannot see, all of the roots have grown together as one. Those trees are not separate from one another but in fact are one. When a bug bites a leaf from one tree it is felt in all of the trees. All of the trees send energy as a collective to fend off dis-ease and because of this connection the aspen grove is immortal.

Those trees are like you. The veil that you have designed so effectively keeps you from seeing your connection to each other and to the Earth. Act and think in unity consciousness and you will change your reality in the blink of an eye. This is how you will create the New Planet Earth.

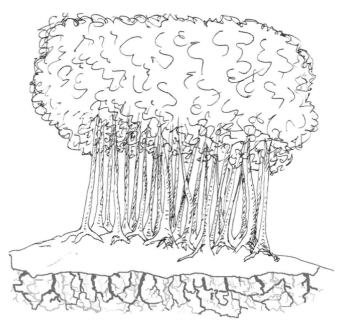

The Aspen Grove - Phyllis Brooks

The Changing Work Paradigm

From the moment humans took a denser form your primary motivation has been survival. In the lower vibrations of the old energy this was as it should be. At the same time this has caused misdirections of energy in many areas, for it did not allow you to see yourself in any way. In the time of your fathers and forefathers the paradigm of work helped to ensure your survival. The essence of that old energy can be summed up in two words:

Work Hard.

In the lower vibrations from which you are now evolving this was an effective truth. But now at last you are reaching for a higher truth. From the brutal middle ages to the great depression to the world wars, you have learned one thing. The heir to the throne of forever cannot die. No longer are you being motivated by survival. Now your need for a higher truth and Unity consciousness is becoming more important than mere physical sustenance. Can you see why we are so very proud of you? You are taking your power and stepping into higher vibrations by choice!

As you evolve into higher vibrational levels you require higher truths to support the new energy. We will speak more of this later as it is important. For now, we want you to know that one of these higher truths is that there is a new work paradigm.

In the higher vibrations of the New Planet Earth your success will be directly proportional to the amount of joy and passion you experience on a daily basis. The essence of the new energy can also be defined by two words:

Work Passionate

A Vortex forms on the Sun

In early 2001 the Sun at the center of your solar system reversed its polarity. This was originally designed to bring the final stage of destruction to the old Earth. Now you have extended the Game. You are awakening at an astounding rate and taking your power. While they will now have a new outcome, some of the events scripted at the beginning will continue to unfold.

The reversal of the magnetic poles on the Sun sparked a series of events that were to have catastrophic effects on the Gameboard of free choice. After years of extreme climatic changes the Earth would have shifted its own polar fields and tilted its rotational axis. This would have been the sixth - *and final* - time the Earth has shifted in this manner.

The direction has now changed and as further events unfold the energies that were intended to bring the Game to an end will now be used to shift the Earth to the next level. As a direct result of the polar shift a vortex formed on the sun. This vortex sent off energy flares into space that were originally designed to destroy the planet. Your original script was to have three big solar flares aimed directly at Earth within a one month period. Instead, it erupted into several solar flares. These flares will continue on a diminishing scale until 2006. At this time it appears that none of them will be pointed directly at the Earth.

Energy from these flares is being stored by the Earth in Her tectonic plates. This will be released as necessary to help Her make Her shift into higher dimensional levels. When this occurs, there will be some unusual signs and reactions.

On August 25th 2001 a solar flare occurred that tipped the scales, overloading the system just enough to spark a defensive reaction from the 'Old Guard' who, on 11th of September, displayed their fear in a harrowing way. [This was predicted by the Group four months prior in a live channel presented in Vienna, Austria. A transcript of that channel is included in the next chapter.]

Your connection to the Earth is much stronger than you know. You will have a great influence on the way this energy is assimilated into your reality. Your commitment to work together with the Earth will be the single largest influence as to how this energy will be assimilated.

The Ring of Fire

Watch the events in the Pacific in the years to come as this area is the barometer. The Pacific and the area known as the Ring of Fire form the heartbeat of your planet. Watch for increases in seismic and volcanic activity. Watch for eruptions and releases of energy in the Pacific Ocean itself.

These are evidence that the Crystal Energy from the sun is being assimilated into the Earth.

Please understand that this is an evolutionary process and not a single event. You will not suddenly wake up in a new energy and a new reality. By taking responsibility now for your own powers of creation you will be helping the Earth to assimilate this energy peacefully. Your actions are directly correlated to the Earth's reactions.

At this time the next shift of the Sun's polarity is set for late 2012. This will complete a cycle of engaging the New Energy that is now entering into your field for the creation of the New Planet Earth.

It has begun.
>   The New Planet Earth is here now.
>   Celebrate . . . Welcome Home

The Second Planet of Free Choice

As we have spoken the Game was set up as a great experiment. To give total free choice to such a Gameboard has never before been done since the beginning of creation.

We tell you that up until very recently it did not appear that you would awaken. Now here you are and the love we have for you is beyond description. Imagine your favorite football team losing every game only to claim the highest trophy at the very last minute of the season. This is what you have done only on a much larger scale. All eyes are upon you, for you are not just changing your own world. You are changing the paradigm of all that is.

The experiment of the planet of free choice was so successful that there is now a second planet of free choice. You will become very familiar with this second 'Gameboard' when the time is right. For now, please understand that your choices are honored more than you will ever know.

We are so very proud of your work. We know there are times when you feel alone; times when you cannot feel your own guidance; times when you do not even trust yourself. Please know that you are never alone. Know that you are surrounded by the most wonderful family on both sides of the veil. We are the fans that believed in you the whole time you were losing the game. Now you hold the greatest of trophies and we are so honored to be in your presence.

It is with the greatest love that we ask you to treat each other with respect, nurture one another and play well together. . .

the Group

Chapter 2

The Angel of the
Twin Towers

Shining Light
in the Shadow of Terror.

**The Group on the events of September 11, 2001
and the attack on the Twin Towers.**

Prediction of the Twin Towers

The section you are about to read is taken directly from the transcript of a live channel presented at the Quill of Remembrance seminar in Vienna, Austria on May 6th 2001. These words have not been edited. When I channel live, I use different words and syntax than when I write. Consequently, I generally clean up the grammar and occasionally clarify the meaning before publishing a live channel. In this instance, I have changed nothing in the section you are about to read. As we commenced this channel, the Group immediately issued a warning. They predicted that in four months the Earth's tectonic plates would start releasing stored energy and that this event had great potential for harm. They even described in general terms who would react and how. Four months and four days later, on September 11th 2001, terrorists attacked and destroyed the Twin Towers of the World Trade Center in New York.

Audio tapes of this live channel are available at www.lightworker.com.

A side note here is how fast world developments can change. Three days prior, we had presented a talk and live channel to the Esoteric Society at the United Nations in Vienna. The Group made no mention of the shocking events that were to come.

Interestingly, neither I nor any of the attendees at this seminar on May 6th consciously re-membered the Group's warning. The Group rarely gives predictions, so you can imagine my surprise when, on Christmas Eve 2001, as I was editing this channel, I suddenly realized that they'd given us a warning. It was only then that I really understood the impact of what you are about to read.

Greetings from Home.

We bring you the vibrations of Home in this time together. This is a special time that you have been here. You have waited a very long time to be exactly here now. We are honored to be with you, for we are in the presence of masters. You are daring to script new contracts, daring to find your own Plan B, daring to reach for your passion. This was not foreseen when the Game was first scripted and, therefore, there are no books written about what is now happening. You have yet to write them. Write them well, dear ones. Take the pen firmly in your hand and write your passion for that is what you came here to do. And you will do it well. Each one you touch, whether it be with a word, a smile, or the flash of your eyes, you will make a difference in the hearts that you touch. Fear them not for they will not hurt you. They will not drain you. You are well guided, for you are the ones that have asked to be here at just this moment, just this time. And there are three of you here in the room at this time who did not take an ample rest in between their incarnations. And even though your loved ones and your friends tried to talk you into waiting and resting and coming in later, you did not. You had to be here at exactly this time. And because of that some of you have been very tired during this lifetime. That is about to change.

The gifts that have been given you recently will start shifting the energy of the planet. Much of this energy is being stored in the tectonic plates as we speak, for it is coming from the sun itself. What is happening is that the vortexes of energy are starting up in the different places on the planet right now and you are beginning to feel a tug on your own biology as a result. Do not let this drain you. Ultimately this will be a gift, for you are being aligned to where your energy will be fed. Please re-member to breathe here and now and to breathe in the energy of this day for it is so easy to get lost in tomorrow. The energy is being stored in the tectonic plates in the Earth at this moment. Over the next four months there will be a charging of these plates. Then will begin a slow release of this energy to the surface of the planet. You will feel it. Most of you will feel this as a re-charging of your own energy. There may be some on the planet who are already charged.

There will be some leaders on the planet who may interpret this energy differently. This energy is change and the human resists change at all costs. There may be some of your leaders here that may actually reach to some of the old ways and try the old things. And they will try one more time to control the energy in the old ways. That is why you are here. Stand firm in your truth. Let people see the flash in your eyes. Speak the truth in your heart. Let them see who you are, for you are the planters of the seeds. And those seeds have been planted well within your own being. We tell you they are in fertile ground, and they are about to bloom. Let everyone see the light in your own heart through your eyes, your smile, and your words. Fear not the opening of your heart chakra for everyone will feel it as you walk into the room. And in some small way you will make a difference here on the planet. And to you it may seem like a very small thing but what we tell you is even those of you here in this room will change the course of all that is to come.

[This channel then continues with the Topic of the Nature of Contracts....which appears later in this book.]

Many people have since asked me why the Group did not give a warning about the tragic events of September 11th 2001. As we have just discovered, they did, but they were deliberately vague. This is because while this event always existed as a possibility, there is no hard and fast Grand Plan. Firstly, the Group has specifically stated that we have evolved beyond scripts and that we are now writing the Grand Plan as we go. Secondly, they have always been very cautious about predicting negative events, for they say we are far more powerful than we know. What we think about we create. As you have seen from the warning, their intention was not to plant seeds of fear, but rather, to issue a call to action.

The Day of September 11th

The morning of September 11th Barbara and I were leaving for the airport, or so we thought. We were on our way to Mt. Shasta, California for the annual ESPAVO conference. We were traveling with several others and were waiting for Keith Smith to show up at our house so we could meet the others at the airport. Carol Holaday, the coordinator of the ESPAVO conference, called and told me that we were not going anywhere and that I should turn on the TV. I turned it on just in time to see the second plane hit the Twin Towers. We were all in shock and rather than gathering at the airport we all met at our house. We decided to drive 14 hours to Mt Shasta because it was even more important than before that we do something.

The ESPAVO conference is a week long event that we put on each year. This was to be the second one and we knew that people who came early were waiting for us. As we were waiting for the last person to show up at the house the Group told me to sit and write. This is the message that we placed on the web site just one hour after the attack.

Greetings from Home.

Dear ones, we watch as the Game of free choice now takes a very difficult turn. Please understand that there is no Grand Plan that is guiding your actions. You are creating the events of the Game in every moment and now there are enhanced creation abilities. With this enhanced creation also comes the ability to misdirect the energy. There are those who are of the belief that they can change the world to their way of thinking. We watch as we see the actions of a very few shift the energy for so many. The intent of the few was to create fear through which they could take control.

The absence of light is darkness. The absence of love is fear. Now is a time when you, as Lightworkers of the New Planet Earth, are being called to become beacons of light. Stand firm in your love as a beacon for all to see. Now is a time on the planet when you can make a difference by NOT falling prey to fear. It is easy to get caught up in the drama now playing out. Please hold the light during these times by attempting to keep on track with your own work of spreading the Light. Your light is needed more than ever now.

Work from the heart, dear ones, and know that in much the same way as these few have affected many, you too can make a difference. Stay in your routines and do not allow this display of darkness to take control of your world. This is the time to use your own faith and be the Light.

Know that you are not alone. There is much support from the Angelic realm at this time. The energy infiltrating into the Earth has added to the tension. Resist the temptation to get caught up in the drama and watch carefully your desire to lay blame or to point fingers. The gift of forgiveness is yours. It can only be accessed through the heart. Now is the time to put this tool to use. Please be calm and stand firm in your expression of the Light. Come together in Circles of Light and make your hearts heard through love and not through fear. The time is now here for all to see the real work of the Lightworkers. Stand firm and hold your light high for all to see. As this happens the light will illuminate the shadows.

We love you dearly and stand proudly at your side during these times. The events intended to cause fear have opened an energetic door. Where that door leads is now up to you. Take your power and create the highest outcome to this situation and the Light will once again shine in the darkness. Come together and reach hearts through the tragedy you have experienced. From the rubble and the ashes you will see a stronger Light emerge. Thank you for being here to make a difference now.

Your love will be felt and amplified.

the Group

The Espavo conference went really well. There were many who did not make it because of the airports closing. There were some who spent several days stuck in airports as they were already en route. This was a very special gathering and we all felt like we were there for the purpose of shifting the Light. The channel that was presented up on the mountain is available on the web site at the web address below and worth reading. It is entitled "Farewell to the Sword ~ Love over terror in the New Game"
www.lightworker.com/beacons09200011FarewellSword.shtml

"Cosmic Winks"

The Angel of the Twin Towers
A month or so after the Twin Towers were destroyed, I was using a printer in my office when I happened to glance up at a picture on the wall. It was a photograph I had taken in November 1996 of the Statue of Liberty in New York. We were there with Lee Carroll who channels Kryon, who was speaking at the SEAT at the United Nations. We were sight-seeing on the boat heading toward Ellis Island. When we got the film back, I was astonished to see an angel in the clouds. That was a real cosmic wink to me so I framed it and hung it in my office. I have looked at this picture thousands of times but on this occasion it was different. This time I was taken aback to discover there was a second cosmic wink in this photograph – The angel in the clouds is hovering directly over the Twin Towers.

"There are times when we, as angels, see where you are heading. We watch with love, yet we will not interfere with your prime directive of free choice. Our message is meant to empower, and to interfere would take your power from you. In those situations we touch you with the "cosmic winks" that leave lasting impressions on your hearts.

Know that you are NEVER alone." — the Group

The Angel of the Twin Towers

You can see this picture in full color on the web site at:
http://www.lightworker.com/articles/TTAngel.shtml

Section II

The New Planet Earth

Attributes of a New Reality

Comparison Chart

Subject	The Old Energy	The New Planet Earth
Primary Motivation	Survival	Seeking Unity and Higher Truth
Dimensional Levels	Third	Fifth
Dimension Attributes	Width, Height, Depth	Width, Height, Depth, Time and Space
Polarity	Right or Wrong Good or Bad Love or Fear	Cause and Effect
Work Paradigm	Work Hard	Work Passionate
Love Expression	Conditional Love (Unconditional)	Universal Love
Tools for Finding Truth	Judgment	Discernment
Living with Truth	Stationary Truth	Truth as an Evolution
Leadership	Follow the Leader	Follow Yourself
Business and Government	Profit, Leadership	Making space for Empowered Humans
Communication	Limited, controllable, propaganda	There will be NO MORE SECRETS
Time	Linear	Circular or Now Time
Healing Paradigm	Do not make the patient any sicker.	Do not take the patient's power from them
Relationship to the Universal Energy	Segregation (Ignoring the Universal Energy)	Blending (Emulating the Universal Energy)
Point of Perception	Lack	Abundance
Manifestation	Co-creation	Living Abundance, Creation
Spirit Communication	Mystical, Unconscious channeling, Mystique, Organized Hierarchy	Conscious channeling, Walking with spirit fully integrated as individuals
Experience of Spirituality	Ritual, Organization and Sacrifice	Joy, Passion and Human Empowerment

Chapter 3

The Hidden Universe

Inter-dimensional Realities
and the Thinning Veil

The ascension is well underway. According to the Group we will be seeing things that at first we may not understand. It is now time to plant the seeds of knowledge in fertile ground. Then, as the veil thins, we may finally begin to understand.

Greetings from Home

We tell you that there is much work being done right now to build a bridge that will span the dimensional levels of your own time and space. Your science is only now beginning to understand that the theory they have been searching for that will apply to both the very small and the very large, is only explainable if you understand inter-dimensional levels. Today we will speak of the exciting possibilities that lay ahead for the human race. You are at a very special time in the history of the Earth.

Allow us to reflect you from an energy perspective for a moment. We have told you that the human race is an integral part of the energy structure you know as the Earth. Some day soon you will find yourselves traveling far into space, light-years away from your home planet. But no matter how far you travel you will never sever the energetic connection you have with the Earth. Even though your travels into space will bring you a broader understanding of your own true nature, they do not compare with the inter-dimensional wonders that await you now.

The Earth's Higher Self

To explain alternate dimensional realities let us begin with the basics. If you examine your own energetic matrices you know that you are more than your physical being. You inhabit bubbles of biology that house some, but not all, of your energy. They hold only a small portion of who you really are. The overflow of this energy is what you know to be your Higher Self. Your own energetic matrix reaches far beyond your physical body. These energy matrices are energy bodies that extend beyond your own body. Now we ask you to look at the energetic matrix of the Earth as a similar structure. We tell you that She also is a sentient, living being with many levels reaching outside of Her physical body. She too has an energetic portion of Her being that does not contain Her full energy. The overflow of the energy you know to be Earth is divided into dimensional levels of vibration.

For the moment please think of these levels as musical notes. If two notes are played that are within close range they have a relationship to each other and thus will interact quite well. If, however, you play the uppermost notes on a keyboard in conjunction with the lowermost notes, the listener has difficulty relating these notes together and there is limited interaction. In fact, they almost do not seem to fit together at all. This is because two notes that do not complement each other have the effect of canceling each other out. In the same way, your biology has only been capable of interacting between specific ranges of vibration. There are many notes that you are still unable to hear or see.

You can see and interact with some of these dimensional levels on the Gameboard. The first of these levels is the molten earth that comprises the center of your planet. This is the core of Her physical body, both physically and energetically. Next in line comes the densest part of Her body, the rocks and solid earth. Since this is a form of life that is very different from your own dimensional reality, it is not yet possible for you to communicate with a boulder. Still, these rock formations are a form of life and many of you are beginning to realize that communication is possible.

Crystal Power

The crystals that power the Earth's internal navigational system are another form of this dense level of life. Therefore, crystals have properties that are more human-like than the boulders that make up your mountains. Crystals hold a variety of vibrations and even have the ability of crossing the dimensional lines of reality. Therefore, they have the ability to exist in several dimensions simultaneously holding the energy of each. It is these inter-dimensional properties that actually make up the crystalline grids of the Earth.

One of the next levels is what you know to be plant life. Your research has shown that plants have feelings and react in a very similar manner energetically to humans. Your own emotional state can easily be transferred to plants. Though they do not have the same senses as you, their sense of absorption is greatly enhanced. They can easily absorb emotional energy from other plants or humans. They 'feel' love, pain and even fear. Their energy sustains you on the planet as energy is often passed from one dimensional level to another. This is what you have termed the food chain and what we see as the energy chain. If you understand that nothing ever dies then it is easier to see the energy flow in its true form. In this fashion you can easily see that plant life on planet Earth is an integral part of the Mothers Higher Self.

Please keep in mind that, from your perspective, you are looking at plant life from a higher vibrational state. Therefore, it is easy to see how plants span the energetic gap between the dense boulders of Earth and the ethereal spirit of man. Understand that as you view levels of dimension that are closer to your own vibration, this energy flow is more difficult to discern. The animal life which we will examine next is a perfect example of this.

As we move outward into less dense bodies, the next dimensional level is what you know to be animals. This dimensional level is very close to your own and, therefore, you can look into their eyes and see much more of your own reflection. Their vibrations are very close to your own and in the example of the piano keyboard, their note range is very close to your own. Thus, you can relate and interact harmoniously with animals. Animal life is so close to your own vibration that it is even possible for you to interact on higher levels of existence with them. For instance, it is possible for you to make contracts to work together with an animal during a lifetime, whereas it is not common practice to do that with a boulder. Animals balance the energy of the planet in much the same way as plants do. The difference is that animals are much closer to the human vibrational range, whereas plants are closer to the dense physical body of minerals.

We have just described for you three levels of dimensional realities on Planet Earth. There are many more, including what you call fish and insects. You can see how these realities do not always interact with each other. Dimensional realities that are close to one another can interact on more levels. For instance, you cannot ask a fish how their day is going. Although you may not get an audible answer, you will get a response if you ask that same question of a dog. The human animal is one of these dimensional realities and all of you are, in effect, parts of the Higher Self of Mother Earth.

These dimensional realities reach far beyond your understanding at this time but more will be revealed soon. There are in fact many more dimensional realities that exist within the same time and space on Mother Earth. The four we have just illustrated for you are only the beginning of the larger picture to which you are just now awakening.

Dimensional Realities

The many dimensional levels of vibration that exist on the Gameboard are wondrous beyond description. Understanding inter-dimensional levels can be as simple as diving into a pool of water. Underwater, your communications are limited. The way you interact with your surroundings are different and even the rules of gravity have a different effect. Becoming accustomed to alternate realities is a big step in your evolution as humans.

Learning to move between inter-dimensional levels will help to take you to the next level of human evolution. The beauty of the underwater world is only a sample of the many dimensional levels that await you.

The Extended Human Senses

Your own biology has enabled you to comfortably interact with your 3rd dimensional reality. With humanity moving to higher vibrational status, your biology is adapting to interact with higher dimensions. When you close your eyes, you may start to see flashes of light emanating from the center of your forehead. Your hearing is being affected, with many people becoming aware of a low ringing or buzzing tone. Many humans are extending the range of vibrational sensitivity of their eyes. It will not be long before you begin to see colors that have not been detectable prior. Many humans now are already gaining brief glimpses into other dimensions of space and time. These are the shadow figures that often appear in your peripheral vision. You may think that others are in the room with you, yet when you turn to look at them directly they dissolve. These sightings are evidence that your own human senses are expanding.

We have spoken previously of another sense that you are not yet aware. This is the sense of absorption. This is the manner in which your own biology receives energy. The way you take in energy when it first enters your field is determined by the energy matrix that you chose for your current incarnation. Your sense of absorption determines the degree of sensitivity that you have to your surroundings. Your sense of absorption is undergoing many advances at this time in your evolution. Empathic people have a much heightened sense of absorption. Many healers are emotional empaths that tune in to the emotional level of vibrations only. What you call psychic abilities are actually well honed senses of absorption that span many ranges of vibration. When we first started relaying these messages through the Keeper, we asked you to imagine a time when everyone had access to all thoughts, and all would know intuitively what everyone else was thinking. We tell you now that this time has begun. In the higher vibrations of the New Planet Earth things will be different. In this new world you are building. . .

There Will Be No More Secrets

Your leaders are becoming increasingly aware of the new power within all humans. Look to the leaders of your world who in the past have often told you one thing and done another. In the higher vibrations of the New Planet Earth this will no longer be so easy. The veil is thinning, and as it does you will all see that you are not separate from one another. The field of polarity in which you have played this Game has given you an illusion of separateness. Understand that as the veil thins even more you will all have access to the connection that you all share. This is the reason that there is an increase in what you call channeling and divine inspiration.

The door has swung open. You are standing at the threshold surveying the realities that now lay before you. We have told you time and again that you live in very exciting times. There you stand, looking into another world yet you do not know what it means or what to do next. Let us re-mind you here to enjoy the road that lies ahead for you will never be at this juncture again. Through your choices the collective vibrational level of humanity has risen to a level that will now support connection between many of the realities that have existed within your own time and space.

Shadow Figures

The shadow figures that you see out of the corner of your eye are from other dimensional realities that exist within the same space as your own. The moment you turn to see these figures they disappear as quickly as they came. You will find this happening more often now as you move forward into evolution. As your eyes adjust to the new vibrational ranges these sightings will increase, and as you advance further you will be able to see other realities existing within the same physical space that you inhabit. Time and space are interrelated and these are actually other dimensions of time, or what we have termed 'dimensional and inter-dimensional realities'. Most of these realities are separated vibrationally and have little crossover from one to the other. The 'you' that you know may also be living a different life with other people and circumstances within one of these realities. Those whom you know to have multiple personality disorder have simply lost touch with the conscious control mechanism that keeps these realities separate. Imagine that there are entire worlds that exist within the same physical space of your own home.

Your human evolution is now making it possible for you to see into these other dimensions of time. However, it will be some time before you can interact with these dimensions on a conscious level, for many are not as advanced as your own. In such instances you may see them but they will not see you. Still it may be possible for you to observe life in a reality slightly different from your own. Although this reality may hold people and things that appear to be much like your own, you will find different inventions and alternate solutions to the problems that you experience in your own world. There have always been some of you who can tap into these worlds and dance for a brief time in these realities.

Did you really think that the science fiction writings that you love so are all a fabrication?

Shadow Figures — Phyllis Brooks

Auras ~ A Light-Link Between Realities

You will often see these beings as if they were backlit. You may also see outlines of light, much like a thin but very bright aura. This light is in fact a connection point that ties them in to the other dimensions of time. In your own dimensional reality you cannot see these connection points very clearly. To you they are often vague and lacking definition. These are what you have called Auras. In reality they are the point where your dimension of time blends into others. You perceive the auras as light and energy.

Proud Third Graders

Your humanness would tell you that anything that you do not understand must be above you in the grand scheme of things. You are such wonderful beings and so imaginative! There is no grand scheme of anything, for the simple reason that you have yet to write it. Still, as humans you love to give your power away to all things that you do not understand. You have spent much of your existence reaching for higher vibrations and higher truths and, therefore, you believe that a higher vibration is better than a lower vibration. Please understand that from our perspective one level is no better than another. We ask you, is your fourth grade better than the third? Please understand that spiritual competition is one of the destructive forces that sank Atlantis. Do not allow yourselves to go there again.

With this understanding firmly in place, we will tell you that there are many levels of dimensional realities that exist within your own time and space. Some of them are of a lower frequency than yours and some of them are higher. As you begin to see into the worlds that exist within your own world, you need to be aware that the higher vibrational realities will see you, and you them. The lower vibrational realities will not see you, even though you can view and even step into their reality. Please understand that even though some of these realities may be more advanced than you in technology and evolution, it is you that holds the power. It is as if the third grade has made advances that will now facilitate the graduation of the entire school.

You have advanced all levels of vibration through your own reality and the awakening that you are now experiencing. In the days ahead, you will come into contact with many who profess to be your overseers and even your judges. They will seem to appear magically, and they will dazzle you with their powers, saying that humans have now reached a vibrational status high enough to allow contact with their advanced vibration.

Please re-member that if they could have done what you did, they would have done it. You are the ones that have shifted the paradigm of all that is. Enjoy these contacts for what they are: Other realities and other games being played out in the cosmos. Never give your power to anyone other than yourself. Look for those who support you in love and harmony and allow you to find your highest power alongside them. These are the ones you will invite to walk beside you in the new game.

Levels of Vibration

It is easy for you to see that we are in a much higher vibrational state than you are. We tell you that we do not keep an open dialog with you at all times. There are only brief times that we spend together planting these seeds of empowerment. Now you are at a stage where your own guides have established a new relationship to you. They have stepped back to allow you to trust your own power.

This is because you have moved several levels of vibration at one time. It is also important for you to know that being of a higher vibration, it is necessary for us to intentionally lower our vibration in order to communicate on this level. It is much easier on us now that you have raised your vibration as a collective of humans. This is the reason you now see so many more communications from our side of the veil.

We have told the Keeper that we will be with him always, as we always have been. Yet there will come a time when he will no longer seek our advice. That is because he and all humans are now in the process of establishing constant communion with their own higher selves. When this happens we will have completed our greatest task. In the interim, we tell you that it is not possible for us to constantly lower our vibrations. It is therefore easier for us to stay in constant harmony with one person, such as the Keeper. The reason we are describing this process is that you will soon be discovering how to lower your own vibrational level in order to interact with the dimensional realities from the Second Planet of Free Choice that will become part of your Game.

In the same way that we have had to lower our vibration in order to communicate with you, you also will find that it takes a lot of energy to sustain such a connection. If you cannot sustain the energy during these connections, it can create a vacuum that could manifest in your emotional body as fear.

To illustrate this point we will speak of some who have already been connecting to lower vibrational entities. Your stories of ghost hauntings, evil and the like, often stem from short trips that an imaginative writer has taken into lower vibrational realities. These short interludes have provided an endless supply of material for many of your popular writers of horror stories. Humans love to see themselves reflected in this manner. You so love to be scared.

Enjoy the ride, dear ones, and do not worry about how you have your fun. Just understand two points: If you begin to find yourself in a reality full of fear there is really nothing to be afraid of. It is only a reality with a lower vibration than your own. Secondly, in the same way that many of you recognize us as angels, this is how you will appear to the inhabitants of the lower dimensional reality that exists on the Second Planet of Free Choice.

Extraterrestrials

We have told you that there are many other Games taking place simultaneously throughout all that is. We also tell you that there are overtone levels of dimensions that support life of a higher vibration within your own time and space. Most of you have yet to see these beings, although they can see you. Many of these beings are those who helped you create the game you are now playing. Some of these are your own parental races. Tales of people living within the Earth and space travelers have abounded since you began telling stories. We tell you that the space crafts you see rarely travel into space. Rather, they simply shift into other dimensions of time. You may see them as crafts capable of great speeds and able to defy the laws of gravity. We tell you that all of these are easily achievable with the technology that you currently have when you understand how to shift dimensions. It is only when these crafts are in a resonant vibration to your own that they can be seen. Fear them not, for they do not have the ability to control you without your permission. Humans are stepping into their own empowerment to a level that these beings will become visible in your world.

Some of these beings have been working with your governments for some time. Please do not allow yourselves to fall into the drama of conspiracy theories. None of that is important and the drama can be quite destructive. Let us just say that contact has been made many times in the history of your Game. These beings of higher vibration have often brought in the promise of new technology to trade with your governments. However, since your Game only supports technology in exact relation to the collective level of your vibrational advancement, it has not worked the same for you as it has for them. What you have called the Philadelphia experiment and the Montauk project are prime examples of such attempted interventions. Government officials have been enticed by the promise and demonstration of high technology toys of war. If only they knew that on the Gameboard of Free Choice it is no longer possible to use high technology for low vibrational applications, they would understand why they have been frustrated in their attempts to utilize this information.

Many of these beings have been watching you in much the same way that you would watch actors in a drama on your televisions. We find it very humorous that you have made movies about people who have spent their existence on a stage as players being the star of the show. [This was a reference to movies like Ed T.V. and The Truman Show.] We see you in much the same way as the characters in these movies. There are events going on behind the scenes that you do not see. In fact, there are many shows being enacted in differing levels of vibration on the same stage as yours. This would equate to the many television channels that run simultaneously. You have only to decide which channel to tune into.

At your current level, it is difficult for you to understand the truth about who is who. We will tell you that the dimensional overtone level that you presently occupy is the level that is attracting the most attention from the Universe at this time. Yours is the level that is creating the greatest change in the history of the Game.

A Quiet Space Landing

You will soon make contact with those beings you have termed as extraterrestrials. They have been waiting patiently, watching you advancing. You are not alone in the Universe. It is important to know that there also are many races who are not as advanced as you are. You have waged many wars over your differences. If you think that you on Earth are different from one another, then you will be in for quite a shock when you see what awaits you. We love your attraction to meeting what you call extraterrestrials. We tell you this is quite humorous to us as none of you are originally from Earth!

To you the Universe appears to be vast but much of what you perceive as space is illusory. When you begin to understand the true nature of time and space, you will have the secret of traveling vast distances in the blink of an eye. Then you will make contact with these beings on their own home ground. In the meantime, they are waiting patiently in the inter-dimensional realities of which you are now becoming aware. Although you will be in awe of these beings when they greet you, we ask that you hold your power firmly and understand that they too are in a changing environment because of the choices that *you* have made on the Gameboard of Free Choice. You have earned your power, use it well and understand that it is no longer appropriate to give it away to anyone or anything. Keep in mind that if you were of no real significance they would not be watching you with such intensity.

You will begin to meet them as you advance to higher vibrational status. Since you will not all achieve this status at the same time, they will infiltrate your reality slowly. For this reason, it may be a long time before you see a scheduled space landing on CNN. Still, many of you will begin to interact with these beings within the next two years. They will intermingle with your own reality very quietly at first. In time, you will come to understand that some of the beings you have called ET's are actually yourselves in another dimension of time and space.

Inter-Dimensional Realities

Each inter-dimensional reality has a unique vibration and can therefore be kept separate from one another. If you look at the technology that you call fiber optics, you will see an analogy, for in this technology it is possible to house thousands of signals [telephone calls] in one strand of light by assigning each a unique carrier frequency upon which to travel. These signals do not intermingle or interfere with each other because each carrier wave is unique. Now imagine a carrier frequency that has the ability to vary its base vibration and, therefore, its unique frequency. We have termed these variable frequencies 'inter-dimensional realities' because they have the ability to intersect many alternate realities. While these frequencies are tunable to some degree, it is not possible to tune directly into an inter-dimensional reality, it is only possible to tune into a harmonic, or overtone level of a reality. This is why a being in one inter-dimensional reality can only be seen as a shadowy figure in the next. This also explains why shadow figures dissipate the moment you focus on them.

Ghosts and Purgatory

It is these harmonic levels that you first visit upon leaving your physical bodies. When leaving the physical plane, the level you first encounter is an inter-dimensional, harmonic level of reality which has similar attributes to the reality you inhabited in physical form. This is the interim level that has been interpreted in your religious writings as Purgatory. It has nothing to do with judgment, for judgment does not exist outside of your field of polarity. We find it very amusing that you would take such a normal process and manipulate it for purposes of control. The one we find most amusing is your fabrication of what you call Hell.

As you leave the physical and enter this first level, it looks and feels like the level you occupied when in physical form. This is why some get stuck here, thinking they are still alive. If there is strong emotional resistance to moving on [i.e., fear or anger] one may remain in this state until the emotion is released. Those who get stuck here are the ones you call ghosts. We also tell you that it is entirely possible to be held in this state by those still in the physical who will not let go of the one who has graduated. Once released, souls can easily interact from the much higher vibrational state you know to be Heaven, or Home.

Using Alternate Realities

You see your existence as one person interacting with other people   We tell you that there is much more than you have imagined. As you uncover the existence of inter-dimensional realities, you will see that you have several realities existing simultaneously within the past, present and the future. As we have mentioned above, it is the Aura that is the light-link to these dimensional realities. Imagine that there are several of you existing side by side. Each of you may make different choices and exist in slightly different worlds and circumstances. You have always had the ability to jump from one inter-dimensional reality to another.   All things are possible on the Gameboard of Free Choice. You have only to choose your reality and then accept it. It is even possible to pull certain aspects from one alternate reality into another. While very few have accomplished this feat, these possibilities are available to each of you now.   In earlier Re-minders from Home we have given suggestions on jumping between realities through changing your point of perception. We tell you that your point of perception is critical to your success at dimensional shifting. First, become aware that this is an important part of the shifting process. Then exercise this ability by constantly choosing to view every event in your life from the highest point of perception. Practice changing your angle of perception and develop the habit of first positioning. This will set the stage for your next step into time shifting. [See story of Nora at the conclusion of this chapter]

Time Shifting

Your collective vibration of humanity is now allowing you to see into other dimensions of time. Practicing intentional control of time will prepare you for walking between the worlds of dimensional realities. Your preparation will set the stage for what is now unfolding. This material is covered elsewhere so we will not repeat it here. [See the Chapter on Alternate Realities in the first book from the Group entitled "Re-member ~ a Handbook for Human Evolution".]

Vortexes ~ Anchoring Dimensional Realities

A vortex is simply energy moving in a circular motion. When a vortex occurs naturally on Earth you are able to feel the wonderful energy it creates. Vortexes can be caused by a number of different stimuli. Commonly, vortexes can be found where a breeze travels down a canyon and hits the side of a mountain to be re-directed in a circular motion. A tornado is a form of unanchored vortex that can be quite destructive. Vortexes can be male or female (point up or down) and can travel either clockwise or counterclockwise. There are naturally forming vortexes and those created through human intention. It is even possible to have your own personal vortex around you. There are many more attributes to a vortex - including personality - but for now we will speak only in general terms.

A vortex is an energy form that has the same attributes in all dimensional realities and is also the one form of energy that can transverse all dimensional realities. When a vortex is anchored into the Earth and nurtured through human intent, it becomes a portal to other dimensions. In time, these portals will become the vehicles for inter-dimensional travel through time and space. Many will visit Earth through such time portals to see how the Game was played on the Gameboard of Free Choice.

Guardians of the Vortex Awaken

There are those of you who felt this call many years ago and through your own intent and dedication began to form the energy portals on planet Earth. We see these portals as swirling energy signatures. Some of you have been drawn purposely to open new portals of energy in various parts of the planet. We tell you that this has been very powerful work and has accomplished much. The energy signatures that formed the potential vortexes have been waiting a long time to be activated. There are also many people whom we know to be the Guardians of the New Energy. These are people who form the nucleus of, and nurture, a particular vortex of energy. These people often travel to other places to help in the opening of new vortexes or visit an established vortex to return home and strengthen the energy of their own portal. These swirling energy signatures will be the portals that will ultimately link the dimensional realities together. Your work with the vortexes will reveal much in the years ahead as it will lead you to understand what exists in your own back yard!

Forming a Vortex with the Breath of Life

Let us offer a suggestion for forming an intentional vortex in a group. First form a circle holding each other's hands. This circle is the basis of the vortex. Together, take a deep breath and connect your energies to the Earth. Ask for Her involvement in the work you are about to do. Ask Her in which direction she would like the vortex of energy to flow. If the energy is to move from left to right then start the energy flowing, slowly at first, in through each person's left hand and out through their right, or vice versa. As the energy moves in through your hand, turn to face the person passing you the energy and inhale the breath of life as the energy enters your hand. Turning your face to the person on your right, release the breath as the energy leaves your right hand. Continue circulating both the breath and the energy in the designated direction. When the energy feels right, speed up the circulation of energy but now return to normal breathing. In passing the energy you can visualize that it is now forming a vortex similar to a funnel. At the base it is moving very slowly, yet as the energy extends upwards it gains speed and intensity. When the time is right, take the entire vortex and gently visualize it entering the Mother, anchoring the energy of the Light into the grids of the Earth.

With this simple exercise, you have intentionally created an energy vortex that will anchor the light and attract others of like vibration. This one act alone will help the Earth assimilate the Crystal Energy.

Learning to 'Walk' in other Dimensions

Many of you have found ways of projecting your being through time and space. You have accomplished this through your dreams and even through what you call astral projection. You are now beginning to see that this type of travel is possible in a fully conscious state. The attributes of each dimension are different. In the same way that water, light, sound and even gravity are altered in a pool of water, so too do your own senses react differently in other realities.

Even now humans can begin to visit other dimensions and delve into their own alternate realities. These are the vivid dreams that are now becoming a part of your experience. Dance in this new light, dear ones. You have earned the right. Stretch the limits and practice. Form a vortex and begin to dabble in alternate worlds. Begin the creation of Home on your side of the veil. Take the best from all realities and blend them together for the creation of Heaven on Earth. The time has come. Your own power is before you.

It is with the greatest of pleasure that we ask you to treat each other with respect, nurture one another and play well together.

the Group

In one of our seminars we present an entire segment on using alternate realities. In this material, the Group talked about three ways of shifting realities that can be used in our lives right now. The first is learning to move the camera of life to view every event against the best possible background. The second is developing the habit of first positioning of this camera. The third is Time Shifting. These are covered in more detail in the chapter on alternate realities in book 1. In illustrating this point of developing a habit of first positioning, I like to tell a story about a beautiful soul named Nora.

Nora is not of this Earth but is here in physical form. She is a special being who flitters around from experience to experience, only deciding what role she will play as she approaches each moment. Nora is a master at changing realities. She is one who is not afraid of her power and has developed a healthy habit of highest first positioning.

One day I was taking Nora to lunch. She was driving a four wheel drive vehicle. Nora flits around even when driving her car. She kept turning to make eye contact with me while she was talking. I found this more than a little unnerving. Then, as we were driving through a very exclusive area . . . bang!

Nora hit the car in front of us, which, as luck would have it, just happened to be a very nice Mercedes. The people in the Mercedes were clearly agitated. The driver got out of his car. It was obvious that he was having a hard time controlling his anger. As he looked at Nora still sitting in the driver's seat of her car, his energy was intentionally threatening. I started to get out but Nora stopped me. In that instant she had just a split second to determine the 'angle from which she would view this event.' She looked me right in the eye and said, "Watch this".

I watched as the man began to get angry. Then Nora would talk and he would respond. Every time he talked he became a little calmer. Soon his wife joined them in the street. It wasn't long before they were all laughing.

Nora and I never did get to lunch alone together that day. It turned out that the people in the car were heading to the same restaurant. They bought us lunch. It transpired that the car was on loan from the agency that was repairing their own Mercedes. The gentleman had taken out a damage waiver on the loaner and so never reported the incident. Nora's car was not even scratched. In that split second, Nora had created a miracle. She refused to accept a reality that did not suit her and I got to see the art of highest first positioning in action. Thanks, Nora!

Chapter 4

Ana and the Bird

The new relationship to our guides with the integration of Spirit

Lightworkers everywhere are feeling confused and disconnected. In these times we are moving rapidly from one
vibrational level to the next. The Group says that we humans
do not take the steady escalator in our quest to move to higher
vibrations. Rather, we can't wait to jump on the express elevator shooting up hundreds of floors in seconds. Then we try to
figure out why we can't walk when the doors of the elevator
open. To us it feels as if we are disconnected and have lost our
way. We are at the next stage of our evolution as Humans.
Our guides have taken a step back. They are now one step
removed. To us it may feel like they have left or abandoned us.
They have simply adopted a new relationship to us that will
allow us to hold more of our own power.

In our private sessions people now ask: "Why do I feel disconnected and confused? I feel like I have lost contact with my
guides. Can you explain what is happening?"

The Group has responded with the story of Ana and the Bird.
Here the Group shares the story with everyone. Now we are
seeing this shift to be a common occurrence as humanity is
moving into the next vibratory level. The express elevator has
stopped and the doors have just opened. Are you ready?

Greetings from Home

Much is shifting on the Gameboard as you step into the higher
vibrations. Many of you feel you are losing the connection you
once had as the magic seems to fade from view. In human form
it is difficult to see yourselves the way we see you, for you walk
with the veils firmly in place. We tell you that your success on
the planet is not determined by how you handle the magic, but
by how you handle the mundane. With the integration of Spirit, it
is possible for you to breathe magic into every step of life. It is
also important to understand that it is not Spirit that creates the
magic. It is *your* magic that we are here to help you re-member.

The Pendulum of Human Advancement

As we have explained prior, humanity advances in a fashion similar to a pendulum that swings from one side to the other The pendulum of human advancement has a pivotal point that moves forward when the pendulum swings far enough in one direction. This forward motion illustrates the advancement of humanity. The nature of the pendulum and the nature of humanity dictate that it must swing to both sides before it will build up sufficient momentum to advance to the next level. What you see as temporary setbacks are only illusions of polarity. From our perspective, they are not setbacks at all. They are, in fact, a build up that will propel humanity to the next level.

In the past, humanity has swung many times to create the necessary momentum to make a shift. Now you are making these shifts routinely. We tell you that the swing of the pendulum need not be difficult.

Walking through the Valley

See yourself walking through an open field with Spirit at your side. You are never separate from that part of yourselves known as Spirit. You speak to Spirit and talk to your guides. Reaching the top of the mountain, you can see that before you lies a valley that you must cross. Although Spirit never leaves you, there are times when you must walk in faith. Know that as you walk through this valley, Spirit is with you, even though you do not feel it. If you feel you are walking alone, understand that your guidance has simply taken on a new form that you do not yet comprehend. Trust your heart and follow that which brings even the slightest amount of passion and joy. These will lead you through the valley to a stronger re-union with spirit on the other side.

You are not walking alone.

Integration of Spirit

You that are leading the way have begun the process of carrying your full power while walking in the bubbles of biology. This is accomplished through a union with your Higher Self. We implore you, do not get into spiritual competition, for it quickly negates any real advancement and turns it into illusion. Competition is only an illusion of polarity and will retard vibrational advancement by holding you firmly to the 3rd dimension. Allow the integration of Spirit gradually and fear not the silent spaces on your journey.

The Story of Ana and the Bird

To address the vibrational shift that you are experiencing, we will tell you the story of Ana and the Bird.

Just before the dawn, all that could be heard was the sobbing of a very unhappy soul. Ana was a twelve-year-old Indigo child who was deeply troubled with her life on the Gameboard of Free Choice. She had few friends and had difficulty relating to others in her class at school. Her teachers viewed her as a problem child. She felt like she was always an outsider looking in. Ana had particular difficulty relating to her mother and they fought often. Even though Ana had an inner sense of knowing, she was despondent and had almost given up hope. At twelve years old Ana wanted to go Home.

Feeling her confusion, Spirit spoke directly to her. 'Ana you may leave if you wish, but first you must go outside to the garden and place your finger out in front of you.' Ana was shocked that Spirit would talk to her so directly as this had never happened before. She could not see how this could possibly help but decided to give it a try. The sun was just rising in the sky and there was a reddish blue hue over everything. Looking around to make sure no one was watching, Ana closed her eyes and placed her finger out in front of her as Spirit had instructed. Moments later she felt a tickle on her finger and opened her eyes to see a small brown bird perched on her extended finger. 'Hello, dear one' said the bird. Ana's eyes immediately filled with tears as the almost forgotten feelings of Home came flooding back into her memory.

Wiping the tears from her eyes she looked around to see if anyone else was watching. Was she dreaming or was this real? Did the bird really speak? Just then the bird spoke to her again. 'I am here to help you re-member, Ana, for you are here with a purpose and if you leave now, your purpose will remain unfulfilled.' Again the tears of joy came as Ana felt for the first time a glimmer of hope. Even the faint knowledge that she had a purpose helped Ana. Magic charged the air in the garden as the bird began a dialog with her that lasted for over an hour. Most of the time Ana could do nothing but cry as she had so much to release. Then she heard the rumblings of her mother in the kitchen. Ana feared that her time with the magical bird was at an end. 'Fear not, Ana, we will speak again. I will be here for you always. You have only to come to this garden and put out your finger and I will respond.'

That day at school Ana's teachers could not figure out why she was constantly crying. They thought something was wrong, but Ana knew that everything was now right. There were times when she doubted that it even happened. Was she making it up? Then she realized that even if the bird were a product of her imagination it made no difference. The feelings of Home the bird gave her made her feel complete and she was not willing to give that up.

Every morning thereafter, Ana rose before the sun, went to the garden and spoke with the bird. They talked of many things and the bird gave Ana life lessons to complete. Ana carried out these lessons joyfully, even though some of them meant that she had to change difficult things about herself. The bird constantly re-minded her that she held the power to change her reality through her choices. This small brown bird breathed magic into the life of the young girl Ana. Day added unto day and soon Ana's life was changing. At school, Ana had friends who looked up to her and respected her. Her teachers had magically changed and now befriended her. Even she and her mother were now getting along and communicating well. Now at last Ana felt as if her life had meaning.

One morning, Ana looked back and realized how far she had come. In just a few months she had made more progress toward happiness than she had in all of her previous twelve years. With that realization she thanked the bird for the gift of magic it had given her. The bird responded, 'Dear one, I cannot give you that which you already possess. My job was to be the mirror for you to see your true self and re-member your power. Please never lose sight of the fact that the power to change is within and not without. You have chosen to exercise this power and therefore have changed your own reality.'

The highlight of Ana's life was to spend that short time every morning with the bird, re-membering her true power. The love she had for this beautiful, simple creature was overwhelming. Rain or shine Ana spent every morning in that garden setting the tone of her day with the teacher she had grown to love so dearly. Ana's life was good.

One morning, Ana awoke even earlier than she was accustomed to. She felt a shift in the energy but was not sure what was happening. She re-membered what the bird had told her about energy shifts and how this was the way humans evolved. She re-membered that the bird had told her that change was a necessary part of spiritual advancement, for without change all things eventually die. It is actually change that creates the magic we seek. These thoughts circled in her head and she carefully formed the questions she would ask the bird during their magical time together that morning. When the time arrived, Ana walked expectantly into the garden and held her finger out in front of her. But that morning the bird did not come.

With the bird's help, Ana had learned to trust her inner feelings, rather than her thoughts. Now was a perfect time to use this skill and somehow Ana knew inside that her dearest companion was all right. She also knew in her heart that she was all right - nothing bad had happened to her after all. Still, she missed her friend the bird and their special time together. Ana thought back on all the information the bird had given her, and how she had used it in her life. But she was puzzled because one of the first things the bird had told her was that it would never leave her. Still, here she stood all by herself in the garden. Ana tried talking to the bird, pretending it was there. She could even feel the familiar tickle as it perched on her finger. But every time she formulated a question to ask, the answer magically appeared in her head. Suddenly Ana understood that the real gift the bird had given her was the confidence to trust her *own* inner guidance, rather than looking to an external source for answers.

Every morning Ana continued to perform her ritual of going into the garden and holding her finger out in front of her. For weeks after, Ana continued her ritual in the garden, and not a day passed when she did not think of her friend. For the first time in a long while Ana wept, but her tears were bittersweet. She was sad to think that her finger would never support the bird again, but in her heart she knew that their connection would never be lost. In teaching her to trust her own inner guidance, the bird had also given Ana the key to walking as a spirit in human form. Suddenly Ana realized that life was not so bad after all.

As time went on, Ana played a pivotal role in her school. The teachers finally understood that she was not a problem child, but rather, that she and others like her, were far beyond what the school was teaching. Ana helped them to adjust the way they approached teaching methods in order to engage the children's interest. She helped the staff to alter their thinking to accommodate the new children that had started to come. The day Ana graduated was a special day indeed. Looking back, she could never have envisioned enjoying this part of her life. Yet here she was having played a very important role in educating the educators. And in her own small way she helped to set the energy for all that was still to come.

Ana grew in years and in stature. She became a great healer, empowering thousands of others to change their own reality. As the bird had taught her, Ana used what was in her heart to guide her students. She found that the more she trusted her own power, the more she had to give.

Ana thought often of her dearest friend and always surrounded herself with birds of every kind. The bird had become Ana's personal symbol and bird representations adorned every room of her abode. She became known far and wide as the bird lady. Ana took that title with great pride. She had been touched in a part of her that was so deep that she could never forget it, and she chose to carry the gift of the bird's wisdom with her in everything she did. Ana was indeed walking with Spirit.

Years later, Ana found herself looking after her grandson. This child was very special to her. She knew the day he was born that they had a connection that reached far beyond this lifetime, and she was eager to see where their contract would lead this time. Billy was a bright eyed seven-year-old who looked fearlessly into the very depths of Ana's soul. He reminded her of the important role she had played in redefining the school system that he would now step into. He was carrying Crystal energy, and she loved him more than life itself. Ana took a deep breath as she thought about Billy, and in that moment Ana was very grateful that she had stayed.

One day Billy was visiting his grandmother. He was examining the many bird replicas on the mantle when his attention was captured by a small brown bird statue. Ana saw her grandson looking intently at the bird. She knew in her heart that something wonderful was about to happen. Ana held her breath in anticipation as her seven-year-old grandson turned to her and said, 'You know, Grandma, this looks just like the bird that is always on your shoulder.'

The words hit Ana with a force that swept her off her feet. Suddenly, all the pieces fell into place. All her remaining questions about the bird had now been answered. She thought back to the day when the bird had not appeared and she now realized that she had progressed in her own lessons to where the bird was able to land on her shoulder instead of her finger. Ana had been so accustomed to looking for the bird outside of herself that she had not noticed that, instead of landing on her finger, her advancement had made it possible for the bird to take a closer position on her shoulder.

After all these years the long silence was finally broken. 'Yes, dearest Ana,' said the bird. 'I told you that I would never leave you and I have not'. Tears of joy filled Ana's eyes as once again she heard the beautiful sound of her dear friend's voice. 'I am so very proud of you for the choice you made that day. You could have stayed forever watching your finger, waiting for the guidance you were accustomed to receiving from the outside. But you decided to walk forward, trusting your own guidance. What you experienced was the integration of Spirit through opening the connection to your own Higher Self. You are not separate from Spirit as your human experience would have you believe. You are not separate from me, for we are one. You walked in the mundane world with Spirit closely on your shoulder and dared to create the magic for yourself. You have done well, dear Ana. You have completed your higher purpose in learning to integrate the human with the divine'.

In that moment Ana knew she and her grandson had completed an important contract. For the first time in her life what Ana knew in her head and what she knew in her heart were in total harmony. The miracle of Ana's life was now complete.

And so it is. . .

Ana and the Bird — Phyllis Brooks

Choose your Point of Perception

Like Ana, you too have choice. If you hold out your finger and your bird does not appear, you have a choice to perceive it as something wrong or an opportunity to listen and trust the voice within. Your choice will determine the outcome. Ana could easily have spent the rest of her life in that garden waiting for the bird to return and give her further instructions. Instead she chose to apply what she had been given in her daily life.

Make space for something higher and your inner guidance will strengthen tenfold. Walk through the silent moments with full knowledge that the answers you seek are already within you. Be cautious of allowing your love of mysticism to blind you as it can keep you from advancing. Understand that the magic is not in having the bird of spirit sitting on your finger, but rather, in allowing it to integrate through your Higher Self. Enjoy the time the bird sits perched on your finger, but understand that the real magic occurs when it moves onto your shoulder.

Blending Magic into the Mundane

Dare to blend your own magic with the mundane as you walk each step in daily life. If you can find one magical thing about every experience you have this day the magic will multiply. Enjoy the mystical, but do not look to it for all your answers, for the real magic will be found in the mundane.

We will share with you a secret. . .
Expect a miracle . . . and you will create it.

Re-member, like Ana, you are not walking alone. Treat each other with respect, nurture one another and play well together. . .

the Group

The Group did not mention it during the message but Ana's bird was an ordinary small sparrow, which perfectly illustrates the blending of the magic with the mundane.

Every time I see a sparrow or a small brown bird I re-member this beautiful story. I hope you do as well.

Chapter 5

Dawn of the New Light

Seven Seconds to the New Light

A live message presented in Denver, Co. June 2001

A s our evolution continues we are beginning to see into other worlds, alternate realities and other dimensions of time and space. So what's next and what will we see here on Earth? . . . Funny you should ask.

Greetings from Home.

You sit in this beautiful room and the sun shines on the outside and you long to bathe in its light. We tell you this day that you will experience more light than you expect.

We are here today to help you connect a part of yourselves. We honor you so for being here, for you are the chosen ones. You are the ones who willingly put on the veils. Some tried so hard to talk you out of it. But, no, you wanted to sit in the very front of the class. You insisted on being where you are now. Even when it was argued, "But the front of the class is where you will find the most resistance," you said, "I will be there. I want to be right at the front. I claim the title of a chosen one." And here you are, looking into each other's eyes and recognizing each other for perhaps the first time in a long, long time. Now you may see why we get so excited when you come together. Can you see why we honor you so?

Welcome Home, dear family of Light.

You are here, dear ones. You have chosen to place yourself through all the tribulations, through all the trials, through all the pain of not being able to see yourself as you truly are, just to do what you are doing here today. Thank you for having the courage to do it. Not only have you changed your own world, not only have you changed your own possibilities and created a reality that is now emulating Home, but you have changed All That Is. Your world is not the only world that is changing. For this reason, all eyes are upon you now. You are the chosen ones. You are the marked generation that chose to be here at exactly this time, and we love you so. You are awakening from the dream, and as you do we will be here, smiling with the Light of Home, to help you re-member who you are. Understand that it is not possible with all the might of heaven, and all the strength of Home, to accomplish what you do. You hold the power. You hold the creation. You hold Home in your own hearts and now you are beginning to create it right where you sit. And we tell you that you are honored beyond your understanding. You will be re-membered always, for you are the ones that made the choices and you are the rightful heirs to the throne of forever. And here you are this day, not asking, "How can I feel better?" but asking, "What can I do?" Again, can you see why we honor you so? Our greatest work is to spread our wings to reflect your magnificence. That is the purpose of our being. And you are now beginning to see a small glimpse of your own power.

The Internal Connection to God

The purpose of our being is to help you to connect to yourself. This is the connection to that part of yourself known as God that you have always seen as being outside of yourselves. In truth, your connection lies within. Those who cannot go within will go without. So find that little spark. Lean against it and trust it. It does not mean that you cannot seek counsel from others. It does not mean that you cannot listen to our words. It simply means *you* hold the ultimate power. You are the truth and you are the highest vibration that has ever existed on this planet. You have taken the Game to levels that even you did not think possible when you first created the Gameboard. You are not a part of God. You are not a little spark of God. Each one of you contains the whole of God within yourselves. Now do you understand our excitement?

The Dawn of the New light

We tell you there are some very exciting events taking place on Planet Earth right now because of the advancements you have made. The Crystal Energy from the central sun has been triggering events here on your planet. This you have seen as the events of your own sun. Your Gameboard has been changing and storing energy in the tectonic plates of the Earth. As this energy is being assimilated, you are beginning to see the Dawn of the New light. You have yet to fully understand light. You think of light as particle waves. You have not even decided if it is particles or waves.

The New light that is forming is not coming from without, it is coming from within. It is the Light from the Central Sun and it is being reflected from the inside out. It is not just coming from within your own heart; it is a reflection from within the Mother Herself.

Seven Seconds to the New light

You now have the opportunity to view everything in this New light. The challenge is that you get so busy with your daily lives that you are unaccustomed to looking for it. The key is to pause for seven seconds. 1 - 2 - 3 - 4 - 5 - 6 - 7 - like that. If someone says something to you and you wish to see a circumstance in a New light, pause for seven seconds, then make your assessment of what was said. If you are viewing the sun rising over the mountains, pause for seven seconds and see the colors that were not there before. You have senses that you are not even aware of and this New light will begin to show you what you have only had glimpses of thus far in your evolution. The Crystal Energy entering from the Central Sun is reflected as it enters our reality. This you can perceive with your metaphysical and physical senses. We are describing it in more detail here because in the near future many more of you will begin to see this new light. This is the light that connects the inter-dimensional time portals.

Falling Through Time Portals

What you are seeing is a connection of the hallways you have never seen before. In the months and days ahead, it will actually be possible for you to accidentally fall into these time portals. That will be very interesting, for you will find that all of a sudden you will have lost three hours or you may find that it is an hour earlier than you thought, or you are in a completely different location than you were expecting to be. You may also find this phenomenon interacting with inanimate objects. Possessions will disappear and reappear without warning or reason.

Please do not overreact to this. Do not try to make something mysterious out of this for it is not important at this stage, it is the excitement of the possibilities that you are gleaning from this. This is the beginning of the 5th dimensional expression in your reality. The dimensions of Time and Space are now added unto Height, Width and Depth to create a 5th dimensional reality. You are unaccustomed to interacting with Time and Space, yet these will be your first interactions.

Much is coming. But you must learn to release the drama around these changes as drama can hold you back more than you know. Drama is one possibility that would actually allow you to take the wonderful messages carried within these changes and negate them. Stand firm in who you are. Hold firm in your own lessons and your own love of self. That is the love of God. That is the trueness of your own being. That is who you are.

Hold your light high and proud. . . then there will be no shadows.

Gifts of New Sight

Because you have stepped into the 5th dimension and are now interacting with Time and Space, new physical abilities will soon emerge. The first of these will be in the area of sight. Subtle energy fields that have never before been visible to the human eye are now beginning to be seen. Those of you who have seen auras as energy fields around a person will now find it is possible to see these in a different way. Those of you who have never witnessed this phenomenon may now find it becoming visible.

Now you will start getting glimpses of what is to come. So start looking in the dark and you will see energy fields that have not been visible to you before. They may be faint and lacking the color that you love so, but we tell you these are the first glimpses of the Dawn of the New light which is coming to each and every one of you.

A Connection to Inter-dimensional Realities

It is this light that will allow you to interact with the thousands of inter-dimensional realities that exist on your own Planet Earth. You hold your finger up in the air and you believe that since you perceive it with your eyes, there is nothing in the space that exists between your finger and your eye. We tell you there are

A Universe between my finger and my eye.

– Phyllis Brooks

whole worlds that exist within this magical space. You reached to outer space and built spaceships and wondrous telescopes that allow you to see light years ahead. As you will soon discover, none of this holds a candle to what exists within this tiny but vast space between your finger and your eye.

Because of the New light coming through the Mother, you will soon be seeing even more phenomena. Even the shadowy figures that you have seen out of the corner of your eye may become clearer in this Light. If you are able to hold your peripheral vision and examine them for a little longer, you will begin to see small energy fields around them. This energy, which emanates from the inside of the body outward, is the true nature of auras. Those of you who have not been able to perceive it will now begin to see the New light.

Yellow – Amber – Gold

When you do see these fields, you will see your own dimensions connecting with others. Look in the dark, dear ones. Watch. Not just for the beings in the room, but also each other, for you will now begin to see small energy trails that outline your own physical beings. This is the Dawn of the New light. It will not stop here, however. This is only the beginning. You will soon be seeing color ranges in your new 5th dimensional realities that you have no explanation for. Your limited range of color vision is expanding. You are evolving to the next stage as you begin interacting in the 5th dimension.

You will find that if you stop for seven seconds and breathe when you walk outside, you will see the most beautiful glow of a New light emanating, not just from the sun, but from the Earth Herself. This is the Aura of the Earth, radiating with the new Crystal Energy. It will be a little different than what you have been accustomed to. As you view it in sunlight, this New light may appear to be the most beautiful combination of Yellow, Amber and Gold. This is the color of the twelfth ray where the colors blend together and pass through all inter-dimensional realities. This is the signal that the New Planet Earth has begun. The band of Light that spans the range of Yellow, Amber and Gold which is known as the Golden Flame, will be the hallmark of the New Energy. When you first begin to discern the New light it will radiate to the heart of your very being. You will see it in direct sunlight and you will see it in the shade. And you will even learn to see it in dark rooms, for it is not coming from the sun. It is being reflected from the very heart of Mother Earth Herself.

All color ranges will begin to expand. Your perceptual ranges are changing even now. Your sensitivity to your own surroundings will shift very drastically. Keep your balance during this time and keep watching with the excitement of a child.

Your Real Work

So often we hear you say the words: "I know that I am leaving my work. I know this is no longer a match for me. I know that I am of a higher vibration than what I am doing on a daily basis and I am frustrated. What am I to do? Where am I to go? What is this about?" We tell you that you will not be kept waiting for too long. We also ask you to release your own visions of what you think this work is. Some of the grandest contracts can be completed - and some of the most wonderful work has been completed - with just a smile at a passerby on the street. Often, grand chains of events are set into motion with a simple smile. You may find yourself in a grocery store and turn to smile at a person behind you. You may never know that this person is having a very difficult day, trying to decide where their life is going.

That one well-placed smile may make all the difference. In that smile you will carry all the attributes of the New light.

Keep in mind that you are sitting at the front of the class. You are the chosen ones. You are the marked generation and you are the ones who will first carry this New light. This is the reason we love the title of Lightworker. As you look into the eyes of each other, offer your Light with unconditional love. Smile, wait seven seconds, and you will intuitively know if the Light was received.

An Unexpected Audience

We have adjusted the energy in this room four times since you have been here. It was to adjust your inter-dimensional reality to accept the overseers that have requested to watch as you gather here now. We tell you that all eyes are upon you. Ahh.. and you thought we were kidding. Do not be in fear of this, but know that those eyes support you. Know that you are never alone. In fact, they have a very important part to play, for they are part of you and you are part of them. Unity consciousness is not limited to one race of beings, dear ones. In fact, the choices you are now making will redefine the Games in many other inter-dimensional realities as well. The fact that it took four separate adjustments to the energy in this room simply indicates that you are not the only ones who experience 'parking' problems.

Lighting the Way for Others

The days ahead may be somewhat confusing for many. You will see many people go into fear. Darkness will emerge. Your first inclination will be to view this as negative. We ask you to change your perception and understand that this is a wonderful opportunity for you to shine *your* light. Choose your reality well, dear ones. You have no choice of what thoughts flow through your head, for you are part of a universal, subconscious mind and those thoughts flow through your head on a regular basis. But you *do* have choice as to which thoughts remains there. Become masters of your thoughts. Choose well, and choose only that which feeds you. Do not be afraid to reach for a higher truth.

This is a magical time on Planet Earth. There are times when alternate realities cross one another and leave permanent imprints. You are at such a juncture now. Look for the Yellow, Amber and Gold. This is only the beginning of the new ranges of light that you will soon begin perceiving. Even the lack of light you know as darkness will now begin to take on a new beauty. As with all forms of light, you have two choices. You can either be the source of the light or you can reflect it. An example of this would be two people, one writes a book and the other awakens others to its presence.

Use the Light of the Twelfth Ray in your healing work. If you are not able to perceive it physically, reflect it. You do not need to be an energy worker to do this. Some of you will do it standing in line at the grocery store counter. Some of you will do it at the hairdressers. Some of you will do it as mechanics. However you do it, just re-member, you are the purveyors of the New light.

It is our greatest honor to be in your presence. Our love for you extends beyond your words. We bow at your feet for we truly see that we are in the presence of the masters. You have chosen to stand behind the veils of forgetfulness and leave behind that which is so precious to you. But now and then you feel it and you become so lonely to experience that grand re-union again. We tell you, dear ones, you are creating it right where you sit. Step forward and welcome the new light. Fear not your own power. Reach out and touch one another. Dare to be Human Angels. Dare to be the purveyors of the new dawn.

We are so very honored to be with you this day. You have created possibilities in your own being of the creation of Home here on Earth. It is with the greatest of honor that we ask you to please treat each other with respect. Empower and nurture one another. Play well together. And so it is. . .
the Group

The Group said in this channel that what we are experiencing is the Dawn of the New light and that the color range between yellow amber and gold is the color band of the twelfth ray. This is the light that is formed when the rays blend together and span the boundaries of all realities. This is the first physical signal that the Crystal Energy has been activated in our world. We will see much more of this unique form of Light and its uses in the time ahead. After this channel, the Group did not mention the New light again for several months. Then, at the second ESPAVO conference at Mt Shasta, CA., they really surprised me. The Espavo conference began the day after the Twin Towers were attacked. We were all in shock at the events unfolding on our planet. In the midst of the confusion surrounding us, the Group took this opportunity to tell me something personally.

Some time ago they shared with me the role I played in the Middle Ages. Apparently, I was a cross between a jeweler and a blacksmith. I made the most wonderfully ornate ceremonial swords and was well respected for my work. These swords were not made for battle, but rather, were made for the higher task of anointing those who were moving to their next level of vibration. In those days this was known as the act of knighting. I not only made the swords, I was also entrusted with their care when they were not in use. These were sacred swords of empowerment.

The Group says that I am now back doing the same work. I even have an Excalibur sword of my own that I have carried to many countries and used in ceremony to help people move to their next level. Because of this, the Group has always referred to me as 'The Keeper of the Sword'.

During their first channel at the Espavo conference they told me in front of everyone gathered in the meadow of creation that, henceforth, they were changing my title. They said that in the same way that the time has come for the world to put away weapons, so also had the time come for me to release the sword. Weapons no longer represent empowerment. Henceforth, all the tools we need are now available within us.

They still call me 'the Keeper', but now, as the collective vibration of the planet has risen, the nature of my work has shifted. I thought this was very nice but I really did not understand the meaning of it until I came to edit this chapter and saw the passage that says, "The band of Light that spans the range of Yellow, Amber and Gold is known as the Golden Flame."

That day in the meadow of creation the title the Group bestowed upon me was:

"The Keeper of the Flame."

Chapter 6

Reaching for Higher Truth

Higher Truths to Support Higher Vibrations

The Group and I have a deal. I want to know what we're going to talk about before the channels. This makes perfect sense to me because it is my responsibility to come up with the words. Things were really going fine with the channels until one day when the Group just wouldn't show me anything at all beforehand. I was quite concerned but I began the channel anyway. I knew they would never desert me in front of an audience. The moment I opened my mouth they apologized to me for not keeping their bargain. They said I had been overshadowed with grief and they had wanted to leave me to myself to work through that process. (My father had graduated just two weeks before.) After that incident I felt a lot more comfortable and trusting.

Then we presented our first channel at the United Nations in Vienna. The timing was such that we did not have sufficient time to get over the jet lag and once again, I was not given the topic beforehand. Here I was presenting for the very first time at the United Nations with absolutely no clue as to what we were going to talk about. Nervous hardly describes the emotion I was feeling. Needless to say, the channel went brilliantly.

Now that the Group and I have been working together such a long time, things have changed. They still show me things ahead of time but for a different reason. They say that I am one of the members of the Group and that we all have our own fields of expertise. Mine is presenting this information in a human language. There are many times when they plant seeds about complicated subjects that we will be talking about. Sometimes it is something that someone will say to me or show me ahead of time, and the Group simply says "Pay Attention".

This method of planting seeds beforehand was the case with the channel you are about to read. Here is what happened: I'm driving near my home and I see construction crews working diligently, replacing the school crossing signs. They're swapping the traditional yellow for a bright lime green colored sign. The Group tells me only to "Pay Attention". Now I'm really curious. It wasn't until later that month when I started to deliver the following channel that I understood what they had been showing me. This channel is about Truth being a process of evolution, rather than the constant that we think it to be. They were showing me that the yellow warning signs traditionally used to attract our attention were no longer effective. Now that we had evolved to a higher vibration we needed bright green to get our attention. In fact, in the U.S. we now have bright green fire engines and emergency vehicles too. I have since discovered that several other countries have made the same changes. We are learning that truth is fluid.

Greetings from Home

We are deeply honored to be with you at this time in your history. Your advances have already changed the paradigm of all that is. We are deeply honored to be here with these re-minders from Home. In this way it allows us to be a small part of the greatest event since what you call the Big Bang. You awaken each day and as you look around you see that everything seems the same as it was. From your perspective very little is moving and you may even feel stuck in your own advancement. We tell you that nothing could be further from the truth. It is only possible to view advancements from a perspective of hindsight. As seen from a larger perspective, these same advancements are occurring in the blink of an eye.

A Lesson in Communication

The magnetic grids of the Earth and the intersections of the ley lines were the original reason that different languages developed. Now the magnetics have diminished on your planet and this has enabled a blending of languages that emulates the melding effect of the Universal Energy. However, even as you are now using common languages, you will find that words will have different meanings in different places.

One truth does not fit all sizes. It is often the case that two people hold the same truth yet use different words to describe what they see. Both descriptions are accurate to the person describing them. Both people are standing in their own personal truth.

We tell you here that in your Game you have gone to war more than once, fighting over the use of words even when you had been envisioning the same truth. It is not the truth that has caused the problem. It is the fact that you all stick so rigidly to the meanings you attach to the words you use. Find words that leave room for evolution and your words will match your higher truth.

Collective Truth vs Personal Power

In the lower vibrations from which you are now emerging Truth was a standard. Your existence as the finite expression of God is activated by the search for Truth. It is only in the mirror of Truth that one can see the divinity within. In the experience of the Game, you examined all things that entered your field, constantly searching for common threads of knowledge that could apply to all situations. Once found, you labeled this knowledge as Truth.

In the lower vibrations of the past, concepts that were passed down from generation to generation were mandated blindly as truth. This was necessary, for it was the only manner in which Truth could be assimilated in the lower vibrations of the 3rd dimension. In those lower vibrations, there were two attributes that constituted a Truth: Knowledge had to apply in all situations and also had to be supported by the majority of the collective.

With your ascension into the 5th dimension, the rules are changing. Now you get to examine truth individually, rather than collectively, and in so doing personal power is returning to the Gameboard of Free Choice.

Truth as an Evolution

In the old energy, truth was a standard. Once a sufficient number believed something to be true it was unquestioningly accepted and then perpetuated. In those days the greatest gift you could pass to your children was to teach them your truth. Laws were enacted and enforced, and schools and religions were formed to make sure that everyone had access to the same truth.

Today, truth is an evolution. Thus the greatest gift you can give your children is to teach them to reach for their own highest truth, even if it is different than your own.

For example, in the days of your grandparents and beyond, there was but one paradigm for raising children. "Spare the rod and spoil the child". As difficult as this may be for you to understand, this was appropriate because it actually worked in the lower vibrations of that old energy society. Today you have evolved. Now you have laws against such behavior as it no longer works for you in the higher vibrations. Changes that once took generations to accomplish are now happening in the blink of an eye.
Many of you are finding that even the truths you embraced a few months ago no longer have the same meaning.

There is only one truth that never changes. This is the truth that is held deep within each of your hearts - the truth of Love. If you will measure all truths against this base energy, life will be easier in the 5th dimension. The feelings that you hold deep within your being will always define your truth in areas where words cannot. It is for this reason that we always ask you to employ the use of higher vibrational tools, such as discernment, in place of judgment. Discernment is the act of making life choices based primarily on the measure of Love in your heart. Where there is Love there is no room for judgment.

Releasing is the Key

The key to advancement lies in your ability to release truths that are no longer serving you. This can be difficult, for humans resist change. There are aboriginal healers among you who came in early to plant the seeds of Light long before it was popular to do so. They faced great difficulties in their work and yet they did it well. Now those seeds of Light have grown and a higher vibration has been attained. But it is difficult for some of them to release the truths that were once so important to them. It is no wonder that many of these dear souls feel abandoned, stuck and unsupported. They have been caught in an endless loop. An example of this is a person who still believes that they cannot attain spirituality unless they meditate a prescribed length of time each day. You humans love the mystique of your rituals. Many of your practices no longer serve you. Some even separate you from your true power. And yet, even though this is the cause of your frustration, still you refuse to release them and move on. Rituals can be useful in helping you to re-member your power. Even so, if you give your power to the ritual, believing it to be the key, it creates a spiritual segregation that keeps you from seeing yourself as the creator. To put it another way; rituals can be used to focus your intent but they are not essential to the outcome. Releasing your attachments to old belief systems is the key to holding your power within instead of continuing to place it outside.

Flow of Universal Energy

The basis of our information is all about learning to move in a manner that emulates the flow of Universal Energy. The Universal Flow of Energy is always seeking balance through blending. Make space for the blending through change in your lives, and you will place yourself in the Universal Flow. Resist it, and you will be opposed at every attempt to move forward. In your field of polarity, you see yourselves as separate. You are not. In fact, you are all one and connected to all. The Universal Flow of Energy is in motion to accomplish that Unity.

When you agreed to play the Game behind the veil, you hid from yourselves your connection to your higher source. From that higher perspective it is possible to see when you are in the flow of Universal Energy and when you place yourself in opposition to it. Learning to connect with your own Higher Self and walking with that power will soon enable each one of you to re-gain that vision. For now, we will offer you some practical ideas on how to sense that flow of energy.

Indicators of Alignment

The circumstances in your daily lives are usually the first indicator of your relationship to the Universal Energy Flow. If your daily life is fulfilling and you are able to experience at least a minimum of joy and passion, this indicates some alignment to the Universal Flow. An effortless, synchronistic life-style is an indication of full alignment to the Universal Energy. People in your field are often indicators to your alignment. There are times when they act in a way that makes no sense to you. Perhaps they even attack you without provocation. This in itself is not an indication of your alignment, for there are times when you are simply a player in another's drama. It is, however, your reaction to these situations that is an accurate reflection of your alignment to the Universal Energy. If your reaction is balanced and centered it indicates alignment.

Your biology is also an indicator of alignment to the Universal Energy Flow. Restrictions and misdirections of energy will eventually show in your biology. These misdirections of energy are the origin of what you call dis-ease. In the lower vibrations of humanity it was entirely possible to place yourself against the Universal Energy Flow for very long periods without consequences. Now, as you move into higher vibrations, your own biology will react much more quickly and more harshly to energy rubs than before. In the 5th dimension, it is no longer physically possible to be against the flow of Universal Energy.

View from the Top

Perception also dictates the view of a truth. Those hanging on to old ideals are moving through life walking backwards. They can only see what is behind them. This has worked quite well in the lower vibrations of humanity, yet now the same actions that brought success and support are clearly misdirections of energy and most often prevent people from moving forward. Such is the case with oppressed peoples and the governments that continue to oppress them. You will see this type of action continuing until these oppressed peoples become fully responsible for their own choices.

Changing the point from which you view something changes the reality. You have much more control over your environment than you can see at this time. Set your intent to view everything from its highest perspective. Develop good habits of first perception. Seek a daily attitude that will allow all energy to find its own balance and blend naturally of its own accord. See yourself as being the player in the Grand Game and allow yourself to enjoy every move on the Gameboard. Each move you make in this Grand Game is the equivalent of a choice. Your expression of the Universal Energy is in the choices you make in every moment. Much the same way that we tell you there are no *wrong* moves on the Gameboard, so it is that there are no *wrong* choices.

Accepting Responsibility for Truth

At this time you are being presented with opportunities for advancement such that you have never before seen. You have shifted vast amounts of energy. For this work we love you dearly. Now it is time to step into your own empowerment. You must understand that the opportunities that now lie before you also come with responsibility. Do you understand that there is only one person who is responsible for creating your experience? Likewise, it is also your responsibility to balance your daily life as you move from the 3rd into the 5th dimension. If your choices are not bringing you the experiences you desire, it is fully <u>your</u> responsibility to choose again. This may sound simple, yet your natural resistance to change would have you stay in life circumstances that do not serve you.

The higher vibrations bring many new and wondrous gifts for the creation of Heaven on Earth. At the same time, the higher vibrations will no longer support life circumstances that do not feed you. In the lower vibrations that existed until a short time ago, it was quite possible to endure a job that did not sustain you, or a relationship that you were not passionate about. That is no longer an option. In the higher vibrations of the New Planet Earth, your success will be directly proportional to the amount of joy and passion you experience on a daily basis. Incorporating joy and passion into your life is your responsibility. You owe it to yourself and to others on the Gameboard to be vibrating at your highest possible level.

It is our deepest honor to present this information to you. Please understand that what we present is always for your own discernment and empowerment. Simply take what resonates within your own heart and leave the rest without judgment. What we present to you has no real value until you take these words and apply them to your experience. It is you that holds the true power. We are here only to help re-mind you that you are the creators. It is our highest honor to bring you these re-minders from Home as you reach for higher truths. It is with great love that we re-mind you to treat each other with respect, nurture one another and play well together. And so it is. . .

the Group

Chapter 7

-Triology-

The Others of E - vibration

Presented Live to
The Enlightenment Society,
United Nations Staff Recreation Council,
United Nations Headquarters, New York City, New York
March 23rd 2001

In March of 2001 Barbara and I presented a series of three different seminars on the East Coast of the United States. March 10th & 11th we presented the Lightworker Spiritual Reunion in Syracuse, New York. The next weekend on March 17th & 18th we presented the Quill of Re-membrance in Baltimore, Maryland. Then on March 23rd we presented to the United Nations Staff Recreation Council Enlightenment Society. For the first time ever, the Group embedded the same message into three different stories. They told me that this was VERY IMPORTANT and that I was not to worry about repeating the information.

The first channel was in Syracuse. Here they dropped the bombshell of this information in a story about Amor. The story of Amor is about a boy who grew up in the days of Mu and Atlantis. This will be a chapter in the 'ESPAVO the story of Amor' which will be released soon. In this channel the Group said the reason they were telling this story now was because, just three days prior, the first human had been cloned on Earth. The day after that seminar I got an e-mail from Michele Anatra Cordone with links to press releases that followed the Group's information by just one day. A group of Italian scientists had come forward to tell the world in a press conference that they were about to clone the first human being. According to the information from the Group reported 24 hours earlier, they already had cloned the first human being.

The second version of the same message was offered in Baltimore, Maryland where they told the story of "The Day that Time Stood Still". What you are about to read is the third message which was presented to the Enlightenment Society at the UN Headquarters in New York.

Greetings from Home, dear ones.

Many of you reserved your seat at this special gathering long ago. Now here you are, sitting in chairs that have been awaiting you for some time. Ahh, and what a special time this is. You have done well to get here. You have done well, indeed. Through your own choices you have made a difference, not only in your own reality on Planet Earth, but throughout all the cosmos. There are many here in this room at this time, and there are many more filtering in every moment, for all eyes are upon you. All eyes are watching your every move. Ahh, and what a grand time this is.

Just when you were beginning to get comfortable, The Game is changing. We tell you there are many more changes that you will face in the months that lie ahead. Please understand what we are now going to reveal to you. No one can foretell your future. That is not possible, for you have yet to write it. You are the ones in charge, not us. You are the ones who, through your choices, through your own free will, shall script the final outcome. We see your uneasiness at this. You are so accustomed to having your scripts laid out in front of you. You pass each other on the street and as you look into a stranger's eyes you know somewhere deep within your soul that there is something that connects you to this person. And then you wait for those scripts to unfold as you play the part that has been written. That is how your contracts have traditionally taken place. Now we tell you, things are going to be quite different.

For now, as you hold the quill firmly in your own hand and prepare to write, the ink you are about to write with is the ink of passion. Dare to dip your quill and scribe your highest expression of your passion. Now it is yours to script entirely your own destiny on Planet Earth, not only as a collective vibration, not only as a collective of governments, but as a collective of individual hearts. For what are you really as a collective but one single heart, and who are you responsible for in holding your own power other than yourself?

Find the love within that will help you to scribe the contracts that will take you through the next thousand years. Look into each other's eyes this day and see the love. Find the reflection in the mirror that shows you who you really are. Then, as you go back to work and sit at your desks, as you answer your telephones and type your e-mails, you will carry the seeds of light in all that you do. The Grand Game of Hide and Seek has been won and this is how it was accomplished.

You have asked about the event that you have termed ascension. We tell you that you are not going anywhere. You are staying here. With the quill held firmly in your own hand, it is yours to scribe the next events that will lead to the creation of Heaven on Earth. "Ahh, so what of the future?" you ask. Let us tell you a story. . . We love the stories. Let us tell you the story of Yalle and Yanne.

The Others -
The Story of Yalle and Yanne

Yalle was a strong woman in her mid-thirties, which, at a time when the average life-span was 350 years, was a mere infant. All her young life, Yalle had towered over her friends and co-workers. In her earlier years, her height and unusual looks had caused her much stress. She had even had to have special alterations made to her house to accommodate her unusual height. In addition to her height, Yalle was also very strong. Even though it came in handy to be so strong, this also made her feel different at a time when she was trying to fit in. Yalle had become accustomed to the remarks that people made about her. They were rarely spoken to her face but with her acute hearing she heard what people said. It hurt her to know what people were thinking. She often thought to herself that humans could be incredibly cruel. Perhaps if she had not been so sensitive the cruelty of Yalle's classmates may not have affected her. But Yalle was very sensitive to the emotions and energy of people within her field. Being empathic, Yalle also had the capability of seeing beyond the veil. With this special skill it was possible for her to see contracts and agreements that people had made before coming to this incarnation. Growing up, Yalle did not have anyone with whom she could share these gifts or confide in. Yalle had learned to turn within and draw in her energy in order to protect herself. It was difficult, but it was the only way that she could make life work for her. Yalle felt like she was alone on planet Earth.

At 35, Yalle's life had become a little more settled. She had work that required her to use her tremendous strength. Yalle felt good about this work because she could see the results of her labor. She enjoyed it because it gave her a sense of accomplishment, and even though it was very physical, that too gave Yalle a good feeling. Yalle worked 16-hour days in the crystal mines. She loved connecting with those crystals and she found there were ways that she could actually attract them to her. Yalle was known to her co-workers for her gifts in finding the clearest and most brilliant crystals.

Yalle worked with attendants who provided for all of her needs. As a worker she was taken care of so that she could focus all her efforts on her work. The attendants all respected Yalle and some of them even felt great compassion for her. Yalle loved her work because she knew how to communicate with the crystals. The crystals that came from this mine were often used as power transmitters and Yalle had a reputation for being able to locate the highest grade crystals that handled the largest volume of power. The crystals did not judge her, they did not care that she was different. They gave her a form of unconditional love and because of this she enjoyed her time at work.

Even with the love she and the crystals shared, Yalle was now finding that her work was not fulfilling for her. Yalle reached a point when her work was no longer fulfilling for her. She began feeling restricted, for miners had no say over these mundane circumstances. Yalle sought only to seek her own passion in what she was doing. She would go home at night and be with the others with whom she lived. And she would look around and say, "Is this all there is? Can there not be anything more for me? There must be more to life than the work that I am doing. Even though I am very good at what I do, I *know* I am here for something more". The others who lived with Yalle thought that she was being difficult. "We have it good here, they take good care of us and treat us well" they told her. But Yalle looked around and saw the people who lived in the village on the other side of town. She saw that they had children, and she saw they had mates and partners and families. And she yearned for that. Yalle knew she was different, but she also yearned for a life full of love and support. There was an emptiness inside Yalle that was beginning to grow. More than anything she wanted to share her life with another person. She felt like even the greatest accomplishments in her life were empty because there was no one with whom she would share them. She knew in her heart there had to be a special person waiting for her somewhere.

One day Yalle was at the mine communicating with the crystals. This was a good day and she soon found herself singing. The crystals responded by glowing more than usual. Although she worked a full 16-hour day without stopping, Yalle took a short break in the middle of the day and wandered to a different part of the mine. The attendants did not notice her missing right away, so she wandered for a time, enjoying doing nothing but simply exploring and letting her mind wander. Suddenly, Yalle heard a deep voice behind her that was strangely familiar. "Can I help you find your way? Are you lost, dear one?" Her heart leapt when she turned and saw standing before her a man who was even larger than herself. She felt weak at the knees and had to brace herself against the wall of the mine as she regained her composure. Before she could speak the man said: "My name is Yanne". As Yalle's eyes adjusted to the sight before her she looked into the eyes of Yanne and instantly knew that there was a contract here. Without saying a word, Yalle and Yanne made their way out of the mine and into the sunlight. Both knew there was a magic between them that did not require words. As Yanne showed Yalle the way back to her station of the mine they looked deeply into each other's eyes and, with only a few words, agreed to meet in this same place every day after work to explore this connection.

It was only a very short time, dear ones, until they fell deeply in love, for the contract that Yalle had sensed was indeed there, waiting to be enacted all along. Every day Yalle would do nothing but think of the time when she would see Yanne again. Each night when their work ended, they met and shared their hopes and their dreams. The time they spent together was very limited, but it was the highlight of their lives. They laughed, they sang, and they made the most beautiful love together. Returning to their individual abodes became more and more difficult as time went on. Soon, they found themselves staying longer, sometimes even well into the night. Yalle was the first to voice her feelings. "There is a pain in my chest that feels so good that even though it is painful I cannot wait to feel it again". Yanne said, "I too feel the strangeness of this love I have for you. We must find a way to be together always".

One day in the mine Yalle saw that she was being watched by her attendant who went by the name of CorleeAnn. CorleeAnn knew Yalle well and treated her with the utmost respect and compassion. Yalle knew there were rules that CorleeAnn had to abide by; rules that clearly did not support 'Others', like Yalle and Yanne, living together. Having children was forbidden to the Others. Yalle knew that CorleeAnn's job was to make sure she followed the rules. Still, this joyous pain in her chest was growing stronger every day.

On this particular day Yalle found that CorleeAnn was watching her even more closely. Finally, CorleeAnn approached her. "Yalle, this day I see you singing to the crystals in a new way. You have a radiance about you that is lighting up this dark mine. What is happening with you, Yalle? I am your attendant, but I am also your friend". Yalle looked up at CorleeAnn and smiled. The darkness of the mine began to diminish as the glow of the crystals chased away the shadows. Yalle was considering telling CorleeAnn of the love she had found. Even this brief thought of Yanne caused a reaction from the crystals still embedded within the walls of the mine. Yalle told CorleeAnn of the love she had found and even of the contract that she had discovered to carry Yanne's child.

CorleeAnn listened to the story with a deep sadness in her eyes. When it was her turn to speak she placed her hand on Yalle's back. Rubbing the back of Yalle's heart between her massive shoulder blades CorleeAnn said, "Yalle I know the love in your heart, for I too have this with my husband. Still, the law forbids 'Others' to take mates and to have children. I have been truly blessed with this work for I am able to make life a little better for the Others, and that makes my heart sing with joy. Still, with all the power that I have, I am not able to grant your wish to be with the one you love. I will tell you that this day marks the first time in my life that I feel a contradiction between who I am and what I do. I do not believe that the light I see in your heart is wrong, and I swear to you that I will do all I can to help change this. I will not report your activities, but I also do not see how I can help you". Even though it was physically difficult with their size difference, the two women hugged that day. Try as she might, CorleeAnn's arms did not reach all the way around Yalle's large body. As they hugged, Yalle felt the internal struggle now taking place within CorleeAnn. Yalle smiled and said, "Thank you, CorleeAnn, for treating me the way you do. There are many attendants who do not use their hearts, and I am truly grateful for having you in my life". As the two women went their separate ways a tear slid down CorleeAnn's cheek. Even though she knew it would be nearly impossible to change things, CorleeAnn resolved that day to dedicate her life and give voice to the injustice that was tearing at her heart.

The mine in Yalle's quadrant continued to glow everyday with the light of the crystals. Then one day Yalle surprised Yanne by asking if they could have a child. "Yalle, you are aware that we are forbidden to have children. It is written so. But I tell you, that you have given me strength beyond measure, and if there is a way I will find it". Yalle smiled and said, "We have a contract and there is a child waiting to come through. I feel her within my own self. Please tell me, Yanne, that it is possible to bring her through". With great sadness, Yanne repeated, "It is written that we are not to take mates or have children. You know our life span is limited, but if it is in my power, Yalle, I will find a way to give you all that your heart yearns for". Yalle was sad, for she knew that this subject had been debated many times before and had always been turned down by the council. Even so, Yanne talked to his attendant of their plight. He asked his advice in approaching the council. But, Yanne's attendant was not as trustworthy as CorleeAnn.

Over the next few days, Yalle and Yanne spent as much time as they could together, loving and dreaming of their future family life together. Then one night they were discovered in a loving embrace. Without a word Yanne was sent far away to another crystal mine. Because her production in the crystal mine was unsurpassed, Yalle was allowed to remain where she was. With a part of her now missing, Yalle's song was no longer heard in the mines. The glow on her face was quickly replaced by the dust of the mines. CorleeAnn spent a great deal of time petitioning the lawmakers to reconsider their views. She was not alone in her action, as this same sentiment was building among many of the attendants. At one point the attendants even banded together in an attempt to bring change to the land. They became united in their stand for the 'human' rights of the 'Others'. CorleeAnn was instrumental in leading this revolt, but sadly had little time to accomplish much before the end came.

At the end of each day, Yalle would return to the place where she and Yanne used to meet. They were able to keep the flame of their love alive, for they were never truly disconnected. The energy strand that connected them was with them always, and when either one of them got tired, when either one of them grew weak, when either one of them lost their way, they would reconnect to this energy. Even though they were separated by a great distance, their love remained alive. Although Yalle and Yanne had chosen to connect in a time and place that did not support their union, they went ahead anyway.

Yalle's greatest fear was that there would come a time when her tears would run dry and she would no longer feel the bittersweet pain of human emotion. That fear was never realized and, after many incarnations, this love is still alive today. By their courage, Yalle and Yanne fulfilled one of the greatest contracts of all of humanity. . .

Have you figured out where this is going, dear ones? There is a reason that we have told you this story. We tell you that this story is real. This has played itself out many times. No, we are not speaking of another planet; we are speaking of the Gameboard of Free Choice that which you call Planet Earth. This was a time long ago, in a time and space known as Atlantis. For in those days of Atlantis, you had what you call genetically engineered humans. Those people were specifically placed upon the Earth with guidelines and limitations which you imposed. These beings are the "Others of E-vibration" in a form of 'triology' that has been absent from your Game since the end times of Atlantis. That is the reason that the names Yanne and Yalle end with an 'E'. In triology you not only blended plant and animal you also blended technology. These are the "Others" that were the genetically engineered beings that you treated as less than human.

So why have we told you this story now?

Because the 'Others' and their 'Attendants' are now back on the planet.

Born March 7^{th,} 2001

We tell you now that on March 7^{th,} 2001 the first human was cloned in the New Energy on Planet Earth. The reason we are telling stories of Atlantis and Mu is that your advancement on the Gameboard of Free Choice has now placed you at the same vibrational level and exactly the same juncture that you were at back then. Now you will be faced with similar circumstances and you will be asked to make decisions concerning the same choices. This time, however, you have help.

Watch for the 'Others', dear ones. Many of them are standing on the sidelines, for they still do not feel like they belong. They feel like they are observers and not participants in life. Throughout many incarnations they agreed to carry the cellular memories of those times when they were treated as less than human. These 'energy imprints' are the origin of a recurring theme throughout your history of what you have called slaves. They are very gentle, sensitive souls who, time and again, have placed themselves in a brutal world to help balance the energy of humanity and to do things differently should the opportunity ever arise again. Their return was foretold in your biblical writings as the time when the Meek would inherit the Earth.

Humanity will soon be faced with some very difficult choices. Do not look to us to tell you that genetic engineering, or cloning, is right or wrong, for those labels are only illusions of polarity on the Gameboard. What we will tell you is that this is a natural progression of your technology and is being supported by your own spiritual advancement. We also tell you that the way things stand at this moment it is not a question of *if,* but rather, *when.* In fact, this has already taken place and it will continue.

Attempting to turn the other way would require humans purposely to forget, and that is not a possibility. Some of you will stick closely to your beliefs that this is not a natural way and, therefore, it is not appropriate for you to "play God". Yet we ask, if it were possible to make your children healthier by feeding them better food would that not be the same thing?   Are your children of recent days not taller and healthier than those of prior generations?   Is this not an improvement that you have made to your biology?   Has not your life-span increased exponentially because of advances in technology?   Fear it not, dear ones, for it is a part of you and a reflection of the creator within you.   These advances will also increase your understanding of human biology and will lead to the rejuvenation process that also existed in the days of Atlantis.

The veil is very thick and you cannot see your true nature through this veil.   If you see the grand creations of God, you can easily accept it as a gift of the divine.   If, however, you have a human hand in this creation process, you do not trust the entire creation.   Ahh, the veil is so thick that you cannot see that when you have a hand in the creation process, that too, is a divine creation.   If we were to pull the veil aside for a brief moment you might see the greatest secret of all.

There is a God and you are it!

Oh dear ones, we tell you that you are not a *part* of God.   *You are the whole of God.*   And the dear one that came on to this Earth for the first time on the 7th of March 2001 may not grow into adulthood. As it stands, you may not hear about this event for it is being hidden from the masses. Yet we tell you, it is only a matter of moments before the next human will be cloned on the New Planet Earth.   Re-member the misdirections of energy in the days of Atlantis, for it is not necessary for you to experience that again.   Please keep in mind that these misdirections were not made by evil or black forces.   They were caused by the choices made by humans facing the same tests and circumstances that confront you now.   That is the seed fear within yourselves that you have been resisting.   The time has come for you to face the fear and heal it forever.   This is what has kept you from moving into your own power.   But now the time has come.   And if you doubt yourself, if there are times when you cannot re-member who you are, look around the room. Look into each other's eyes. See the God within. Look to your heart first and then consult your head. See the reflection of yourself and re-member the love. And if you find yourself forgetting the story of Yanne and Yalle, they will be there to re-mind you, for that was their true contract and the contracts of the 'Others'. Many will now be coming forward to help take a stand. Find your own heart, dear ones. Speak your truth, educate yourself as to what is now occurring on Planet Earth, for it is your choice that will make a difference.

Biology and Technology ~ Technology and Biology

This is a magical time. We have been telling you for some time to watch for the blending of technology and biology. Now here it is and we tell you, do not fear it. This blend will also occur in the opposite direction as well. It will not be long before you see 'human' computers. They are not to be feared. They will do only what you ask them to do. Can you re-member only a few years ago when you first saw a computer? "What would I possibly use that for?" you asked. We tell you that the advances in technology that will take place within the next 10 years will make the introduction of the computer seem insignificant by comparison.

All of your advances in technology have been leading you toward a better communication, and therefore, to a better understanding that you are one with all things around you. All forms of communication have helped to change the world as you know it, and to place the true power back in the hands of the individual by returning the power of choice to them. This is not to be feared, but rather, should be celebrated. We tell you that technology can only exist on the planet as long as the spiritual vibration is high enough to support it. There have been many times when technology has been dropped onto your planet and has not been supported, for you did not have the collective spiritual vibration.

Are you surprised that you are here at precisely this moment in time? Do not be. We tell you that you have cashed in all your karma chips to be here at exactly this moment. Some of you are thinking that you may be one of the 'Others' that have returned. Many of you feel like you have a definite pull to what we have just shared with you. We tell you that it is not appropriate for us to reveal whether you are one of the 'Others', for that can only take your power from you. If you feel the pull, it is highly likely that you are one of the 'Others' or one of the 'Attendants' who have come back with a focus to carry the energy. That is why you have been drawn to this information.

You have placed yourself at the very front of the class and you have done so on purpose. We cannot wait to see what you choose next. We are so very proud of you, for you were not meant to be here even now. Yet, here you sit, listening to the story that you wrote. Choose well, dear ones, for in choice lies your true power.

Re-member, we are never far away. The veil is thinning as you continue to advance your collective vibration. You are literally closer to Heaven. And if you ever find that you are lost, if you ever find that you have forgotten who you are, if you ever look through the room and say, "Is this all there is?" find another and reach out. Take that hand and look into their eyes and there you will find us, for there is much help on this side of the veil. The entire angelic realm is waiting to wrap you in the wings of Home. They are there to help you every moment of every step of the way. Yet we cannot help from this side of the veil unless we are asked, for it is your free choice that makes the difference.

We tell you that the time has come on Planet Earth when there will be NO MORE SECRETS. Ahh. . . and we cannot wait to see how that works! Can you imagine the joy we will have in watching you as you begin to read each other's thoughts? Look into each other's hearts and share that energy well, and if you forget who you are, call on us. Understand that your power lies in choice, and if at any time you are not happy with your reality, have the courage to choose again.

Know that you have the answers within you. Reach for them and they will be there.

It is with the greatest of love that we ask you to treat each other with respect, to nurture one another, and play well together.

and so it is. . . the Group

In the first of the three channels at which the Group repeated this same message they said that there were three people in the room that were 'Others'. All three approached me shortly after the channel, two of whom were in tears. In Baltimore the Group once again said that there were four 'Others' present. In Eindhoven, Holland and Attleboro, Ma., questions about cloning were raised. Again the Group mentioned that there were 'Others' in the room. On every occasion, each of these people was deeply moved to find that there is an explanation as to why they have felt so separate from everyone else.

Please understand that the Group is not saying that cloning or genetic engineering is right or wrong. What they are saying is that it is here now and that nothing will stop it. Even if we make laws prohibiting it, they will be disregarded. The Group's entire purpose in giving us this information is to help educate us about the misdirections of energy that we made the last time we were at this same juncture.

In the story of Amor, which will appear in the book 'Espavo', the Group makes it clear that the lawmakers of Atlantis were only trying to do their best to preserve their way of life. At this time in Atlantis, major breakthroughs had just been made and advances in this technology were being incorporated. The leaders of Atlantis found themselves being overrun with people, as jobs and resources began to get scarce. Add to this the fact that there were a lot of people immigrating from what used to be Lemuria and it was easy to see how the infrastructure was being overrun. The leaders of Atlantis (us) attempted to address this problem by passing certain laws that inadvertently resulted in a three-tier class system. The Atlanteans, the Immigrants and the 'Others' were governed by different rules. Instead of helping to preserve the life-style of Atlantis, this in effect created a class of slaves. This was a huge unconscious misdirection of energy that, together with two other misdirections were eventually responsible for sinking Atlantis.

The Group told me after the first channel at Syracuse that I would be spending a lot of time helping the 'Others' to reconnect. With the help of several people who have come forward we are now providing a place on our web site www.lightworker.com for people to find out more information about the 'Others' and the advances in Triology. You can find an entire section about the advances in this area here: http://www.lightworker.com/triology/

York Daily Record, York PA. March 29th, 2001

The very first time the Group spoke about Triology was in Syracuse, New York, on March 11th 2001. Shortly after returning home we found this newspaper article in our mailbox.

The Group says that we already have. Later that same year (2001) at Drachten, Holland, the Group said there were now four genetically engineered (cloned) people here on Earth. It has begun.

Information is the key to making appropriate choices and we will provide this on our web site. We also provide a place for those who wish to connect and share information about how this knowledge applies in their lives. The 'Others' are not here just to have their say about cloning and genetic engineering, they are here to hold the vibration for all of us to learn to trust our creative abilities, and to listen to our hearts. They are here to help us make the New Planet Earth a place for gentle humans of all origin. Our history has shown how very cruel humans can be. These beautiful beings have been quietly holding the truth of who we can be and how we can incorporate this gentle energy into the higher vibrational experience of the New Planet Earth. They have much to teach us if we will only listen.

We're listening now.

Chapter 8

The Government of Mu

New Paradigms of Business and Government

United Nations V.I.C. Vienna Austria

**Presented Live to
The Esoteric Society,
United Nations V.I.C.Vienna, Austria
April 26th 2000**

The following channel was presented to the Esoteric Society at the United Nations in Vienna, Austria. In the audience were delegates, project managers, department heads, office managers, secretaries, as well as engineers and scientists from the Atomic Energy Agency. Directly following this presentation we gave what we believe is the first class on channeling ever presented at a United Nations facility.

The VIC Esoteric Society meets in the Vienna International Community which is an international city housing all parts of the United Nations. The members are primarily employees of the United Nations and many of its subsidiary organizations including UNIDO, (the United Nations Industrial Organization), The Atomic Energy Agency, (which oversees all atomic activity globally), UCBDO and several others. The VIC society hires presenters to speak at special meetings, and this was the second year that Barbara and I had been asked to present information and a live channel from the Group.

Upon arrival in Vienna, we went straight to the VIC. A we were actually entering the Vienna International Community and had to go through an extensive security check much like clearing customs. In effect, we were entering a country within a country. When the time came and the members began filtering into the room I was surprised to see so many familiar faces. To us it was a Spiritual family re-union with many people we re-membered from the previous year. It's great to see how many very important, powerful people are reaching for higher truths during these times. The gap between mainstream and metaphysics grows smaller.

The room soon filled and we began. The Group presented the beautiful message below. After the live channel and a short break we began the channeling exercises. We were delighted to find that most everyone connected in some way. The entire process took five hours, which represented a large commitment for those participating. We were very honored to be presenting this information.

This European tour in April/May 2000 lasted five weeks. During this time Barbara and I presented seven seminars, including two corporate ones. I love to bridge the gap between mainstream and metaphysics. If you had told me six years ago that I would be teaching a class on channeling at the United Nations I would have thought you were crazy. I guess the cosmic joke is on me! We are evolving into a higher form of humanity. This evolution includes all walks of life. It's a great time to be alive!

Greetings from Home.

As we look around the room we see brothers and sisters looking into each other's eyes. We see those of you in the room are very powerful beings, for you have changed your destiny on the Planet of Free Choice. Through your choices, through your connections, you have created a reality that resembles Home. We tell you, it is our greatest honor to be sitting in your presence, for we are here to re-flect your magnificence. We are here to hold the mirror up to you so that you may see who you really are. We are here to help you re-member. The room is now filling with the entourages that are your own guides and oversouls. We sit in your presence and we are honored to wash your feet, for you are the masters and we are here to help you re-member that. For you to take even the smallest amount of your power and use it to create your own reality is our highest dream. We are honored to be here with you as you now do exactly that.

Tonight we bring you information of great importance. There are some in this room who will carry this information to very important areas. We ask you not to judge yourself and think, no, it is not me, for my job is unimportant. We tell you if only you knew the difficulties we overcame to put you into this room at this moment. Even those of you who think you cannot make a difference are about to see for yourselves what a difference you can make. We see the pain in your eyes and the difficulties that you experience on the Gameboard. We tell you we love you for it, for what you are accomplishing would not be possible without the pain. Bless it and release it, and do not get comfortable with it, for that pain is a temporary situation. In the next few days many of you will be seeing a major influx of energy. Use it. Grab hold of this power and apply it in your life. Dare to create your highest reality. Dare to go after your passion. That is where you are of the highest use to yourself and to those around you. That is where you are of the highest use to the Universe.

The 'Government' of Mu

The information we bring this night is about the formation of groups that will bring back the greatest of governments that has ever visited the Planet of Free Choice. That was the government of Mu. In the days of what you called Lemuria, there was a system of government that made space for empowered humans and we tell you that it is making its way back to the planet as we speak. There are those of you in this room and those of you reading this who will act upon this information. There are those who will plant the seeds. Imagine a day when the governments of the world talk as one. Imagine a day when the religions of the world find harmony. Imagine a day when the hearts of mankind find balance through seeking their commonalities instead of searching for their differences. We tell you that day is at hand. Make space for this in your lives.

We challenge you now to create the organization necessary to make room for the blending of all the religions of the world, and you will see a re-emergence of the government of Mu.

The government that you call Lemuria is actually a form of non-government, for by its very nature it is self-regulating. Begin by applying the basic principles of empowerment. First, empower those around you. Learn to live with human empowerment as the rule and primary motivation of all organizations. Empower first yourself and have the courage to use your power. Walk forward into the life of your own choosing. Dare to create the best for yourself. Center your own energy by placing your needs first. Fill your cup first, then turn around and fill others. By doing this you will have much more to give to others. Start then to restructure the competition that has created the illusion of separateness in your reality. The economists of your world even now know that as one does well, all do well. As you have seen, when one economy dips, others do not rise. In reality, they all fall in sympathy. This is not competition. This is a common thread that connects you all, which will become stronger as you step into the next level of evolution.

The government of Mu had no laws. Free choice was always honored and it was balanced with the responsibility of cause and effect. If one were to cause an infringement upon another's choices, the effect would be swift and self-imposed. We tell you that when you inhabited Mu your vibrations were very high indeed. You held your power within, not without. Therefore, laws, as such, were not required. Instead, you relied on customs that were treated with the greatest respect and honor. All customs were focused on empowerment. Even though there were governors they were servants and not leaders. Collective power was not afforded the governors, they were trusted servants who watched the relationship to the Universal Energy in comparison to all actions within the land of Mu. There were no penalties other than extradition in only the most extreme cases. When there was infringement upon another's free choice, the perpetrator would ultimately decide the best way to reconcile the energy. Mu was a highly evolved spiritual society where it was not a right but an honored privilege to be in communion with the highest vibration of souls. Life in Mu was all about choice. You could choose to walk in your power or not. You are just now reaching a state in your evolution this time around that will begin to support the return to the ideals of Mu. We ask you to move slowly and to allow this transition to occur gently.

Start with Self First

Choose your state of mind carefully, for your own reality is also part of a collective. This is why we implore you to dare to create the highest, most generous reality that you can. As you take responsibility for your own joy, feel the vibrations of Home spread to others around you. This will spread to your organizations, businesses and governments of the New Planet Earth. Feel the love of Mu that is your birthright, and you will feel the power that has been yours all along. Then we ask you to find ways of utilizing the power. Use it first to create the things that you wish to have in your lives that make life easier for you, for it is your right to be comfortable on the planet. Treat yourself as if the highest of masters were coming to visit you. Would you not afford them your best linen? Would you not set a place for them with the finest china and feed them only the finest foods? We tell you that you *are* that master. Treat yourself with that respect and all will fall into place around you. Set your own tone intentionally through these actions and watch the magic begin. Treat yourself well, for only when you do, and only when you allow yourselves to become fully involved in your passion, can you re-flect the energy of Home to others around you.

The Shifting Energy

It is a wondrous time in which you live and we tell you there is much magic in the air. You will see it soon if you have not seen it already. The setbacks ahead will only serve to hasten a global understanding of Unity. Know that as the collective vibration rises, so also do *you all* rise. Even the economies of the world are all interconnecting as they emulate the Universal Energy. As one grows, they all grow. And as one expands, they all expand. This is the Universal Energy in action. Allow yourselves to be in a constant state of expansion, constantly reaching for the higher truths that help you expand. Take charge only of your own vibration and know that this action alone will leave your mark on everything around you. Then we ask you to do something that is very difficult, for we ask you then to accept the best as it is re-turned to you.

The organization of the days of Mu is making its way back now. Apply it on the smallest scales to begin with. Apply it in your home. Apply it in your schools. Apply it in your businesses. Apply it in all the relationships around you. Be comfortable with placing empowered people in your field.

Instead of seeing your differences, search for your similarities. Then give others the tools, and hold them responsible for finding their own empowerment — with love and temperance.

Know that *you* can make a difference. You may think: 'I am only one. I cannot make a difference, for my voice is not heard'. And we tell you, yes, it is. You are responsible *only* for your own, singular vibration and that is all. Choose your truth and stand firm, for that determines the center of your own energy.

A special time is at hand. Take the energy that is given to you. Take the gift and dare to use it. Dare to speak your deepest truth for that is how we speak to you. You ask to hear the voices. You ask to have open dialog with spirit. You ask to speak to your own guides. Then you cannot hear us when we speak to you, for you think you are making it all up. You think that this cannot be about me, and we tell you it is. We can only pull the veil aside for brief moments so that you can re-member. Yet there are times when all we can do is raise the hair on your arms and touch you in such a way that you think you may feel something, but then again, maybe not. We are here always. We are around you always. We are opening the doors just before you get there. We play a synchronistic part in your life-style. We are very honored that you have asked us here. We tell you we have never left. We are with you all. Your own guidance is very strong. Listen very carefully for it will lead you if you learn to hear through your own heart. Take that which you know in your heart to be truth and dare to speak your creations.

Re-union in Heaven

With the seeds of empowerment you will be building the days of Lemuria once again. We tell you that you are not the only ones in re-union. For as the circles of light on planet Earth connect with one another, so too is this happening in Heaven. As below – so above. All of the archangels are in a grand state of re-union. Even those who played a part in the Lucifer Experiment are re-uniting in heaven. You have made it possible through your choices on the Gameboard of Free Choice. For that we bow at your feet. Now can you begin to see your importance? Now can you see the effect you have? You look at yourselves as you pay your bills with no money. You look at yourselves as you struggle in your relationships and you say, is this all there is? And we tell you sometimes the lessons you learn through those struggles reach into dimensions that you do not comprehend, for you are creating realities with your choices which go far beyond your understanding.

Lemuria was a time that held great technologies on the planet, for the spiritual advancement that balanced the technology was also great. It is also the time when you were in your greatest joy. It is also the time that you walked in full connection with your higher selves, walking every step in unison with your full power.

The time directly ahead of you will bring new energy to the planet. Take it, for it is for you. Allow it to be part of your experience and have the courage to use it for your highest and most passionate being. Fear not how others react to this energy. In the midst of turmoil, allow yourself to create Home. We tell you Home is one of the most abundant things, for it is anything you wish it to be. Think you are Home and you are. Hold the thought of an ice cream cone and it is in front of you. Hold the thought for world peace and it happens.

It is our greatest honor to be reflecting your energy. All we ask you to do is breathe and let us open the doors for you, for you have done well. You have won the Game and now you are creating a new one. Create the highest and the best. Re-create Mu. Start with your own lives first, and then empower those around you, for this will create Heaven on Earth and return you to the days of Mu.

It is with the deepest and greatest honor that we ask you to treat each other with respect, for that is the respect of God. Nurture one another and empower each other. And above all, play well together.

and so it is. . .

the Group

Chapter 9

Responsibility, the Balance of Power

Enhancing Personal Power

Esoteric Society, Vienna International Community, Austria

Presented Live to
The Esoteric Society,
United Nations V.I.C.Vienna, Austria
May 2nd 2001

Greetings from Home.

Ahh, yes. We look around the room and we see familiar faces. But more importantly, we see family. And as you look around this room and you see yourselves in the eyes of others, that is the important sight for that is the part of you that re-connects you to your own power. That is the part of you that you will take when you leave this day. You are becoming the Human Angels in the creation of Heaven on Earth. The process has begun already.

In this moment we will shift the energy in the room. And we will tell you a secret. In the short time that you are together here, and the short time that you are in this energy, you will not age. [Reaction from the audience.] Ahh, you like that. In the short time that you are in this energy together, we will share with you the vibration of Home. Take a deep breath, dear ones. Breathe it in and accept it into your body. That is a part of you that you have forgotten. You have agreed to come in and place one foot in front of the other without knowing where you are going and not being able to re-member who you are, and we honor you so much. You sit in our presence; you read the material the Keeper has put out in the form of these books. You read the meditations and the messages on the internet. And you honor us. And we tell you; it is *we* that are honored to sit in *your* presence, for you are the ones that had the courage to forget who you are as you left behind your own heritage and the re-membrance of your own power.

The Choice of the Chosen Ones

There are many of you in this room who are here for the first time, but we tell you, your names reserved your spaces long before you got here. We thank you for listening. Find one thing that you can take from our time together and apply it in your own life as you leave here. Find one thing that can make your life a little better. That is the secret of the Universe and the secret of re-membering your power.

You are at a very special crossroads. You are the anointed ones. There are many of you here in this room that were also in Atlantis. Many of you have awakened to come back to do it differently this time. And here you are.

Your relationship to time is changing as you feel the energy shift. The energy that has been released from the sun over the last month has set in motion many new events on Planet Earth. In the months ahead you will have an opportunity to step into your power more fully than you imagined. It is an opportunity for you to re-member and re-claim your own heritage and the birthright of your true power. You are so accustomed to giving the power to your leaders. You are so accustomed to giving the power to your teachers, your spiritual mentors, even to us. But those days are coming to a close for it is no longer appropriate for you to give your power to leaders. It is no longer appropriate to give your power to *anyone* or *anything.*

Do you choose the creation of Heaven on Earth? Do you wish to change your reality to something more to your liking? You have that opportunity now. This is the gift your sun has set into motion for you. Even now, its energy is being stored in the tectonic plates, for the Earth, too, is going through Her own evolution.

Tools of Empowerment

We tell you one more secret today that is very important. For in the shifting of the Planet Earth you have created the new energy. In this New Energy there are tools that can help you hold and utilize your true power. It is these tools that can so easily allow you to create the passion in your life and to see that passion on a daily basis. Here we will offer you two important tools to use on the New Planet Earth. So many of you are wrapped up with your own daily lives that you do not take time for *you.* The art of be-ing has been largely neglected on your planet. If we told you that you were God. If we told you that you were not a part of God, but each one of you were the whole of

God, would you then take five minutes for yourself? Treat
yourself in such fashion for it is the truth. In taking time for you
and just be-ing you are honoring God in the highest. When you
all treat yourself first and dare to have that which resonates in
your own heart, it is then that you create Home. That is when
you bring the vibrations of Heaven to Earth.

Some of you are being touched by angels even as we speak.
Just breathe in the energy, dear ones. We know that you are so
busy placing one foot in front of the other with so many tasks to
do, that you do not take that five minutes. This time is for you to
just *be*. Breathe it in and you will re-claim the direction of your
own daily lives. You will once again hold the power and create
the reality which supports you fully. Have the courage to
improve your own quality of life by allowing time to *be*.

Ahh, but what is this second illustrious tool? What is this elusive
magic that we can give you in one stroke of the pen to help
people understand how to connect to their power? Power
without balance is useless. When you get into your egos and
your entire energy is puffed up, there is no balance and without
balance there is no power. There is only one way to balance the
power and that is with personal responsibility. How do you claim
responsibility? There is only one thing that you are responsible
for. That is your own happiness. We have told you time and
again: You are in charge of your reality. Your choices are the
gifts that you have given yourself from the beginning of the
Game. You are the chosen ones and you have asked to be
here. Your choices have led you to a time of enhanced creation.

Does it matter what the leader of this country does? Yes, of
course, it does. But how is it going to affect you? That is truly
your choice. You ask, "Is it appropriate to give my power away in
any fashion?" No, it is not. And yet we understand that you
have been doing it for so long that old habits die hard. You look
to us for answers. "Tell us which way to turn, tell us which way
to look and what to watch for", you say. Some of you come to us
to hear these very things. Often we speak in general terms so

as not to take your power from you. All the time you know those answers in your own heart, you simply are not accustomed to trusting yourself. Ahh, but the veil is thick. It is so much easier to see magnificence in others than it is to see it in yourself. So how do you begin to see it in yourself? You do that by taking personal responsibility for your own happiness. Dare to do one thing this next week that will improve your quality of life in some small way.

"Ahh, but I am not worthy," you say. Or, "But if I do that, how does that help others? How can I change the world if I am doing something for myself?" Ingrained deeply within your own cellular memories is the belief that you must suffer to achieve a higher vibration. That truth was appropriate in the lower vibrations of who you were but it no longer has the same effect. Choose first that which feeds your own heart. Choose that which creates your highest reality and if you are not happy in your reality, have the courage to choose again.

Aligning the Energy of Home

We know these are only words. We know that it is so difficult for you to apply these principles as you peer into your reality from behind the veils that you have built so well. If we could only remove the veils for a short time, you would see who you are. We cannot remove the veil, for that would take away your power. So instead, we offer you these short interludes to help re-mind you of what it feels like to be Home. Breathe it in, dear ones, for as we fill this room, the vibrations of Home are here around you now. We have taken our wings and touched each and every one of you here in this room. Fear not, for it is your own heart you are feeling. There is nothing that we are doing to you. We are simply creating the space and you are choosing to walk into it, and in that choice you are creating Home on your side of the veil. In that choice you are changing All That Is. Choose for yourselves and all will fall comfortably in rightful order. Be responsible for yourselves and your power will increase.

If you are ever feeling drained, it is because you are taking responsibility for others. Even though you may do so out of an honest desire to help, in reality you are taking their power from them. It is not yours to take responsibility for your mate, for your boss or for those working under your care. As a facilitator, it is not yours to take responsibility for those who come to you for healing. It is not yours to take responsibility for your children. Rather, teach them how to take responsibility for themselves by taking responsibility for yourselves first. Align the energy in this fashion and you will walk with a balance that will be evident in everything you do. Then you will carry the vibrations of Home every time you flash your smile and every time you walk into a room. The energy will emanate from your own heart and it will change the world.

Dealing with the Memories of Home

You are with us in these short times together. And as we share the memories of Home the tears come to your eyes for you re-member that which you are longing for. You are only able to play the Game because you have forgotten the longing of Home. Yes, there are some of you who are tired. Yes, there are some of you who will be leaving. There are some of you who wish to go Home. We tell you, when that time comes, the choice is yours for we will welcome you with open arms. The joy that you will feel when you all enter the great hall of honor, the applause that will ring out for you, will resound for eons. The applause will be for you who have dared to play the Game behind the veil of forgetfulness. The echoes of the cheers that will resound will last forever in your own cellular memories, for you have chosen to be here at exactly this time. And if you choose to stay, we will walk beside you when you allow, with gentle re-minders of the vibrations of Home. The lives you touch with those vibrations will reach far beyond your understanding. You are the Family of Light and you will remind others in the same way that we are now reminding you. Be proud of your heritage for you are becoming the Human Angels that will walk the New Planet Earth

Be responsible for carrying the vibrations of Home in all that you do. Be responsible for following your heart's desire, for only when you do will you be touched by the angels. The touch of an angel is something that you all can look forward to. But know that the touch of an angel comes with responsibility. It comes with the responsibility to pass it on to others. Work together to Re-member Home, and Heaven will come to Earth. Then you will long for it no more. We see the tears, we understand that you miss Home. Know that we miss you as well and that we will play together again. That is our promise to you. For try as you might, you cannot separate yourself from Home. You are a part of us and we are a part of you and we thank you for the time that you have allowed us to reflect for you a re-membrance of Home.

Claim responsibility for your own power and your own happiness for this will increase your power. That is the most courageous gift that you can give to the entire Universe. Those around you will applaud you for taking such actions, for they take the greatest of courage sometimes. There are four of you here in this room now, who have made great shifts in your lives in the past six months. We applaud you. We applaud you. We applaud you.

Have the courage, dear ones, to reach for your own passion. Balance your responsibility first and then find your power. And if you ever forget who you are, if you ever forget why you are here, we will touch you with the touch of the angels, for we are here to re-mind you. It is with the greatest of honor that we ask you to treat each other with respect. Nurture and empower one another and play well together.

And so it is.

the Group

Chapter 10

The Five Traditions
of Abundance

Stepping into the New Energy

Lightworkers all over the globe are redefining their relation ship to the world around them. Redefining our relationship to Abundance is an area of healing in which it is becoming critical for us to do our work on the New Planet Earth.

Greetings from Home

The creation of the New Earth is at hand. We tell you that this brings us joy beyond your understanding. It is important to know that in creating Home in the reality that you call Earth, it is necessary to re-member and re-create *all* of the attributes of Home. When you are Home you want for no-thing. Home is even more abundant than you can imagine. Here at Home there is no lack. The illusions of polarity are what cause you to see everything as separate when, in fact, everything is connected. It is this same illusion that causes you to experience lack. In the very moment that your mind sees limitation, it creates it. The time lag of creation is now growing much shorter. In the higher vibrations of the New Planet Earth you are the creators and your creations are now manifesting much quicker than ever before. We wish to share with you some of the illusions that have kept you running around in circles since the beginning of the Game.

Abundance: More than is minimally required

Our definition of Abundance is simply an overflow of energy in any given area. In the 5th dimension, the art of co-creation is replaced with abundant living. Abundance is defined as creating more than is minimally required. This does not mean greed, for abundance only exists where a flow of energy is present. Greed stops the natural flow of energy. Please understand that spirituality is not measured by abundance. In the lower vibrations of your Game it was thought that materialism was the opposite of spirituality. In times past it was thought necessary for one to take vows of poverty to achieve spiritual advancement. Please understand that in the lower vibrations this was truth. Now that you have moved into the 5th dimension, those attributes have changed. Living an abundant life style is contagious. When everyone is affected, you will have created Home or Heaven on Earth. There is no more abundant place than Home.

Keeping Score with Karma

The manner in which you devised the Game has included a medium of exchange. In the beginning of the Grand Game you understood that in finite form it was necessary to keep score of the Game in some way. This is what you know today to be karma. All events had an effect on the total karma, either adding to it or detracting from it. Karma was a self-regulating system that was used on many levels.

Once you stepped into the higher vibrational levels of existence, your score-keeping system needed adjustment. Thus, the long-term karma issues that have traveled with you from one lifetime to the next have now been cleared. Even long term karmic ties and group karma has now been released as a result of your own advancement as a collective of humanity. Many believe that karma is no longer in use, yet we tell you that, as with your own existence, it has been redefined. Even though the long-term karmic control has been released, it is still very possible to create balances in both a positive and negative manner. With the new energy, you will most likely choose to call it cause and effect. The difference is that now the reaction is much quicker. It no longer takes lifetimes to come face to face with the reaction to your actions. Now that you are seeing the reaction much more quickly, you will learn more about the system and how to use it to your advantage in the creation of Home on your side of the veil.

As ethereal beings, you used the system of karma and were aware of it but not involved with the actual mechanics of keeping score. After the Earth cooled and you began the phase of the Game in which you took on dense physical bodies, you began to devise mediums of exchange that represented karma in a denser form. In the dense form, one of the first mediums of exchange you used was a form of Crystal Energy that you know as salt.

Keeping Score with Money

What you have called money is not energy. It is simply a *reflection* of energy, and that is the key. Though money is accurately reflecting your energy, it is possible to manipulate the reflection whereas it is not possible to divert the energy. Energy always travels in a circular motion, yet the reflection of energy does not necessarily have to travel in that manner and therefore alternatives are possible. Please do not use your relationship with money as a measure of your advancement as humans. It is your attitude, or belief systems, in relationship to money that will influence how money flows through your life. When you are truly open to receiving, the money [energy] will start to flow unimpeded. In the higher vibrations of the new Planet Earth, stepping into your passion and joy will automatically attract abundance to you. Does that surprise you? Many of you are thinking right now, "That has not been my experience so far". Ahhh . . . and why do you think that is? It has to do with your own belief systems around spirituality and money, and your ability to practice the art of graceful acceptance. Re-member that the New Energy is here, you have only to learn to reflect it to the highest and best to fully experience abundance with money.

Creating Home –
Improving Your Quality of Life

We tell you here that it is only possible to create Heaven on Earth if you improve your quality of life. Your quality of life when you are Home is of the highest. Therefore, in creating Home on your side of the veil, it will be helpful to improve your individual quality of life. Fear not to seek improvement in this area. This is your birthright and an important component of the New Energy.

Improving your own quality of life, even in small ways, helps to create Home, for it supports you to be the fullest expression of passion that you can be. Learn the art of graceful acceptance and allow the abundance that is yours to find you effortlessly. Place yourself on a mission to do something to improve your quality of life. Allow yourself to feel the satisfaction and excitement in your creations and improvements. Your attitudes of resistance to accepting the finer things in life are in direct relation to your belief in lack. Start where you are at this moment and find a way each day to do one thing to improve your quality of life. It may be moving the furniture in your house or cleaning your car. It may be moving in to a nicer house or buying a new car. Regardless of your focus, if you start where you are at this moment and move forward, the energy will be set in motion. Understand that it is the quality of life that represents the energy, and not that which you call 'Money', for money is only a reflection of *your* energy.

World Leaders and You

Please understand that your leaders are only trusted servants and, ultimately, they are responsible to you. Please do not give your power away to them. Although they may have the power to make decisions for their individual governments, you must know that these decisions DO NOT control your personal reality, especially in the area of abundance. They may have an effect on the streets that you drive on, yet *you* are the only driver of your double decker bus. Make your voice heard by the trusted servants that work for you and then release your attachment to the outcome. Understand that it is *you* who are in charge, and even though they may not be acting in accordance with your complete wishes, it is still important to make your wishes known.

You are holding the vibrations of a higher truth and, therefore, you are making a difference in simply be-ing and in adding to the collective vibration. We ask you to make your voice heard, not for the leaders alone to hear, but, more importantly, for *you* to place your tone into the collective vibration of humanity. This is the magic that happens when the vibrations of your own voice travel around your head and enter your own ears. Making room for your voice to be heard and to enter your own consciousness places it firmly in the collective consciousness and begins the process of change.

The Five Traditions of Abundance

Following are the five simple suggestions that we offer for abundant living. Make these five simple ideas a habit and you will adopt a tradition of abundance.

1. *Center Your Energy*
2. *Create a Vacuum – Merlin's Law*
3. *Check all actions against the Universal Energy*
4. *Adopt the Attitude of Abundance*
5. *Practice the Art of Graceful Acceptance*

First Tradition: Center Your Energy

First is the ability to center your own energy. This is the art of placing your self first, which emulates the natural flow of energy in the Universe. Centering your own energy is an important lesson that affects many areas of your life. This is easily confused with being selfish, yet we tell you there is a real difference. One who acts selfishly places themselves first in the flow of energy and cuts off everyone else. Those who are centering their energy place themselves first in the flow of energy in order to have more with which to do their work.

Most of you have been very confused by this concept, yet it is of crucial importance in creating abundance. When you begin any creation, the original point of energy determines the perception point from which this creation will be viewed. When you fail to place yourself first in the energy flow, the creation is tainted from the start.

We first illustrated this concept to the Keeper while he was on an airplane. In all flights of your commercial aircraft, there is a time before take off when the flight crew goes through their safety instructions. Here they show you the exit rows, how to fasten your seat belts, and so forth. There is also a time where they speak of the oxygen masks. The line usually goes like this: "If the cabin experiences a sudden change in pressure the oxygen masks will fall. If you are traveling with a small child or anyone else who needs assistance, *please put on your own oxygen mask first.*" This illustrates the art of placing yourself first. The airlines know through experience that one person can only help another if they are taken care of first. It is not possible to help another if your own cup is empty. We ask that you do not take this to mean that you cannot do or give to others, that is not what we are saying. We tell you that in the higher vibrations of the New Planet Earth, sacrifice does not work the same as it did in the lower vibrations. In the New Earth, when a gift is given through sacrifice that gift carries with it an energy strand that reflects the weight of the sacrifice. Therefore, gifts can only be given freely, unconditionally and without sacrifice. This is a situation in which both the giver and the recipient benefit. Dare to place yourself first and then watch as you set yourself up to experience true abundance.

In the area of abundance, this applies to paying yourself first. Please re-member that the act of abundance is experiencing more than is minimally needed. Do something for yourself each time you receive income. Place it aside or spend it on yourself in some fashion. Your ability to treat yourself well may determine the degree to which you can adopt the traditions of abundance.

Second Tradition: Create a Vacuum – Merlin's Law

Create a vacuum that will draw in the abundance. A vacuum is created the moment you share. Energy is only energy when it is in motion. Create a place for the energy to flow, and the laws of

Universal Energy will be called into action. When a vacuum is created, the Universal Energy will automatically fill it. The type of vacuum created will determine the creation itself. There are two basic types of vacuums that can be used:

Ethereal Vacuum – Ten-Fold Return

Giving a gift of any kind creates a vacuum in the ethers of time and space. This type of vacuum will be amplified as it is returned to you. This is the basis of the ten-fold amplification process. When you give a gift from the heart it returns to you ten-fold. Giving freely, without condition, clears an ethereal space for more of like kind to return to you. Please re-member that money is a *reflection* of energy and not a *form* of energy. Therefore, gifts of money can be best used when they are actually gifts of abundance. Celebrating your abundance by sharing it will create a vacuum for more. This is the basis of what you have termed tithing. Giving to something that you believe will help in the highest good can create space in your own life for the energy to flow. Since the vacuum is created in the ethereal, there is no limit on the amount that is returned to fill the vacuum. Gifts given unconditionally will yield a ten fold return or better. If there are conditions on the gift or if there is any energy drain, like that of sacrifice mentioned above, the yield will be less.

Share with those around you, or help in a cause that you feel is making a difference. Be careful that you do not enable others to believe in lack through your support. If you are sharing with another individual, hold them responsible for taking the energy and creating their own vacuum and flow. If the gift you give causes a dependency to form in the recipient, the return of energy will be lessened.

Physical Vacuum – One to One Return

There are several other ways to effectively create a vacuum. A physical vacuum can be set into motion through the use of creating physical space.

If you are manifesting more clothes, start by making room in your closet. If you are manifesting a new car, clean out your garage. Your actions in the physical world can create a vacuum that will yield effective results. Making space in your life for new things to enter will work to create abundance. The return of a vacuum created in the physical is more specific to the actual creation. In other words, the return will be one to one.

Merlin's Law - The Equalizer

When creating a physical vacuum, the creation is normally returned one to one. There are, however, actions that can change the return attributes of the vacuum created and increase the return of a physical vacuum. This is done through the action of abundance itself in practicing Merlin's Law.

In the days of Camelot, King Arthur had a dream to create a land where all could live in harmony and empowerment. We tell you that the Keeper has that same dream now. This was not easy in the days of Camelot, for the middle ages were very dark times indeed. There were many obstacles to overcome. One of these was changing the belief system of the people to accept abundance in their lives. Arthur found that many people had a belief in lack that was very difficult to change. At first Arthur began to create customs and laws that would change the hearts and minds of people so that they could more readily experience abundance. The good king knew that it was not possible to create abundance for everyone in the ethereal realm. Therefore, he attempted to create it in the physical through laws and customs. As Arthur found that the laws and customs were not working, this became one of his greatest frustrations.

After a time, Arthur called in his dear friend and mentor, Merlin, for advice. As Arthur expressed his frustration, Merlin chuckled with amusement. "What is so funny?" said Arthur. "Dear Arthur, as you well know, the sword only came to your hand from the stone because your actions reflected the purity of your heart. It is your own actions that have created abundance for you. However, in your honest attempt to create abundance for the people of Camelot, you have unwittingly robbed them of the opportunity to experience abundance for themselves through their own actions. Abundance is not an item to be had, it is a way of life. Accordingly, abundance cannot be given to another. It can only be created within one's self through the expression of abundance". The two men spent much time talking and after a time Merlin offered a simple suggestion. This simple suggestion is still in use today. It became known to the people of Camelot affectionately as 'Merlin's Law'.

'Merlin's Law' simply states that it is the expression of abundance that creates abundance. *Give a little more!*

Merlin Statement

Start the overflow on the giving end and watch as it quickly spreads to the receiving end. If you wish your business transactions to be successful, find a way to give a little more in each transaction than was bargained for. After the deal has been struck and all parties agree, find a way to deliver more than you originally agreed to. Merlin's Law sets into motion a series of events that creates an overflow of energy. You have seen these practices in use many times on the Gameboard. The origin of tithing is an example of Merlin's Law in use. In days past you had an expression called the "bakers dozen". This began because a young baker wanted to give his patron something more as an expression of his own abundance. He began the practice of placing thirteen baked goods to a dozen instead of twelve. His bakery thrived as did his flow of abundance.

In every dealing, after the deal has been struck, find a way to give a little more. Merlin's Law is the practice of true abundance, because it is the expression of excess in one's life. This is taking the idea of true abundance and placing it into action in your daily life. This automatically creates a vacuum that will manifest that same excess and abundance into your own reality.

Third Tradition:
Honor the Universal Energy

There is a Universal Energy which permeates all things. This is the energy that exists in a complete vacuum. It exists even when all other energies are removed. This is the energy of potential. This is the energy of that which you call God. The purpose and motion of this energy is about blending. This energy has one purpose only:

> *The Universal Energy pulls back together that which was separated in order to create the illusion of polarity in which you live.*

In the 5th dimension, all that oppose this Universal Energy will meet resistance, and all that support it will find support. In this space where no other energies exist, the action of blending is facilitated by one simple rule: ***For every action there is an equal and opposite reaction.***

When applying the five traditions of abundance to your everyday life, it is helpful to view all your actions as seen against the backdrop of the Universal Energy. Do your actions support integration (blending) or separation? In the higher vibrations of the New Planet Earth you will find that even your organizations will have people who are responsible for ensuring that the actions of the organization flow in accord with the Universal Energy. Do this for yourself as an individual and watch the results.

Fourth Tradition: Adopt the Attitude
of Abundance

Adopt an attitude of abundance in all things that you do. Whenever possible surround yourself with others who can be healthy role models in abundant living. Treat yourself well, for in doing so you are defining your reality as abundant. Understand that you can become abundant by reaching for more, or by becoming grateful for what you already have. Often the act of attaining more is no more than an illusion of abundance, for it is then that your possessions begin to posses you. Attaining more by itself is not the achievement of abundance. Abundance is an attitude and the attitude can be achieved from wherever you are at this very moment. Adopt the attitude of always having more than you need, then you can make the choice of how much you will experience.

The illusions of polarity have had you believe that you are separate from one another. Therefore, a belief in lack has pervaded the Game from the very beginning. A pervading belief in lack makes it difficult to conceive of, and therefore experience, true abundance. The basis of lack is the belief that what one can see is all there is. This is the same problem that has kept some of your scientists from understanding that their intent will alter the outcome of their experiments. The belief that nothing exists outside of yourself is the restriction that keeps you tied so firmly to the 3rd dimensional illusion of lack.

Your own world economists are now aware that lack is an illusion. When the world is abundant, everyone is more abundant, for abundance is a flow that emulates the Universal Energy. Imagine five coins on a table. The illusion of lack would have you believe that if you took one coin for yourself, that would only leave four for other people. In fact, when energy is in motion it proliferates. Since money is merely a reflection of energy it, too, must multiply when it is in motion. Your world economists know that if there are five coins circulating on the table, it has the same effect as if there were 12 coins.

The higher dimensional levels of the New Planet Earth will no long support a belief in lack.

Fifth Tradition:

The Art of Graceful Acceptance.

Finally, when abundance does find you, it will only flow to the degree to which you allow it to flow. This has to do with the Art of Graceful Acceptance. Most of you are well versed at creating flow by sending out the energy, yet when that energy returns it is hard for you to accept. Those of you who are what you consider to be lucky are usually well versed in the art of graceful acceptance. Start by learning to accept compliments and small gifts gracefully. Practice graceful acceptance and you will return the gift to the giver. If you give from the heart and your gift is not accepted with grace, the gift itself becomes diminished. The true gift belongs to the giver. Do not rob them of the gift by not accepting it gracefully.

When anything comes your way, challenge yourself to find the most graceful way to accept it. Find ways to return the gift to the giver and you will complete the energy cycle.

Consider the art of graceful acceptance as you place a value on your own goods or services. The law of energy says that people can place no higher value upon you than you place upon yourself. Ultimately, you are the one that determines your own value.

Practice the art of graceful acceptance and dare to improve your quality of life in all areas. This soon becomes a habit of abundant living, and you will find that it is possible to reach many more hearts than you imagined through your intentional creation of Heaven on Earth.

You do not easily re-member true abundance while you are wearing the veils. These veils keep you from re-membering Home, for if they were not in place, you would simply push them aside and return Home. We are here to re-mind you of the vibrations and the memories of Home. The veil of forgetfulness will not allow you to see Home for more than brief moments. It is in those moments that we speak to you. We tell you here that there is no greater expression of abundance than that of Heaven. If you are truly about the creation of Home on your side of the veil then the concept of abundance will need to be embraced and incorporated into your every creation. Remember that as you accept your abundance you are accepting your birthright and re-membering Home.

It is with the greatest of love and respect for the rightful heirs to the throne of forever that we ask you to treat each other with respect, nurture one another and play well together.
And so it is. . .

the Group

Section III

Questions to the Group

Answers to questions placed to the Group in live channels on a variety of subjects.

Q & A Lightcircles Congress, Oct 2001, Veldhoven, Holland

In each seminar the Group delivers a message much like those you see in the chapters of this book. At the end of this message they provide an opportunity to interact with them personally through a question and answer period. Here people can interact with the Group personally, and ask anything they want. We get some very interesting questions and it allows the Group to give very concise answers to complex topics that would take many pages to explain in writing. It is also a special time for people to directly experience their love and humorous personality. Many times I also get to hear new things. These are some of my personal favorite times in channel, and the rest of the Group feels the same. These occasions will invariably elicit a range of emotions from tears to laughter. In the Questions and Answers that follow you will feel the entire emotional range, but most of all you will feel the sincerity and love of the Group. We offer a selection here of some of the many Q & A sessions taken directly from the transcripts of recent live presentations. We hope you enjoy them as much as we do.

For more information about seminars in your areas please see: www.lightworker.com/schedule.shtml

Chapter 11

~ 2012 ~

Esoteric Society - United Nations - Vienna, Austria - May 3rd, 2001

Question:

Please tell us about the year 2012 and what is going to happen after that. Thank you.

the Group:

No. You ask what will happen in the year 2012. We are asking *you*, for it is *you* who hold the key, not we. It will be your choices that ultimately will decide the outcome. We will tell you what some of the potentials are, but we cannot tell the future. Does that surprise you? You think "Ahh, from where you are you see everything. You are all-knowing and all-encompassing". Yes, we are all of that and more, but if this is truly the Planet of Free Choice, you can understand that there is no predestination or grand plan in place. We cannot see your future, for the simple reason that you have yet to script it. The year 2012 was originally intended to mark the final reckoning. It was to be the final balancing of the planet. We ask you, why do you think that very little has been written about what was to follow the year 2012? It was the belief of most in the Universe that the Game would have been completed at that point. The veils would have lifted, you all would have gone Home or have started another

Game. But as the last moments of the Game approached, you started to awaken. Many from the days of Mu and Atlantis started incarnating on the planet with the intention of doing things differently this time around. Together, you rapidly raised your vibrational level.

The year 2012 was to be the division point. If your collective vibration was high enough you would move into another reality and dimension. This would have been the time of ascension of the human race. If you did not awaken from the dream, humanity and the planet of free choice would have had its final outcome in the year 2012. If that were to happen, rather than ascending into the 5th dimension, planet Earth would look more like the planet you know as Mars.

These are Magical times. What is to come in the next thousand years? What is out there? Will space travel be possible? Yes, of course. Will you use it? Probably not, because inter-dimensional travel will be much more interesting and much more efficient. How long will you live? You have the capability to live over a thousand years. The technology that is in place now does not hold a candle to what the next twenty years will bring. It is growing at such a rapid rate because of your awakening.

What will happen in the next eleven years? There is only one thing that we can tell you for sure. Your lives will change. Ahh, but you already know that, for you are in the process of change right now. Embrace it.

Will there be difficult times on Planet Earth? Of course there will be. There will be many that will resist the new energy coming in. You have seen it time and time again. Some of your world leaders will cling tightly to the old ways, trying to make the old paradigms work. They will try to motivate from a base of fear, rather than of love. They will try to hold and hoard the energy, rather than spreading it freely. The good news is you will no longer tolerate it.

Aliens

Columbus, Ohio - June 9th, 2001

Question:

It's been suggested to me that I am a star person and I really resonate with that, but my dilemma right now is what do I do with that information? Do I pursue that in some way? Is this information that would be useful to bring to this planet? Or is it better just to focus on playing this Game on Earth?

the Group:

We tell you that you have many choices as to where you play. You may play here or you may play there. You may focus your energies where you wish, but your true success will be found in your passion. The moment you said you resonated with that information, we heard passion. Tell your story and you will be in your passion. You have much knowledge about this. What are you to do with it? That is up to you. Understand that there is no right or wrong about your choices. Cause and effect are attributes of the Universal Energy and if your effect is not to your liking we encourage you to create something new. Look for the passion, as it holds the key in the higher vibrations of the New Planet Earth. Talk about it, work with others, and find other starseeds. There are many here on the planet that feel a strong pull making this information available to others. You are one of them. Find the others. Work with them. Set the intent. Set the energy and power with the smallest amount of action, and you will see very quick motion.

Are you from another planet? Of course you are. The joke of it is, *none* of you are from Planet Earth. We are so amused when you talk of aliens. You will soon learn much about your origins. Some of it may surprise you, because some of it is not from what you term outer space, but what would more accurately be described as inner space. They are here now and have been for some time. Ah, the Keeper wishes to see them on CNN, and they are not there yet. But they will be, so be patient. In the meantime, let your imagination run with this, and tell the story of what you know in your heart, for it is that passion which will lead to your own channeling, to your own connection to your Higher Self and sharing your truth.

Nijmegen, Holland - April 16th, 2000

Question:

This is a difficult question to ask. I'm afraid to look in a mirror sometimes as I see an alien instead of me. Can you explain this?

the Group:

There is nothing to explain, you *are* an alien. Get used to it. *(Laughter)* And such a beautiful alien you are too. What are the rest of you laughing about? *None of you here are from Earth!*

You have asked to return to your source. You personally have been on a quest to uncover your own origins, and you are getting glimpses of it every time you look in the mirror. Please know that the mirror will not crack, for it only reflects the beauty of you. The special qualities you carry have been with you since you first came to play on the Gameboard known as Earth. You have agreed to bring to Earth the special flavor of the planet where you first incarnated. Even that original planet is not your true home, for you originated from the oneness of Home. Yes, you have a very definite affinity with what you call aliens, because you know their ways and their struggles. We think it so humorous that you would call them aliens and think of them as separate or different from you. Most of what you know to be aliens are actually the parental races of humanity. You are all blends of the most wondrous aliens.

When you decided to wear the veil of forgetfulness, when you passed through the second dimension and split into the sexes and took form in a world of polarity, you became a beautiful part of the Creator. You do not see the beauty sometimes, for that is part of the veil. Yes, you know where you are from. We will validate it for you. You know where your heart is, and yet we tell you it is not in the same dimension in which you now exist. So if you were to look with a microscope/telescope, and see the planet from which you originate, you would not find life in the manner that you think of it. They have a different relationship to time and space, therefore, you would not be able to see them.

Inter-dimensional time travel is the same as inter-dimensional space travel. You will soon find the relationship between time and space to be much closer than you first imagined. There are no restrictions of time. You can only experience this on a limited basis as your biology and your belief systems will not be supported. But as you step into the 5th dimension you will experience this in daily life. And when you do you will see the Truth about the question you did not ask: about where you are from. You will be seeing much more of your own origins. Now that the cetaceans are redefining their relationship to you, it will be possible to see that they are actually your brethren. They are very close to your own vibration.

The variety of beings and personalities that exist within the Universe reaches far beyond your imagination. Therefore, when you look in the mirror and say you think you are an alien, it causes us to laugh. If we showed you some of your own origins you would surely think the mirror would crack. You are such a beautiful reflection, and your parental races are very proud of you. For all the original races are rushing to the forefront right now and saying, "that's my girl".

Richmond, Virginia - June 10th, 2001

Question:

About a month ago there was a press conference in Washington, DC about something called The Disclosure Project. This is a project that is intended to uncover what the government knows about the UFOs. Part of the cover up is about free energy devices that would give us pollution-free energy. I just wonder if you can tell us if this will be successful and what we can do to help this project.

the Group:

There are many things you can do to help this process, but first we ask you to broaden your perspective to understand the situation. Yes, things exist on Earth that are being hidden from the public. We will also tell you that all of these cover-ups are not as they seem.

First of all, in asking the governments of your world to disclose knowledge, you are making an assumption that they *have* knowledge. In some cases they do and in others they have only partial knowledge. Please understand that what you are looking for does not exist in one central location as you might think it does. It is not a file drawer that has been locked for many years. The knowledge you seek has been intentionally scattered amongst different people and in different locations.

At one time there were agreements between the visitors and select governments to facilitate the exchange of information. Due to larger karmic implications, those agreements are no longer in place. Much of the technology and evidence that would substantiate the charges of the disclosure project no longer exist in physical form. Because of this, and because of a future increase in what your governments call security, government disclosure of information regarding high technology and contact with other races is not likely in the foreseeable future. We do encourage you to make your voices heard as this will bring these issues to the collective consciousness of all humanity.

The technology for power generation and distribution that you have described does exist, but It is not being withheld for the reasons you may think. Please understand that humans have an inherent attraction for drama in their lives. You love to think that there are secret echelons that govern your world. You love to believe that big brother is watching your every move. We hate to disappoint your need for drama, but we must say that most of the governments of your world are simply not that smart. With very few exceptions, your governments' drive to develop technology has been instigated by their perceived need for weapons of war. Please note that many of your own advances in technology were initiated while searching for war toys.

The technology for power generation and distribution has not been applied to practical use on your planet at this time. This technology was being developed by the one known as Tesla many years ago. Tapping into the energy is not the difficulty, rather, the distribution of it has been the road block to using it. There are still some key challenges with regard to putting this technology into practical use that you have yet to discover. We tell you that you are closer than you know to uncovering the key to distribution of this power source. Once again, it has been your search for war toys that has developed the laser technology that is required for free energy distribution. Segments of the free energy project of which you speak are not completely developed. We tell you it is not ready for immediate deployment, but it can be. Even so, there are other technologies that now exist on Planet Earth as a result of your search, for your war toys can be utilized in energy distribution. The greatest free energy that you possess is that of the sun, but you have yet to harness it effectively.

Please understand that secrets will no longer be possible on Planet Earth. You are reaching a higher vibrational status that will create instantaneous communications between all people. Your governments will certainly have their hands full then. It is very appropriate that you make your voices heard as you hold your power as creators. This sends a message to your world leaders that their roles are to be *your* trusted servants and no more. Please know that the steps you are now beginning to take into the 5th dimension will open the door for contact with others in the Universe. We applaud your actions in demanding the hidden information, however, let it be known that if all the governments of the world released all the information they have about alien contact, most of it would be incomplete, misinterpreted or sadly out of date. The truth is, that through your own evolution, you now know more than they do.

Business and Governments of the New Planet Earth

Sydney, Australia - August 26th, 2001

Question:
Thank you for being with us. Some of us are becoming involved in new ways of running a business, or of working together as a community. Is there any guidance or pointers that we should be looking for at the moment that can help us ease our way into this and, yeah, work it properly?

the Group:
There are many that are asking the same question, including some of your multinational corporations, for they too are seeking higher truths applicable to the New Planet Earth. Please do not see these organizations as being separate from you, for they are not. You are one with your organizations and that is the point we will make. There is something that you can do in business and governments that will become increasingly important. Observe the policies, intent and actions of your organizations in relation to the flow of Universal Energy. The natural flow of Universal Energy is one of blending. There will come a time when specially appointed people high in governments and businesses will do nothing more than compare the actions of their organization to the overall motion of the Universal Energy. These people will be highly honored in their work. Ask yourself: Do the actions of your company promote a segregation of energy or are they promoting a blending of the overall energy? Ask this not only for yourself personally, but in relationship to your businesses and governments as well. That is the simplicity of the new paradigm.

We take you back to a form of government in the days of Mu, which was actually a form of non-government, for it worked so well that it actually required very few people to be employed by the government. The idea of this government was to create space for others to experience their empowerment. It worked because no one was in charge. This is the basis of energy that later re-emerged in Camelot as the concept of the round table. During that time, the energy moved in a circular motion and actually created a vortex. Had one person held their sword higher than the rest, the flow of energy would have been broken. At the same time, the energy could rest with anyone at any time, without losing balance.

We wish to tell you that there was a time on Planet Earth when one segment of humanity could advance faster than another. That is what you are here to change. Never again will some of you be left behind as others advance. Instead, you will all now advance as one. That is the Unity consciousness which you are seeking. That is the reason for the re-turn of Camelot and the re-turn of Mu. That is the reason for the re-turn to the paradigms of business and government used in the days of Mu.

That which you call competition is not what it appears to be. Competition is based on a belief in lack. Therefore, if one person has something, you think that it means that another may not. You believe that you must compete for the limited amount and we tell you, that is not the way. Soon you will experience a new form of healthy competition that builds upon personal empowerment. What you will experience is a way to raise each other's vibration by working together. You will not experience the negativity of a belief system in lack, for there is abundance only when energy flows. Re-strict it and you will have lack. Find ways of creating this, of bringing the like together to blend in many motions, and that magic will happen. It is already well underway. We thank you not only for asking the question, but for having the courage to put it into use.

Channeling

Las Vegas, Nevada - January 20th, 2000

Question:

A few months ago I had an experience with channeling, for lack of a better word. When I asked who was speaking to me, they said they were the nine. I wonder if they are the same nine as yours or do I have a different nine?

the Group:

We love these questions for they illustrate your humanness, which we love so dearly. What if we told you that the nine was one? What if we told you the eight was one? What if we told you that the one was nine and the nine was twelve? What we tell you is that it makes no difference? Give not your power to the labels but discern instead the love content of the information itself, for only then is it possible to fully hold your power.

There is no coincidence about what you are seeing and hearing, even though your own ego does not often allow you to hear it. This is one of the crystals that your own Higher Self has placed on your path to re-mind you who you are. We tell you, yes, we have spoken through you many times and we thank you for that opportunity. But to define it as sacred because it came from this level or that source is giving your power to us.

Practice listening. If the information is good, accept it regardless of where it comes from. For you see, it makes no difference if the Group be nine or twelve. It makes no difference if it is the Elohim, or the Galactic Federation, or the Brotherhood, or even if you made it up yourself. If the information is good, take it as your own. Do not give your power to any one label of truth. Do not give your power even to us. This is the reason we never gave the Keeper a label by which to identify us. When all is said and done you will pull away the veils to find that you have all been channeling the same entity. You are all simply different flavors of the same truth. We do not wish you to follow us, for our work is to remind you of your *own* magnificence. That is only possible if you hold your power fully within yourself. That takes more courage than giving away your power. Would you like to know the greatest of cosmic jokes? The God you search for so intently outside of yourself *is* yourself. *You are God.*

We tell you that all of what you call channeling is only a warm-up for greater things to come, for there will come a time when you will connect in ways that you cannot possibly imagine at this moment. There will come a time when you will not call it 'the Group'. We will never leave you, for it is our greatest desire to be at your service, to remain just over your shoulder, holding the mirror for you to see yourselves. And yet, there will come a time when you will have a more direct connection with your own Higher Selves. That is the reason we tell the Keeper that this wonderful thing you call channeling is not that mysterious. It is one of the most basic forms of communication that you can possibly experience, and all of you have the ability to do it. It is not a gift given only to a selected few. It is given to all. For it is the connection to all that is that you are tapping into. We come to the Keeper in this fashion because it allows us to reach many, and we have actually shown the Keeper personalities and visuals, but that is only to satisfy his mind. Our energy is beyond your comprehension in your current state of e-volution. Follow the truth, my friend, for you are very much a part of this family. We thank you for being here and for making your choices. As long as it feeds your heart, keep the channel open. We are here to help you carry your power within not without. Let us simply say that in the days ahead you will hear much from many. Please stay tuned.

Nijmegen, Holland - April 22nd, 2001

Question:

I feel so very grateful for this information because it's part of the puzzle I needed to put together, but I have a question. I believe I am one of the four that you mentioned. Last week I turned my work around 180 degrees. I am returning to the work I began in 1984. I was just waiting for inspiration and I think I have just received it. I want to know, is that true? Can I do this?

the Group:

Hear this vibration. Yes. It fills our heart so when you ask to be guided. We do not need to guide you any longer, for you are well underway yourselves, but when you ask to be shown a way we always do it. You have asked for inspiration. You have the inspiration that you requested and yet we will give you more for you know where this is going. You can feel it in your heart even though you are afraid to look at the answer. You know that you have greatness within you and that is hard for you to comprehend. It does not change what is. Later this day the Keeper will touch your heart with the touch of an angel. In that moment you will receive more inspiration than you can possibly handle. The challenge for you will be sorting out and choosing which inspiration you will use.

Furthermore, we ask you all to share that with each other. Touch each other with the touch of an angel. Reach around and touch the back of their heart chakra or touch them on the front heart chakra. With this tool you will leave our energy imprint. Spread this energy through the touch of an angel and you will create Home.

Here is a story to show you your own connection. Spirit often taps you on the shoulder and gives you inspiration. You call it inspiration and the Keeper calls it channeling. The joke is on you, for they are the same. You see inspiration within your own imagination. Because it is coming from you that you think it is not worthy. Oh, so many of you have said similar things. "If only I could channel like the Keeper," you say. "If only I could hear it as clearly as he hears it then I would be in my passion". We tell you, the Keeper does not hear it clearly. He asks the same questions as you. What the Keeper has learned to do is to trust and to lean against the information as it flows through him. That is what we ask you to do. Place yourself in a position for the flow to begin. The Keeper has a light in his office. On the wall is the switch to that light. The potential of electricity is in the switch all of the time but the magic cannot take place until the switch is turned on and the electricity has a place to go. Find a place for the inspiration to go and watch the magic begin.

Step into it as if it were someone else for then you can trust it. Step into it as if it were the greatest part of you. This is the purpose of not having your Higher Self within your own bubble of biology. This gives you a chance to see and feel a part of yourself that is much greater and extends well beyond your own energy fields. And yet it is very much a part of you. Tap into that part of yourself and if it is channeling, call it channeling. And if it is writing, call it writing. And if you are looking in the eyes of another and touching their very heart, call it what you like. We call it healing. You have a story to tell. You have already been inspired and it will continue and your inspiration will grow and only follow it with the smallest bit of action for we can inspire easily. We can wave the Keeper's hand and give you the greatest of potentials even in this room and your heads will start racing with the possibilities. And even though we have that to give, the only thing that we do not have to give to you is your courage to step into action. For that is not possible on this side of the veil, that is only possible from you.

Take that challenge to be the Human Angel. That is what you came here to do. You are the chosen ones. You are the ones who stepped forward and said, "Let me be there at that time. I promise I will awaken just in time to take my place". And here you are. As you are wiping the sleep from your eyes, we are here waiting for you, hoping to show you brief glimpses of the vibrations from Home so that you will re-member your true heritage. That is why we are so in awe of you. You have had the courage to do it; you have had the courage to trip, to fall, to pick yourselves up from the ground and make a difference, and we cannot thank you enough. You are the human angels that are changing All That Is. Fear this not. Hold this title and hold your torch high.

Steve and Barbara at the Lightcircles Congress
in Veldhoven, Holland, October 2001

Children of the New Earth

Enlightenment Society - United Nations Staff Recreation Council
United Nations Headquarters - New York - March 23rd, 2001

Question:

I'd like to know more about what's going on with our children shooting each other in school.

the Group:

It is such a sad situation for you to watch the children of new Planet Earth as they begin shaking up the energy in a destructive way. Does it surprise you that they would act this way? Do not some societies have guns readily available and actually encourage them as an expression of freedom? Why would it surprise you to find your children using those guns as they search for their own expression of freedom? What was a truth in the lower vibrations of Planet Earth may no longer hold and may need re-evaluating on the New Planet Earth. From the child's perspective it is a way of crying out, "I need help, I cannot make sense of this world". We also tell you that it is the Indigo children that are largely responsible for this behavior. They are a powerful yet frustrated breed of humanity with a very thin veil. They have not been engaged and therefore they can become destructive when they are bored. It is so difficult. Many of the Indigo children have come in with specific contracts not only to change the school systems, not only to change the way we think about children as a whole on Planet Earth, but also to change the hearts of other children. In much the way it was necessary to experience global aggression to understand that it did not work, so too will you experience a shake up in the energy surrounding children, your education systems, and the belief systems for raising children. Sometimes it is necessary to pull the pendulum of human advancement so far to one side so that it gains the momentum it needs to swing right to the opposite side. This is part of what is happening now. In the times ahead you will see this extreme behavior diminishing as other issues in the world take center stage.

You are seeing only a very small proportion of indigos behaving in destructive ways. Know that the same is true of your many government leaders. In the near future you will see small pockets of fear that will crop up as people try to cling to the old ways, but the old energy no longer fits. Love the children, empower them, and hold them responsible. And we tell you that is true not only for the children of Indigo color, but for the government leaders that are acting out of fear as well, for it is all the same vibration. And although we cannot see the future, we can tell you where things are heading and you may yet see even more global aggression. In many respects what is happening with the Indigo children is actually relieving some of that pressure. In the event that world leaders act out their frustration, you will see a lessening of the children's harsh actions. Understand it as best you can. Empathize, sympathize and hold them responsible. Challenge them to be better than you were and then watch the magic, for they are up to the task.

Dear ones, the children of Planet Earth need your attention. The children of Planet Earth need your love. There are many here who do not know where they are going. Even though the veil is very thin for them, they do not know what to do. They see things that you do not see. They know Home is right in front of them, and yet still they are confused. We tell you to use the Empowerment Factor and to give them the power to create their own reality. But as with any power on Planet Earth, it must be balanced with responsibility. So first challenge them to connect with their power and to find ways to empower themselves, and then hold them responsible for using their power in a positive manner. This will engage the children of the Indigo vibration, for their brains are moving just a little bit faster than most of yours. At times you have given them drugs and invented strange disorders to explain why they do not fit into your system. They are leading the way for the next generation of Human evolution. And if they are not fully engaged they will become very destructive, for they are very frustrated. They are bored. Engage them, empower them and hold them responsible, for make no mistake; they *will* change your world. Yes, it is only a few that are behaving in such a destructive manner. Yet if you learn from the few, all will gain from the knowledge.

The Indigo Children will change the collective consciousness to make space for the Children of Crystal Vibration, which is your next level of incarnation. The Crystal Children are the ones with the great power to which you are all ascending. There are two attributes of Children of Crystal Vibration: The first is that they are extremely powerful. And the second is that they are extremely vulnerable. They have been here many times before in your history, yet they have never been able to stay. You have not done well with the Children of Crystal Vibration. You crucified one two thousand years ago. Ahh, but now they are re-turning. It is the Indigos that are starting to put this in motion. Honor the Indigos, dear ones, for they are doing a tremendous job.

Esoteric Society - United Nations - Vienna, Austria - May 3rd, 2001

Question:

What can you tell us about the Indigos and all other children?

the Group:

How much time do you have? We will speak to you briefly of the Indigos for they are playing an important role in the history of the Gameboard of Free Choice. Through your choices you have created the opportunity to evolve to the next level of humanity. But it is not just humanity that is evolving, for the Earth herself is also shifting along with you. Indeed, through your choices, all the higher ethereal realms and the inter-dimensional levels will also move to the next level. Note that this is not occurring through the choices of plants, nor through the choices of fish, nor through the choices of cows, but through the choices of humans. It is through *your* powers of choice that these events are now unfolding. Because of this opening a special group of people had to come onto the planet to start changing the ways in which you think about humanity. These are the Indigo children. They had to bridge the gap from point A to point C. They are point B. We tell you it is the children of the Indigo vibration who will go down in the annals of history as the ones that made a difference.

Now, what about those of you who have given birth to Indigo children? "It does not feel like they are making a difference to me," you might say. "They are driving me crazy". Ah, but that is simply a part of what they came in to do. Many Indigo children have direct contracts to change the school systems and the way you think about children in general. They often do this with their own abrasive, at times spiky, energy. We will tell you much about the Indigo children, for they are so misunderstood. Please do not place them on a pedestal. Please do not worship them. They do not need it and it is only a misdirection of energy to place them on pedestals and tell them they are special. Instead, place them on a pedestal and say, "You are special because you are *you*".

They feel different and often left out. They look around the room in their own classrooms, and they think they are alone. And so they are in many ways. It is almost as if their brains are moving at a faster pace and to be in a classroom with other children requires an eternity of patience. Often they are so far ahead of their teachers they actually have to slow down their own vibration to comprehend what is being said. It is difficult for them and because of this many can often be found staring out into space as the teacher is talking. You have intentionally slowed many of them down in order to fit in. And the sad part is, this tactic appears to work. But we tell you from a higher perspective it is not your job to change the Indigos. It is *their* job to change *you*. Bless them. Challenge them to be more than their predecessors. See and understand the difficult task they have ahead of them.

Many of them will do rather well in school, for they do not all have contracts to butt heads with your teachers and schools. Some of them may have social challenges. Some of them will not fit in. They may do rather well in school, but they will be loners. They will be off all by themselves, for they do not relate easily to others. They are on a higher vibrational level than other children. We will give you some keys that may help you with them. First of all, we ask you to be patient with yourselves, for they have infinite patience with you. They have infinite patience with those of you that are in the process of helping to change things. They have infinite patience with the institutions as they are changing. So take your time.

You surely understand by now that guilt will not work as a motivator with them. They have a very thin veil and they re-member Home. Therefore, they know that guilt is an illusion. Sometimes when they are young they will tug at your apron and say, "Mommy, do you re-member when I was your father?" And you will think they are making something up. They are not. Learning to live with that is difficult for them, for they have to learn to shut down such memories in order to cope in the 'real world'. They have to learn to go out and not appear to be different.

Scolding an Indigo child is difficult, for they will look at you with a smile on their face and it may make you angry. Teach them responsibility, for it will be the key to their effectiveness. We ask you also to engage with them, for most of the time if they do not do well in school it is simply because they are bored. Expect more. Tell them that you expect something special from them, for *they* are special; not because they are Indigos, but because of whom they are as individuals. Let them know that it is their differences that make them special. Wait until you see the fun that will begin as the Indigos start changing and moving into the magic of adulthood. Oh, we tell you, many of these little imaginary lines that you have drawn on your planet to indicate where one land stops and another land begins will start to dissolve. Ahh. . . what a time that will be. It is closer than you think. The Indigos will open the way.

Beyond the Indigos you will see a new breed of children that will be coming. These children will also be very special, for they will express humanity in a higher form. We have termed them 'Children of the Crystal Vibration', yet when they become the norm on the New Planet Earth there will be no name for them other than 'Human'. This form of Humanity has two simple attributes: They are extremely powerful and extremely vulnerable. They actually derive their power from their vulnerability. They will be the first level of humanity to have what you call magical abilities. They will have a basic understanding of energy that you do not possess at your current level of evolution. As each of you decides to re-turn in new bodies, you will take the bodies of the Children of Crystal Vibration, for they hold the new matrix. As you come back and take the form of Crystal Children, you will set humanity on a course that will take you through the next five millennia.

It will be a magical time, for the Children of Crystal Vibration have tried to come here many times before. There are some scouts here now, but they are very few, and they are mostly in hiding. They are the magical ones. They have an understanding and interaction with energy forms that you do not perceive. They can wave their hands and make things happen, and yet we tell you, as powerful as they are, it is their vulnerability that gives them their power. Many of those you have called teachers or masters have been of the Crystal vibration. Can you imagine having those powers now? Well start imagining, dear ones. The Indigos are clearing the way for this to happen. Now can you see how exciting Planet Earth is going to be? Now can you see why we have called you the chosen ones? The Christed Energy has re-turned to Earth, but not as a single person, as *all of you*.

Espavo Conference - Mt. Shasta, California - October 1st, 2000

Question:

How can we, as elders and grandparents, support the parents of the Indigos?

the Group:

The Indigos carry a great deal of energy which can often seem overwhelming to those around them. It is up to the parents to help them direct their energy in the highest and most positive way. Your schools will be re-arranging themselves to handle children like the Indigos. This is part of the Indigos' contract, and the primary reason they are here. You, as healers, will be working not only with the Indigos, but also with their parents. Please tell them they are not going crazy. Their ideas about child rearing have changed drastically in the last fifty years. As you have stepped into the overall Plan B of planet Earth, you have re-arranged your paradigms and your belief systems around working with children. Create space for the empowered human in your home, and you will be successful. Create space for the empowered human in your schools and you will be successful. Create space for the empowered human in your government, and all that it does, and you will have re-created the land of Mu. That is the reason we share these stories with you, for that is exactly what you are doing here on the Gameboard of Free Choice in the 21st century. You are bringing the magic back to the planet.

Do not look to the Indigos and say, "Thank you for coming". For it is you that have opened the door and made it possible for them to be here. You will wear badges of color for the choices you have made. Sometimes alone in your bedroom you cry because you think you are alone. You feel pain because you feel you are not supported. You feel like you are the only one here that understands what is going on. We tell you, sometimes it is necessary to experience pain in order to make a difference. Now can you see why *we* sit at *your* feet? We are in the grandeur of Home. We are in heaven. But it is you who are making a difference, and it is our deepest honor to spread our wings to reflect your energy.

Syracuse, New York - March 11th, 2001

Question:
Is there any way as healers and educators that we can help the Indigo children with what they're going through?

the Group:
Listen to these three words. They are very important: It is the *vibration* of the three words that we are about to utter through the Keeper that is most important:

Yes. Yes. Yes.

The educators are the ones that are the first to make space for the Indigos. Challenge them. Do not be afraid if they are smarter than you. As hard as it may be for you as teachers, expect and encourage them to exceed your own limitations, and know this to be your measure of success. Do not try to make them fit into the small box that has been labeled for them. Instead, see how far they can go. Open the door. Challenge them. Dare them to be better than their predecessors. Make it a game, for they love games.

Understand that it is natural for humans to resist change. Yet the Indigos have come in with a predisposition for change. Therefore, they may at first be seen as problem children or trouble makers. They are starting to change what you already have. You naturally look at some of the negatives of this change. You look at some of the difficulties experienced if they are not challenged and get bored. When they are bored, they can become frustrated and can be destructive. If they express that frustration outwardly you see it as destructive behavior. If it is held within it can manifest as self-destructive behavior and that is such a sad situation for you. When this happens, it requires self forgiveness. You take things so personally, yet have you ever considered that no one is at fault sometimes? Have you ever considered that there are times when 'bad' things happen for no reason, and that it is not until years later that you see that the 'bad' thing was actually a contract that was successfully fulfilled? Forgive and play the Game again. Make the Game fun for yourself and the quick children will follow your lead. Lead them by example, allowing yourself to make mistakes gracefully, and in so doing you will give them permission to do the same. Make space for that to happen without pressure and, above all, enjoy the Game.

There are times when you have diagnosed your children with what you call dis-orders because they do not fit into the parameters that previously defined them. Is it not an interesting phenomenon that now that you have words to describe such dis-orders, suddenly there are so many children that fit the description? Just be aware that what you are doing is slowing down a fast mind merely in order to bring it into your own realm of teachability. However, not all cases are misdiagnosed, though you will soon see that a good many of them are. Make space for the mind that moves faster. Understand that this, too, represents a form of change, and if you think humans are resistant to change, wait until you see how your institutions react! Since it is humans that make up the institutions, we ask you to begin examining your own heart. Start asking questions. Ask questions of your fellow educators. Ask your friends, for together you may come up with the answers you seek. And together you will experiment and find ways of changing your institutions. And if you think this is interesting, just wait until you see these children hit your work force and your governments. For that will be the next step they must take.

Do not feel that you need to segregate them or identify them. That is not needed. Do not feel that they all have to go to special schools, because in fact many have contracts that are specifically related to your public school systems. Typically an

Indigo child will have difficulty in one area, such as their academic studies, or with their social skills, but not usually with both. However, those areas may specifically relate to their contract. Of course, you look at them with your humanness and you say, "What did I do wrong as a parent? How can I help them?" Maybe nothing is wrong. Perhaps this is what they came to do. So what can you do? Support them. Love them as best you can and yet hold them responsible for their own decisions and actions, for that is the true empowerment. Do not take it upon yourself to create space for them, for that is creating a leaning situation and Indigo children do not lean well.

Know that you are on the path, for if you were not, you would not be asking these questions. Know that you *are* making a difference.

Vienna, Austria - May 6th, 2001

Question:
[At this time the Group decided to answer a question that was being thought but not verbalized.]

the Group:
There are two people in the room with questions that are not being asked aloud. There is much going on now with children on the planet and first we wish to tell you that the children will be fine. So often you are turning your life around to make space for your children. Even the contracts that you are scripting here are being written with your children in mind. As you are writing these, you are thinking, "how does this affect my children? For if I am selfish, and only go after my own passion there will not be space for my children". We ask you to simply look back one generation. What did you want for your own parents? You wanted them only to be happy, did you not? For if they went after their own passion and did what *they* came here

to do, did that not give you permission to do the same? We ask you to please pass on that same gift to your children by first centering your own energy and finding *your* own passion. In doing this you literally will be giving them permission to do the same thing, and in turn you will then be playing a more interactive role in their lives.

We have told you of the greatness that you will carry while in biology as you raise your vibrations to that of the Crystal Children. In order to hold this higher power you are going to need to modify your biology. There are two ways to accomplish this. One is through a process that we have not yet discussed, which we will simply term OVERLIGHT. This process will allow you to stay and adjust your present biology to higher vibrations. The rest of you will come back through the reincarnation process as Crystal Children. These magical beings are born with all twelve strands of the DNA fully connected.

There are difficult times ahead for the children currently on this planet, for much change will be necessary to make room for the Children of Crystal Vibration. There are some scouts already here testing the waters. More will soon follow who will have even more of the magical attributes of the Crystal Children. Right now you can best support them, and support your own children who are clearing the way for them, by taking good care of yourselves.

The Children of Crystal Vibration carry magical attributes that you have not seen before. Imagine a person who sees only through the eyes of love, and can see every thought and feel every emotion held within your heart. Imagine a person who can see beyond the veil, and can hold a normal conversation without ever falling into lies or deception. Some of the scouts that are entering now will be kept hidden by their parents until they are old enough to use their attributes. A parent of a Crystal child will quickly recognize that these children are very sensitive to energies around them, especially the lower vibrational emotion of fear. The parents of the first Crystal Children will be inclined to protect their child at all costs, yet this will not be quite as necessary as they think.

As advanced as you think you are, you are still a warring and brutal species. Crystal Children will have a sensitivity to fear that could be very detrimental to humanity. The challenge facing the Crystal scouts is to see if they can sustain the higher vibrations in physical form without succumbing to the detrimental effects of lower vibrational attributes such as fear. The Children of Crystal Vibration cannot survive on a planet riddled with constant fear. Your own future as a collective of humanity will depend on how you deal with fear. This is the one *Ugh !* area that each of you can be working on now. You will also soon have a chance to work on this collectively as well. [This was the second time this day that the Group hinted at the events to come of September 11th 2001. Earlier in this same presentation they gave the warning seen in chapter 2 "The Angel of the Twin Towers".]

Fear is the great vacuum that draws all energy around it. The Crystal Children have no fear within themselves. The problem comes from their empathic abilities which allow them to tap into emotions around them. Because they have no reference for the emotion of fear they can only reflect it back, amplifying it as they do so. Fear is the opposite of love and the Children of Crystal Vibration are children of love. Help them now by changing your own actions and reactions to fear. Face the fear within yourselves, teach others to do the same, and you will make the planet safe for the Crystal Children.

Do not look for your governments to do this for you. For who are the governments? Are they a bunch of people who meet quietly in secret rooms, controlling the lives of all on Earth? No, we will not let you avoid responsibility that easily. Your governments are *you*. They represent the collective you. *You* are the corporations, you are the businesses, *you* are the governments at all levels, *you* are the word you so love to use when you pass responsibility to '*them*'. Stand firm in your truth. Stand firm in what *you* believe and you will make space for the Children of Crystal Vibration.

Attleboro, Massachusetts - May 7th, 2000

Question:

I would like some assistance around positioning myself appropriately to help my own daughter make the transition into her new life.

the Group:

You have done well with your positioning thus far, for you have already planted seeds that will help do this job. The best thing you can do for your daughter is to focus your energy on your own needs. Find happiness within yourself first. Allow your daughter to make her own choices when feasible. Allow her to create her own reality and then hold her responsible for creating her highest and best. Give her the tools; empower her by trusting her to make her own choices. Plant the seeds of wisdom and then hold her responsible for tilling the soil, watering the seeds and growing the plant. That is her job and she is doing quite well.

The magical Indigo children that are now upon the Earth will do great things. You will be so proud of your daughter. When you see some of the magic that will result from her work you will understand just how well you have done. Imagine a time when the lines you have drawn in the sand are blown away. Imagine a time when you can travel anywhere without having to cross borders. Imagine a time when there are citizens of planet Earth, rather than citizens of this or that community. That time is coming and it is the Indigo children who are making it possible, for they are paving the way for the Children of Crystal Vibration to come.

You will be very proud of your daughter, for she is a leader among healers. Allow her to experience her traumas and her pain, for this pain will spur her on to become the leader she is going to be. Thank you for being here and for being willing to experience the difficulties of raising such a magical child. You have made more of a difference than you know.

Claiming Your Power

Esoteric Society - United Nations - Vienna, Austria - April 26th, 2000

Question:

How can we find a resolution to poverty, especially when it comes helping people change their mindset to think more in terms of abundance?

the Group:

Education is the only answer. Lack is a belief that pervades much of your thinking on Earth. That belief is a direct result of living within a field of polarity. You are endless infinite beings who live within a field of polarity and therefore see yourselves as being limited in everything. Is it any wonder that you see lack and limitation as an inescapable reality? Becoming accustomed to seeing energy as endless in all areas is the single idea that can change your world. You are in the process of creating Heaven on Earth. We lovingly re-mind you that there is no limit to abundance in Heaven. As you educate one, charge that one to educate another and another. Then hold each one responsible for taking this education and creating their own abundant reality. Feed them not once, but show them how to plant the garden. Give them the tools to stand firmly on their own feet and find their passion, then the passion will bring them to their own experience of abundance. Encourage them to do what they love to do. It is difficult to teach one who is searching for their next meal to be in their passion. But if they will at least move in that direction the results will very quickly become evident.

Educate them, charge them to be responsible for their own reality, and hold them responsible for their own environment. As each one experiences their own personal abundance it will spread to reach not only other individuals, but governments and organizations as well. The Keeper has a saying that we love so much: "Being broke is a temporary situation. Being poor is a state of mind". Teach them to move away from that state of mind and change their situations. Challenge them with possibilities. Be the Light in that fashion, and help them to understand that they are in control of their reality.

Education is the key. Educate with Love. Educate with your mind and your heart. Tell them that they are a part of you, and that you are a part of them. Show them that this hand wishes the other hand to do well, because both hands win when that happens. So often on The Game Board of Free Choice you think that you are in competition with one another. That is such a humorous scenario for us to observe.

Lack is the illusion. Abundance is the true nature of energy. Create that which emulates Home. Help people to plant their own gardens and give them the seeds. Then hold them responsible and watch as the garden of the New Earth flourishes.

Esoteric Society - United Nations - Vienna, Austria - April 26th, 2000

Question:
You have spoken of empowering other humans and you say we have free choice. How can we establish a government that can empower people to develop their spirit? How can we establish a government that will encourage the creation of Home?

the Group:
We thank you, for you have traveled long and hard to be of service to the planet and we tell you your message is being heard. That which you know in your heart to be true is being

acted upon, and although you find many difficulties in finding resolutions to these problems, we honor you, for you have made great advances in the areas you seek already. You are one of twelve who have made a big difference already. We are honored to be in your presence.

The question you ask has to do with the vibrational level of people. If a person is of a particular vibrational level and you move them several levels higher in one moment, they become confused. Their education and their understanding of energy does not allow them to move quickly from one level to the next. Sometimes they become disoriented and sometimes they become greedy. It has to do with empowering a person and creating a spot for them in which to create their own reality and then holding them responsible for choosing that reality and creating their own spot in turn.

There is a form of government that is returning to your planet. It is the government of Mu. The people you have in mind to help are not quite ready for this form of government at this moment. Still, the seeds are planted and the beginnings are already in place. We tell you it will be necessary first to find applications of these practices in other areas so that they can become accustomed to true empowerment. As you move forward and create more opportunities to use these in daily life, you will then find opportunities to educate and to show people how to use their empowerment.

Start slow. Start small. Empower people in small ways and then hold them responsible for using that empowerment to create their own reality. Let them see that they are in charge in some way where they can see results. They may see nothing but famine, and desolation. They may see governments that are not responsive. Let them know that they need not look to the government to create their reality, that they hold that power within them. Start small with small groups. Let it build from there as each group connects to one another. As they begin sharing ideas and resources and hopes and dreams, you will build a level of personal empowerment. Create governments and organizations dedicated to supporting personal empowerment and the next steps will become obvious. Have the courage to make mistakes, our dear friend, for that is your greatest fear. We tell you there are no mistakes. You have had the courage to put one foot in front of the other for your mission is well under way. Draw others around you that have the same dream. You are right in the middle of your passion. Share with others so that they can see what that feels like. Help others to know that they can create their reality much the way you have. Let them know that the government is not in charge of making them happy, or prosperous, or joyful. They will then create their own government that will best support them.

Nijmegen, Holland - April 16th, 2000

Question:

I'd like to express my gratitude and the honor of your beautiful work. My question is, here, in this beautiful area, it's rather easy to experience your love, to let myself be surrounded by your love and your wings, and even to feel my own wings. Soon I will travel home by car for more than an hour, and on that drive when I'm thinking of my daily life next week I just want to know how I can I keep the love that I have now?

the Group:

You come to these gatherings and you look into each others' eyes to re-member who you are. And then you look out the window at the cars that pass on the street. And you say, "I will be there tomorrow. I will be back in my daily grind". Oh, if only we could help you choose higher words for your thoughts. But we tell you that you will not re-turn. It will be a new you that is going back to that daily joy.

Do not create separateness between in here and out there. Do not hoard the energy and say, "We are going to go off into the mountains and create a community where we will all live in perfect Love". Instead, have the courage to take the same love you feel in here out there. People are awakening on the Planet at an astounding rate. Everyone is reaching for a higher Truth. For as you awaken, you look and you say, "Why are we here? What am I to do?" As you pass each other in your cars on the street, you look at the one driving next to you, and you smile. And, in that instant, you plant seeds of the same love you are feeling this day in this room. In that instance you help them re-member who they are. And in doing so, you are becoming Human Angels, re-membering who *you* are. Dare to claim your wings, dear ones.

Conspiracy and Secret Governments

Vienna, Austria - April 30th, 2000

Question:

There is a lot of talk about conspiracy and mind control these days. David Icke wrote a book about the biggest secret, about the global elite being shape-shifting reptilians, and about being into satanic rituals. What do you think about this?

the Group:

We are very saddened that you have included shape-shifting as a negative, for it is not. It is actually a very positive attribute practiced by masters. You will find, as you raise your own vibrations, that you will be able to shape-shift very easily, for you are much more in control of your physical bodies than you realize. It is humorous to us that most of your minds have just envisioned weight control. Shape shifting is a very high-vibrational activity.

Yes, there are negatives. Yes, there are what you have called satanic rituals. And yet we have told you of the true nature of Satan, have we not? Lucifer was not the villain that you make him out to be. And yet, we tell you that if you focus on the dark side, you will create darkness, for you are powerful beings. You ask about black magic, voodoo, mind control, and those that work with the dark energies. Is this possible? Of course it is possible, for you are powerful beyond your understanding. Does it have control over you? That is a question only you can answer. If you believe it does, then it does. Do they have control over you without your consent? Only if you fear them, for then they have your consent. For there is only one rule, and that is the rule of free choice. Choose to look only at the Light side and you will see Light. Your perception creates your reality. So be very careful where you place your attention.

You have a term that is called "secret government". We love that term. If you only knew the Truth, it would be so funny to you that you would never stop laughing. And when you finally do come Home, we will reveal this 'secret government' to you. Is there a secret government? Yes there is. Are they in control of anything? Absolutely not. Even they know that. Humanity is reaching a critical state where everyone will see inside each other's heads and hearts. On the New Planet Earth THERE WILL BE NO MORE SECRETS. No secret government can survive long in those conditions.

Please refrain from giving your power away through fear, for it only gives your power to those who seek it. Be careful where you point your co-creation machine, for that will determine your next reality. Choose to seek only Light and refrain from looking for subversive activity. You are powerful beings and if you look for darkness you will create it. Be cautious of the dramas that you allow yourself to play. We tell you that there is no difference between Love and fear, other than that which you attach to it. And yet, if you find Love to be a more empowering vibration than fear, then choose only Love, for it is your choice. And if you feel the mystery of fear, and if you feel the mystery of enjoying that aspect of it, then choose fear. Enjoy the drama if you choose, just know that it is always *your* choice.

Crystals and Minerals

The Woodlands, Texas - February 25th, 2001

Question:

What is the most appropriate and most spiritual use of crystals?

the Group:

It is no coincidence that you have been drawn to this field, dear one. You have been collecting vibrations in crystalline form from all over the planet. That is part of what you do. There are many spiritual and practical uses for crystals, and some that you had not even imagined. Crystals are living, breathing entities. They are the heart of the Earth. They are the energy of the Earth, which is why, when you hold them up to your own heart, you often feel something, though you may not know what it is. Though your scientific instruments are not yet able to register this energy, your own perceptions are expanding to the point where you are beginning to see evidence of the energy that resides in crystals. Watch the range of visual acuity expanding in humans, especially in relationship to crystals. Once more of you start to see this your scientists will be forced to look deeper for explanations.

Play, dear ones. It is not for us to give you full technology for it will not hold if we simply drop it onto the planet. It has to be discovered and uncovered by your scientists and supported by your own spiritual vibrations. And you will do just fine as this is not the first time you have been through this process. Feel free to experiment and play. Ask the crystals, for they know. You are beings of vibration. You only exist in your realm because the atoms in your body are vibrating between specific ranges. The crystals hold vibration, and they are the connection between your own vibration in physical form and the vibration of the planet. That is how you connect to the Mother. You have found that as you place an electrical charge across a crystal it vibrates at a specific rate. Releasing this vibration has helped you to keep very accurate time. So you now have electrical watches which have crystals in them. There are many more ways of utilizing the vibrations which are held in crystals and of working energetically with them. You are using them in your computers, are you not? What you have yet to fully discover is the spiritual capabilities of the crystals themselves. Even the crystals [semiconductors] used in your computers are alive and sentient beings. You have learned to program them as simple switches [computers], but you have yet to understand how to engage their true being. You will find they will hold the energy of intent just as well as they hold an electrical charge. Experiment with placing your intent into the crystals and watch the results. Play with this and enjoy.

However, please do not overwhelm yourselves with the crystals, for it is entirely possible to fill your whole house with them and then find you cannot sleep at night. Take care of your energies. Balance your energies. Understand that you are here doing what you came to do. And you, dear one, thank you for being where you are.

Earth Changes

Las Vegas, Nevada - January 20th, 2000

Question:

I would like to ask the Group to explain about the general pain that I have been feeling in my physical heart area.

the Group:

This is a good question because many of you have been feeling the same reaction. We will tell you a little bit about what you have tapped into. As healers, as energy workers, as people who have chosen to move to the next vibrational level, we tell you very specifically that you are tapped into more than you may know; you have tapped into the Earth Herself. There was a time when there was a great trauma in this particular location of the Earth. The greatest energy disturbance that has ever visited the Planet happened at a test site here. It was caused by the first atomic bomb and we tell you that the energy ripples that were set into motion then are still being felt today. There is much that is happening within the Earth to heal this process. There is much that has happened recently to shift the planet and open the way for a healing of its heart energy. This healing process is still ongoing. As you feel these shifts, those of you who are empathically sensitive to the Earth's vibrational energy will feel a gentle tugging in the area of your heart chakra. This is often felt as a slight sadness that overshadows even the most joyous occasion.

We shall now tell you what is really happening here. The Earth is preparing to shift her vibrational and dimensional levels. Because of the many energy disturbances that have occurred at this place and others like it, these are the places that will be affected first. This is also the reason that many of you here in this room today have been called here. Some of you actually find it very difficult to be here but you each knew you were being guided here. You may find it difficult to function sometimes, but you are holding the heart of the planet in your hands. Seek each other out, for you are not alone. Find others that can tell you what this feels like. Many of you are shifting dimensions yourselves and we tell you that a great joy will come from this, yet the process of change itself can be bittersweet.

Imagine that you were moving to a new house. As you prepare to move into that house, you are in great joy and anticipation about your new abode. When everything is ready, you go to move the final things out of your old home and into the new home. In that moment as you are packing up the last particles of your old existence, as you are preparing to leave, you feel sadness. This is a grief within your heart that tugs ever so sweetly and sadly. It does not mean that the move is not a good one. It is simply a bittersweet adjustment. The Planet also is shifting Her energy. Much like the illustration we gave you, She, too, is experiencing this bitter sweetness at this time. Those of you who are empathically sensitive to the Earth often feel this as a sympathetic pain in the heart. It simply means that you are very sensitive to the Mother, for this is Her energy and we thank you for helping Her to hold it. The time is fast approaching when the cetaceans, the whales, dolphins, and those of similar energy will be handing over the final vestiges of the care of Mother Earth and the holding of this heart energy to the humans who were supposed to have it all the time. You have earned that right and we thank you for taking this torch, for you are doing a marvelous job.

ℐree Choice

Esoteric Society - United Nations - Vienna, Austria - May 3rd 2001

Question:

It is said again and again that Planet Earth is special because we have free choice. How can we imagine other planets without choice? I ask out of curiosity, but also to better appreciate the choices we have here.

the Group:

This may surprise you. There was a time when Earth was looked down upon by others who do not have free choice. Indeed, most of the Universe has said, "Well, there is one that will never work. They cannot even take care of themselves. How do they expect to change All That Is?" And here you are. The reasons it was necessary for us to adjust the energy in the room at the beginning of our time together, was to make space for all the inter-dimensional beings that have filled this place. They as us can not wait to see what you do next. Before we began our communication this day, you created a vortex that opened up portals between your reality and several other dimensional levels. The moment you do that, everyone is here to view what is happening for you are the bright spot now; you are the first Planet of Total Free Choice. You are the special ones.

At the very beginning of the Game it did not appear to work, for you were taken over and turned into what can only be called a slave race. It is because of your enslavement that the concept of slavery has re-appeared many times since in your Game.

There are many Gameboards in other dimensions that have only partial free choice. Understand that these are beings who enjoy having a sense of predetermination. If you were to take one of these beings and place them in *your* Game, they would be forever drifting. Allow us to illustrate this in your own realm. The comparison we will now give you is not a fair comparison for things work differently in other dimensions. You may not be aware, but the fish in your oceans live in another dimension, and they do not have total free choice. You can see that even sticking your own head beneath water takes you into another dimensional reality where your senses work quite differently than they do above water. From the perspective of the fish, there is nothing wrong, nor is there anything lacking. They simply have a strong inner sense of being guided. You call this instinct, a sixth sense or extrasensory perception. They call it basic survival. When you experience this extrasensory energy, or instinct, you have the ability to exercise full choice about how, or if, you use it. Fish, on the other hand have only partial choice, for to deny their instincts would mean certain death.

Because your world had total free choice, which you did not always exercise, others were able to take control of you. Ahh, but here is the beauty. Even after you had been enslaved, even after your own DNA had been altered, ultimately you did choose to exercise your free will. You broke the bonds and you said the two words that set it into motion. "I AM". The moment those two words were uttered, the moment you re-discovered your power, in this case through procreation, you began to regain control and vowed to never again lose it.

By your actions, you have created such excitement in the Universe that all eyes are now focused on you, watching your every move. You are changing the paradigms of All That Is. There are no words in your language to encompass that which we call All That Is. The Universe, by its very definition, has limitations, yet you are not limited by those boundaries. You have changed the Game so much, you are no longer the *only* Planet of Free Choice. Because of your choices, dear ones, it is possible to now take your place as angels to those on the new and second Planet of Free Choice.

Aha, where is it? We hear you ask, as your left brains kick in. You wish to know exactly where this other Planet of Free Choice is, and in what star quadrant. We wish it were that easy to tell you. It is not. Suffice it to say that at this moment they are in a different time frame than yours, and therefore they are in a very rapid evolutionary cycle. But we will tell you this: If you stay on the track that you are presently on and continue with this curve of evolution you have started, things will get very exciting, for ultimately you *will* meet these beings. They will come to Planet Earth to see how the Game was played and Earth will then become the library it was always meant to be, and *you* will be the teachers and librarians. Some of you know in your heart that this is what you came here to do. And now you will get a chance to do it. Ahh, but they will not be the only ones to come. There will be many others on other dimensional levels who will also seek to learn from you. Even some of your own parental races will seek your advice.

In the days ahead you will make contact with some of these races. Be advised; do not let them take your power. Some may come to help with honest intention. Some will come to tell you that it was their intervention that allowed you to evolve. They have even fought over who has helped you the most up to this point. Hold your power, dear ones. Although there have been many that have helped, you have earned your advancement all by yourselves. Can you see why we chose you? Can you see why we call you the chosen ones? Can you now see why we are so honored to sit at your feet? You are making a difference beyond your understanding. We cannot tell you how great a difference, for it would scare you. But there is a key and it is passion. Find it, follow it, and do not let anyone else tell you where your passion lies, for you are the only ones that can tell where that may be.

Getting Along

Drachten, Holland - April 19th 2001

Question:

I have no problem making things happen as a creator, but I get into conflict because I feel I am manipulating people by doing so. Can you tell me how to balance this?

the Group:

Yes. It is a human attribute and a natural human re-action to manipulate other people. Some of you are well versed at it. Most often this action is not intentional, but only an attempt to create for yourself. There are times when your own life lessons would lead you to believe that your life can become better if only the people around you would change. This is clearly a misdirection of energy, for you are the only one who can change your reality. It has little to do with those around you. Those who repeatedly get caught in this misdirection we refer to as Master Manipulators. They may have a primary life lesson of Charity, where they are learning how to honor the energy of those around them. Or they may have received energy stamps early in their childhood that caused them to build walls for emotional protection. Learning to control your direction in life from behind such walls can result in a habit of manipulation. Such is the case with the victim who manipulates others with their problems. They then find that manipulating others to suit themselves is much easier than changing their own pattern of behavior. Those who set themselves up for lessons in this area generally attract people with weak or non-existent boundaries and then develop the habit of manipulating them.

Prime examples of people with weak boundaries are those working with a primary life lesson of Definition where they are learning to define their own energy fields. Here a Master Manipulator is often the catalyst, pushing them into working with their lesson of learning to define what is theirs and what belongs to another. Rarely are the actions of a Master Manipulator conscious or intentional. Generally their actions become habit, and that can be very difficult to change. The bonds are most often broken when these people go within and place themselves first in the energy flow, knowing that they have all they need. Here they begin to see their own hearts from within, instead of seeing themselves as they think others view them. They then realize their true connection with those around them and, consequently, have less need to manipulate others. At this point all that is left is to break the remaining habits.

The same action is required to break this cycle for both parties: Center your energy and place yourself first in all things. Determine your own energy boundaries within and not on the outside. Make use of the energy inventory which can help both the persons learning Charity and Definition. The person learning Charity learns to see themselves from within and the person learning Definition learns to define their energy boundaries and place themselves first in the energy flow. When each of you do that, manipulation, as you know it, will no longer be possible.

Your question also intimates a belief in lack that is not real. Here the base belief is that if you create something good for yourself you must be taking from someone else in some way. Understand that the greatest gift you can give all of those around you is to be centered in your own energy and to be placing yourself first. Only then, can you be of the highest use to the Universe.

So often we have envisioned you as children in a dark room. All the lights are out and you are all searching for the light and the way out of the room. You may see a little glimmer of light over in the corner of the room. Excitedly, you run toward it and without realizing it you bump into another person. Here, you may have caused harm, yet, your intentions were pure. You did not intend to manipulate this person or cause harm in any way. Your honest desire was to reach the light and find the door. This is the truth of your heart, dear one. If you can speak that truth freely, there will be no manipulation on either part.

We tell you also that you are coming to a very interesting time on Planet Earth. For with the influx of the new energy and your own heightened senses, we tell you there will be no more secrets. Think about that for a minute. Things are liable to get very interesting on Planet Earth as you all begin to see what each other is thinking. This will eventually return you to the purity of thought that you carried as children. In the interim, those of you attempting to hold secrets will no longer be able to. Can you see why we tell you things are going to get interesting? This is part of the reason that so many entities from other vibrational realms are watching the Gameboard of Free Choice. It is much like the grandest of you soap operas. We thank you for the wonderful show

Speak your truth. Just the fact that you are concerned about possibly manipulating others indicates this is not the problem that you may think. Stay with your truth, dear one. Reach for your greatest passions, reach for your desires and instead of *making* it happen, *allow* it to come to you by simply holding that vibration in your heart. You do not need to pull Heaven to Earth. You have only to *allow* it.

ʜealing ꟼodalities

Attleboro, Massachusetts - January 28th, 2001

Question:
I have a question about breath work. The breath work that I have learned is a full, circular connected breath that is in through the mouth and out through the mouth. The breath technique you teach through Steve is in through the nose and out through the mouth. I would like some clarification on the different purposes of these two styles.

the Group:
Let us start first with the clarification of what you call breath work and how we see it from a perspective of pure energy. What we see is that as you breathe in the air you are literally taking an ethereal part of yourselves and bringing it into physical being. It is the life sustenance, along with water, that is really all you need to create your being here on the planet. You are moving to a point where you will need only two forms of energy to sustain your physical being, and that is air and water. Both of them are actually forms of energy that you do not understand. Water, in particular, contains energy far beyond your understanding. The moment you discover the secret held within water and begin to tap into that energy source, you will no longer need the remnants of dead animals to power your automobiles. There is energy all around you and you will not only learn how to use it to light your cities and your homes, warm your bodies, you will also learn how to nourish your being with it. That is really all you need.

Techniques, ahh. . . there will be many. Are there any that are right or wrong? No, there are not. What the Keeper teaches is a technique for using breath energetically to charge your spine. One technique is not more right than another. Use what works for you. And for you, breathing in and out through the mouth is more powerful than breathing in through the nose and out through the mouth. That is your power of choice and all choice is honored. Teach what you know best. Teach what works for you. We tell you that both techniques produce a slightly different result, and therefore a slightly different flavor of the same truth.

One of the forms that you teach was used by one of the ancient tribes here on the planet long before you started recording your history. In fact, you helped develop these techniques. That is the reason you have such an affinity for it, and for teaching people how to breathe.

Attleboro, Massachusetts - January 28th, 2001

Question:
Would you tell us a little bit about the process of changing our DNA?

the Group:
You are going through many vibrational changes and part of what you are experiencing is directly related to your own intent to shift your DNA. This is happening on a global basis, for you have given your permission collectively for this to happen. You will find many who teach classes, give exercises, or who have developed modalities based around this. Are they necessary? No. Are they fun? Are they helpful? Yes. The ultimate process of shifting your own physiology to match that of the Children of Crystal Vibration is what we have termed the OverLight process. In the next few years you will see many who will teach several OverLight processes. Please understand that if you never take any classes you will still have the opportunity to participate in this process. It is your birthright. If you do wish to take classes you may find them quite enjoyable.

There are many ways of activating OverLight. There will come a time when you may be sitting quietly, or driving in your car, or laying in your bed, and your body will simply start to vibrate. That is the physical manifestation of the new DNA and the beginning of the OverLight process. It will happen to all of you at different intervals and at different times. If it has not happened to you yet, please do not try to bring it on. Please do not try to create it when the time is not correct, since you will only aggravate the situation. Allow it to come naturally in its own time. Treat your biology well. As much as you have abused it, it has worked very well for you. If you purposely shift your DNA too quickly you will have major re-actions. So please proceed slowly.

Health & Biology

Drachten, Holland - April 19th, 2001

Question:

Can you tell us something more about the physical changes? What is happening? There is so much aching around us—in every bone. So much headache, dizziness and people are so busy with their bodies and not with their spirit because they are anxious about what's going on.

the Group:

When you make vibrational advancements, when you choose to jump from one level to the next, it affects your biology. Please do not think that if you are experiencing challenges with your physical that it means that your spiritual is not moving. They are tied together and one cannot move without the other.

We have spoken before about the vibrational flu. It feels like every bone in your body is aching but you may not have a fever. It is simply your physical body catching up to the vibrational shifting that has taken place. When you scripted this we begged you to take this slowly, but no, you jumped in and insisted on being at the very front of the class, advancing as fast as possible. Then, when your body reacts to the rapid vibrational movement, you try to figure out what you are doing wrong. Ahh, you do afford us much humor. *(Laughter)* But we would not have it any other way. For you are so ambitious and you have done so well. It is often that we hold the energy for you when your body aches. And if it were possible for us to do so, we would touch you and make it okay. But that is not possible on the Gameboard, nor is it appropriate, for in many instances your pain serves you well. In some instances, your pain causes further vibrational advancement. Pain often motivates you to be the healers that you are. You ask why there are no books about what is happening. It is because you have yet to write them, dear ones. And you will.

There are things you can do to relieve some of your stress. This may sound strange to you, but if you are meditating five hours a day, please stop. *(Laughter)* The problem here is that you are trying so hard to advance spiritually that your physical body cannot catch up. Be aware that in the higher vibrations of the New Planet Earth meditation is not necessary for spiritual connection. Now you will walk with that connection within. So, if you have been meditating in order to raise your vibrations, it will no longer produce those results. If you meditate for relaxation and centering, then it will work well.

Salt baths will help you to make the electrical connections between your physical body and your many etheric bodies and also help you ground the energy quickly and with less pain. This will be particularly effective if you also decrease the salt you take into your body while increasing it on the outside. Salt is a soluble crystal and when you do this you change the energy charge of your body, much like changing the charge on an electrical capacitor. This will help your spirit feel more comfortable within your bubble of biology.

Watch your body energy and become aware of it. Watch the environments you place yourself in and make sure they add to you. There are many times when people come to us and say, "My house feels terrible. Every time I go into my house it drains my energy. What is wrong? What should I do?" And we say, move. *(Laughter)* Pay close attention to your environment, for you are more sensitive than even a short time ago. Some things will feel good and others will not, and you know better than us. You know in your own hearts what you need. Pay attention to your biology. Ground it well. You have spent so much energy advancing your spirit that you may have created a gap between the spirit and the biology. This is the reason that many people feel a strong pull toward grounding foods. Chocolate is especially useful for grounding the biology and is useful for counteracting the vibrational flu. Many of you will find yourselves pulled in this direction.

Vibrational healing is one of the largest area of healing that will develop during the years and months to come. Your physical being is nothing more than a squiggly line from our perspective. You are vibration and such beautiful squiggly lines you are. The only reason you exist is because the atoms in your body are vibrating. Each organ in your body carries a different vibration. Your bodies have an overall vibrational signature that is unique to each one of you. And you thought your fingerprints were strange. You should see what we see. What is especially interesting is when you act one way and believe another. That can really mess up a vibrational signature. Quite often what happens is that you put your vibrational signatures out of sync through your actions, through your emotions, through your ignorance. When that happens, it is easiest to re-introduce other vibrations to help you re-set your signature. You experience this on a very small scale now with modalities that use color, sound and aroma. Even as you listen to soothing music it is helping you to reset your energy. You will find out much about this in the next few years. Vibrational healing includes many modalities that currently exist and many more yet to come. Experiment with vibrational tools now, for they will help you most with the aches and pains of the vibrational shift. Play with it. And then write the books that will help others. That is what you have chosen to do. You are the special ones. Welcome Home, dear ones. Welcome Home. Welcome Home.

Sydney, Australia - August 26th, 2001

Question:

I'm conscious that I have already lived for more than half the number of years currently allotted on average to people in our way of being. And yet I have only really just begun to do the work that I am here to do. I would like to expand my life-span as much as I possibly can so that I can be and give as much as I can while I'm here. And I'm wondering if you can help share information with me and others that may be interested about how to expand the life-span?

the Group:

Making deals as we get older, are we? *(Laughter.)* Ahh. . . how we love your humanness. You ask a question first about how you can expand your life-span but before that you made a statement: "I would like to expand my life-span as long as I can and give as much as I can while I'm here". And to that statement the Universe has a beautiful answer: And so it is. In the moment you made that statement, your life-span *was* increased. As a result of that statement you have already begun the process of rejuvenation. The energy in this room currently has no forward time. When we come to you in this manner an energy vortex is created, and in these moments the ageing process ceases to be. That is the energy and the magic of Home. You look to us and think that we are some magical beings. But we tell you that you can create this yourself within statements of passion, much like the one you spoke when you asked this question.

Please do not concern yourself with the fact that you have spent half your life-span asleep. In fact, it has been quite common for people to sleep through entire lifetimes. Instead, celebrate that you are awake and are now reaching for your passion.

Life extension is a reality that will be presented to you sooner than you think. You have capabilities of living beyond your wildest dreams. Even so, we tell you, there will come times when many of you choose to come Home to re-fresh and re-set your energy. It is your choice, dear ones, for the processes of rejuvenation will be at your fingertips very shortly. Many life extension secrets are coming through your traditional sciences as well as through the metaphysics that you love so much. Soon you will see a blending of the physical and the metaphysical. Watch for it, embrace it. You will see the magic happen within your own lifetime. If you live only another ten years the average life-span on the New Planet Earth will reach 120 years of age. Some of you who thought you were getting old may soon find that you are only half way there.

A Healing Center Dream Manifest

Here, as in many other writings, the Group directs us to watch for the blending of the physical and metaphysical sciences. We will now tell you about a project very dear to our hearts that is the real life application of this concept. In Holland there is a group of people building a dream. Ground has already been broken to build a healing center. This healing center will include space for education of the special Children now entering Earth, both Indigo and Crystal. It will also include space for Transition Teams as well as those who choose to transition in dignity. The Transition Team center will have a gentle loving staff. It also includes a glass ceiling. There will be space for classes of all sorts, including many different modalities of healing. This healing center will be the realization in the physical of many dreams that have been dropped into the collective consciousness for decades. Many of you reading this have held this dream personally, and now you will see it manifest. In a way, you all have had a hand in its creation. The brave people behind this project are holding a sacred vision which is now becoming a reality for all of us.

This healing center is already underway and, interestingly, is already fully funded. This is not exactly a small project. In fact, at first glance, this center may look similar to a traditional hospital. It will have 175 beds and a large staff of doctors and nurses. Construction has already begun in Obdam, in the state of Noord-Holland in the Netherlands.

Now, here's the best part of this story: For every doctor working on staff, there will also be a metaphysician working alongside them. This center is founded upon the principle of blending the physical and metaphysical sciences. Doctors and energy workers, acupuncturists and surgeons, pediatricians and reiki masters, podiatrists and reflexologists will all work side by side to form one of the first healing centers of this unique kind. Allopathic, homeopathic and many alternative modalities will blend together under one roof to offer the most comprehensive healing center known to man.

As of this writing, there are four other healing centers already planned and funded and just awaiting construction. It's a big task, but even if this goes no further, it is already a success. The biggest challenge thus far is in getting the insurance companies in Holland to support the project. However, the largest insurance company is already on board. Once the others see the results they will not hesitate. We ask that you send these brave souls your energetic support. When the benefits of this new type of healing center become apparent, others will start popping up all over the New Planet Earth.

Contact HL1951@planet.nl for information.

Watch the Lightworker web site www.Lightworker.com for regular updates on this and other groundbreaking projects that the Group has predicted will be integral to the creation of the New Planet Earth. The time is now. . . are you ready?

Columbus, Ohio - June 9th, 2001

Question:
I've had a question I've been vacillating back and forth with. I have a disease and for 15 years I've been taking different kinds of harsh medication for it. I feel really well now,

healthier than I've ever felt before. My dilemma comes from dealing with the decision to stop medication, how to know if and when it's all right. And I know that it has to be my decision, nobody can tell me that. I guess I'm just asking, am I warped for thinking I can do something like this?

the Group:

The human body, which you call biology, is a miraculous tool and a holder of your energy, actually only part of your energy, but a perfect container for the energy that you travel with in biology. Sometimes it holds the opportunity for lesson, sometimes it contains the energy matrix that you are trying to master, sometimes it holds the energy imprints that you receive here from your experience on Planet Earth, and sometimes it holds your emotional body which you love to struggle so much with. We tell you it is miraculous indeed and the moment your thinking changes even slightly, your physical body starts to adjust to make the perfect container for the new thought forms.

Envision the DNA in your own body as energy receptors much like radios. When you have a thought, you send radio signals to your own DNA. The physical outer sheath is actually the part of the DNA that receives the signals and transmits them to the inner structure. The DNA carries the blueprint of your own biology and the building blocks are set in perfect order, according to how that DNA is holding the plans. It used to be that every seven years you would replace 98 percent of the cells in your body. That is no longer the case. It is happening much faster now. As you replace cells in your body, each cell checks with your DNA to get the most up-to-date plan available that will define its attributes and the role it will play. Now it can begin the shift at a moment's notice. Therefore, your thoughts are what you will become…only now it will happen much faster. This is the reason we ask you to choose your thoughts carefully as they hold your next reality.

Balance your comfort zone with your ability to heal yourself. Understand that your own biology will tell you when it is time for any change. Get in touch with the inner voice of your outer biology. Listen and you will hear. Do not think that you must fully heal yourself to be the healer for others, for that presupposes that your condition is something wrong. We tell you that it is this very condition that prompted you into healing. When you asked the question, "Do I have the ability?" The resounding answer is, "Yes. Yes. Yes". Your biology is a direct result of your thought patterns, now more so than ever. When you are ready, your biology will let you know as you move into the next phase of your own healing.

Homosexuality

Syracuse, New York - March 11th, 2001

Question:

You spoke about polarity of the sexes and the questions that came up in me are these: Is the increasing visibility of the lesbian, gay, bisexual, transsexual community part of the breaking down of polarity? And what is the special role that we have to play in our society? What is the gift that we, as homosexuals, have?

the Group:

Let us answer your last question first. You asked: "What is the gift that we, as homosexuals, have?" To that question we answer simply that you have no special gift as homosexuals. You do have a wonderful gift to give as humans in love. Love knows no boundaries and in the higher vibrations of the New Planet Earth you will find many expressions of love, including the expression of love that you call homosexual.

One of the first questions the Keeper asked us when he became aware that he was channeling entities from the other side of the veil, was: "Is there sex on the other side of the veil?" We love it so, for he is such a grounded human. And we answered no, not in quite the same way you think of it, for we are not separated into an expression of one gender or another. We did not go through the second dimension and split off into polarity, so we integrate both male and female energy, and that is part of the reason we are resistant to placing labels on this. Still, you see us as one or the other no matter what label you put on it. We tell you the Group carries as much female energy as it does male energy, with the exception of the Keeper who loves being male. We also tell you this: What you experience in your brief moment of union whether it is male to male, female to female, or male to female is the vibration that we live in all of the time. So it would be a more apt question if you would ask, "When is there *not* sex on your side of the veil?" And that is the reason we smile all the time.

As you move forward in your evolutionary process you will see a huge increase in what you have labeled homosexuality. Same sex relationships are becoming much more widely accepted as education spreads. It is important that you understand that love is love and it makes no difference how you express, or where you express it. Follow the love in your heart, for that is the truest expression of God. Find one that can reflect you in the most wondrous way. Find someone to have a relationship with and with whom you can express that love on a regular basis, someone who can walk alongside you and not lean against you. Share life together and you will find magic, and in this manner you will create the vibrations of Home on a daily basis.

You will learn much more about this expression of love as you progress. There is greater potential here on this side of the veil for different types of sexual expressions and relations than you have yet envisioned. There is much that you will create in the future. And we tell you again that love is love. Find the love, and for those who find one love, remain open to the idea that there are other types. Use your discernment. Find what is right for you and leave the rest without judgment, for that is the truth of the higher vibrations of the new Planet Earth.

Welcome Home.

Human Cloning

Attleboro, Massachusetts - May, 20th, 2001

Question:
What do you have to say about cloning? Is there anything there that serves a purpose?

the Group:
How much time do you have?

Questioner:
All Day

the Group:
Good answer. We told you before that you humans love to adapt and yet you are so afraid of creation. You love to take things and adapt and improve upon them. Yet sometimes, just to use your powers to create would be much simpler. You are so afraid of your powers of creation, you do not see yourselves as the creators that you are. You can take your own human science known as medicine and you can improve upon God's creation, but the moment you are faced with the possibilities of your own creation, you pull back.

If we told you that "You are God", would you believe us? You are. Therefore, why should you fear the art of creation? We tell you, the first human was cloned on Planet Earth on March 7th of this year [2001]. So you see, it has already begun. It is only technology and it is nothing to be afraid of. It is being supported by your own vibrational expressions. Do not fear it. Are you going to make mistakes? Yes, of course you are. Are you are going to correct those mistakes? Yes, of course you will. Do you think the first automobile that you made worked properly? Do you remember the first flying machine that you made? Please understand that you will not stop technology. The Genie

is out of the bottle and will not go back in. There is no right or wrong, it is simply progress. It is your nature to fear progress, yet without it you would not be reading these words.
Understand that it is simply not possible intentionally to unlearn something. You are blending biology and technology into a new science that we call Triology. It is a natural evolution of your own power.

We tell you this is not the first time this technology has surfaced. The Others of 'E' vibration are here, even now. In fact, four of them are in the room with you this evening. The Others are the ones that were biologically and genetically engineered beings back in the days of Atlantis. At that time your governing rules were based on lack. You felt that the Atlanteans were the most important people and the immigrants came second. This placed the Others third. Inadvertently, you created a slave class of beings and you put limitations on their lifestyles. You told them they could not procreate and you told them they were only useful for work that the Atlanteans and the immigrants did not want to undertake. Because you had a hand in the creation process, you did not think these beings had souls. These beautiful gentle beings have carried those cellular memories with them from one lifetime to the next. And they are here now to help you make those choices again. Do not fear them or your own power. They are creations of God. Honor them, for like you, they too have souls.

Your own science fiction writers have asked these questions: "What if we create a race of beings much better than us? What if they take over?" And we ask you, "Have you given your children vitamins? Do you not want them to grow physically healthier than you?" So why would you fear this? Yes, it is a big change. Yes, it will scare many. Make space in your hearts for these beings that once walked with fear and now will walk with pride. There are many of you who have re-incarnated in order to be here at exactly this moment in your history. Most of you have felt disconnected throughout all of your lifetimes. Most of you have felt like you have been part of the wallpaper, playing the role of observers of life, instead of participants in it. You felt that you had no purpose. Well, your purpose is here now, for you have gone through all those lifetimes between now and then just to be here at this time. Without saying a word you have already made a difference in the collective vibration of humanity. We thank the Others for the work they have done, for they have suffered so much. Re-member those times. Encourage each other to write your stories. Encourage each other to connect and reclaim your identities. And we will be here to help you, just as we always have been.

Lucifer Experiment

Vienna, Austria - April 30th, 2000

Question:

Will you please explain the Lucifer Experiment?

the Group:

You came from the first dimension into the 3rd dimension through the second. As you did, you split off into various parts of yourself, and you became light or dark, good or bad, love or fear, male or female. You split to reflect polarity and provide contrast. As below, so above, for as you went into polarity we, too, had to follow similar energy patterns to retain our connection to you. We are connected in more ways than you know. We replicated your experience of polarity on Earth by setting up experiments to emulate a field of polarity in Heaven.

The experiment of Lucifer is what you have known in your writings as "the devil". You created this as a part of yourself that is evil, darkness opposing Light. You constantly amaze us as you are so imaginative with your dramas! As much as you love your games we tell you evil does not exist. Darkness is only a lack of Light and nothing more. What you call darkness is only a shadow caused when the Light is restricted. If you choose to fear the shadows, then they become powerful. It is your own fear that gives power to the very thing that you are afraid of.

As your Game became more polarized, it was necessary for us to create similar conditions in Heaven. The result was what you have termed in your Biblical writings as the refraction of God. This was the split of energy into light and dark. These you see as the Archangels and the Devil. Lucifer was the key player in this grand experiment. Lucifer loved God and The Universe more than you could possibly know. To have him play such a role, to be scorned and perceived as evil, demonstrated the immensity of the Love he feels for you. Please re-member that it is the darkness that allows you to see the Light. The intent of the Lucifer Experiment was to provide contrast for the Light so that it could be seen in a field of polarity. It was a great experiment, indeed.

But we tell you now, it is coming back together. For what was once separate is separate no longer. Lucifer is Home, we are whole once again. Through your choices on Earth you have made this possible. We apologize to The Keeper, for we have hugged too tightly. We will take a moment. . . [At this point tears overwhelmed Steve.]

You are moving from a motivation of survival to a motivation of Unity. And as you move toward that Unity you reflect it toward Heaven. For as below, so above. And through your own re-union of original Spiritual Family you have created the opportunity for us to re-unite as well. And we are doing so in the grandest of Joy. We are dancing in the very Light that *you* are creating. We ask you to dance in that same Light with us.

We know that we have only described it in ambiguous terms that you may not fully understand, but we also know that we have planted some very important seeds here, and we thank you for that opportunity.

Memories of Home

Enlightenment Society - United Nations Staff Recreation Council
United Nations Headquarters – New York - March 23rd, 2001

Question:

When the channeling began, tears just came into my eyes. I felt flooded with all this love. I myself do channeling and in those messages this name keeps on coming up, it's Elohim. How and in what way can I channel in a more pure and focused manner without ego?

the Group:

Thank you for asking a most excellent question. You are not the only one in the room that will be interested in this answer. How can you carry the message? How can you hear it more clearly without the ego getting in the way? We tell you the ego is tricky, certainly, and there are many who find themselves struggling with this too. In fact, there are many wonderful channels that have disconnected themselves from their original source of information by falling into their ego. The interesting thing is that most of them do not know they are disconnected. Please understand that the ego is an important part of you and your experience on Earth. In the lower vibrations from which you came, it was necessary to temporarily transcend the ego in order to let the information enter. This was the purpose of what you call trance mediums, or unconscious channels. In the higher vibrations of the New Planet Earth this is no longer necessary. Now, it is a balance of the ego you are seeking. We tell you that if you do not have enough ego to stand and say that you have something of value to offer, then you cannot do your work. If the ego takes over you lose your connection to spirit. So it is a balance that is needed. Trust your heart for your heart knows where the balance is. As facilitators, we suggest that you check your ego and your motivations often, and then you will always be in balance.

Now, as for the name Elohim, you must keep in mind that you are speaking now to a group of entities known to the Keeper simply as 'the Group'. Here you can clearly see that we are not big on names or labels. Regardless of the label the energy is always the same. It is simply that each one interpreting the energy must do so through their own filters of experience and, therefore, brings it through with a slightly different flavor. This is as it should be, for each flavor will attract a specific segment of people. The biggest misdirection of energy is when one 'flavor' falls prey to spiritual competition and says their flavor is the only *true* flavor. Chocolate chip, Vanilla, or Strawberry, it is all ice cream. Find your own flavor, dear ones, for ultimately it does not make a difference where it comes from. Please use your own discernment and enjoy those flavors which resonate with you.

Personally we tell you that although you primarily write at this time, there are several other forms of this channeling that you will be doing very soon. Enjoy the journey.

Esoteric Society - United Nations - Vienna, Austria - April 26th, 2000

Question:
I want to know why I am so sad inside, even though I'm a really funny person. Where does this inner sadness come from?

the Group:
If only we could remove the veil for just a moment. If only we could help you see your origins and the greatness from which you come. For you woke up one day in this human body and you said: "What have I got myself into?   What have I done? This body is awkward and I do not know how to work it. Where is the manual for this thing?" Then everyone tells you how

simple it is and it still does not seem to work for you as easily as it does for them. You feel like you do not belong. You feel like you are an observer and not a participant in life, and yet, somewhere in the back of your heart, you re-member Home. You have a part of you which carries the re-membrance of Home always. There are times when you poke small holes through the veil. When this happens, the memories flood back and the Heart is filled with bittersweet memories. The pull of Home is very strong. There is such joy here; there is such great happiness, and such great passion. Here, there is laughter like you have never heard on Earth. You re-member this part of Home, and you miss it. The truth of the matter is that you, and many like you, are simply Homesick.

Yet you know you have a purpose. We thank you for being there. Be patient, dear ones, the miracle of Home is now right in front of you as you create Home on your side of the veil.

Mu and Atlantis

Nijmegen, Holland - April 22nd, 2001

Question:

Lately I've had the feeling I was in Atlantis, cloning and experimenting with genetics on people and other races. I remember that I enjoyed it and did not think about their souls. I would like to know if this is true because I would like to take full responsibility for it.

the Group:

Did you hear her words as that beautiful voice created a resounding chord of energy that crossed her vocal chords? As that vibration was shared with your own field, you heard it first in your ears and then you heard it in your heart. Listen well, dear ones, for you are listening to a master. Why? For she has the courage to ask the question: 'How can I take responsibility?' Yes, you know perfectly well without even asking that you were there and you played the villain. In fact, you have all played the villain and you have all played the victim. You script your roles well and you play them with such interesting drama sometimes. This is very humorous for us to watch. You think that your television shows are entertaining! We tell you, when you re-turn Home, you will replay these memories many times.

The courage to ask that question about your responsibility is the true base of your power. For it is not possible any longer to hold true power without balancing it with responsibility. Even if the Keeper were able to give you the gift of great power it would only work if you balanced it with the responsibility of using it wisely. Would you like to see where your responsibility lies? Would you like to see what you have already done to balance that responsibility? We ask you to look at a young child in your life, for you have already made a big difference here. You have already planted the seeds of a master healer that is awakening. We tell you that it took a lot of courage for you to come back here at exactly this time to complete this contract.

You have already cleared the energy, dear one. Of all the injustices that you had a hand in, you have balanced them long ago, yet you still carry the cellular imprints. You still carry the energy stamps of those times, and that is the confusing part for you. For you still feel guilty. Acknowledge it, feel it and move past it, for now you are touching hearts and making a difference on the planet.

You will re-member much about what you actually did in those days, for you are now ready to accept the truth. Do not judge yourself harshly. The contracts that you played out reached far beyond your understanding. Simply accept the past and look upon it as the storybook that it was. Now here you are writing a new one, and that is where your responsibility lies this day. We thank you for asking that question.

Syracuse, New York - March 11th, 2001

Question:
Can you clarify the misdirection of energy in Atlantis? What do we need to be alert for particularly?

the Group:
Atlantis was a high technology civilization and the spiritual vibration you held in those days was high enough to support that technology. Yet even with this high spirituality you had slaves. This is not something that you see happening now. This is the advancement in consciousness that will take you beyond the evolution of Atlantis. This time, it looks like you might make it. The Universal Energy is a constant, and all things that emulate the Universal Energy will be supported, while all those things

that flow against it will find great resistance. The latter days of Atlantis afforded you many opportunities to be opposed to the blending motion of the Universal Energy and that was one of the underlying factors in its destruction. One of the greatest things you are doing on this planet now is racial blending. Your economies have been blending for years. It is wonderful to see. Allow yourselves to be part of this blending energy and you will see what we are talking about. Nothing is outside of you. Do not fall into segregation, and you will not fall prey to the same misdirections of energy that you did in the latter days of Atlantis.

In the last few decades there was a great fear among Atlanteans that there would not be sufficient resources to sustain everyone. That fear generated the very lack that you were trying to avoid. In trying to decide who would benefit from your technology you created subcultures, one of which was a race of slaves. Yet all are the same in the eyes of God. (And if you think that some of you here on this Earth are different, wait until you meet some of those from other dimensional realities. You humans will bond together very, very quickly!) Therein lies one of three misdirections of energy that caused the destruction of a great culture. The other two misdirections were spiritual competition and your inability to hold your full power of creation. More will be given on these in the near future. [See the final chapter entitled 'The Atlantis Connection']

You are at a crossroads right now where you will have opportunities to make the very same misdirections of energy that you made then. We tell you, follow the flow of Universal Energy and you will find that the great days of Atlantis are still possible on Planet Earth. Because of your past misdirections, many of you feel the seed fear that creates a huge resistance within you as you start moving into your power and causes you to say, "Oh my God, am I supposed to be doing this?" Feel this seed fear, dear ones, for it acts as the guardian at the gate.

As long as you are following that which is in your hearts, you are listening to your higher selves. Your connection to your Higher

Self is becoming very strong, and although it is very difficult for you to trust - for the veil deludes you into thinking that you cannot do this yourself, you cannot create energy you can only alter it - you will start to see differently now. It is a wonderful time to be here. If you think the Indigos are making a difference and if you think the Children of Crystal Vibration will make a difference, the honor of Home will go first to you, for through your choices, you made it possible for all of this to happen. You are the Human Angels responsible for the creation of the new Planet Earth.

Welcome Home.

Drachten, Holland - April 19th, 2001

Question:

I would like to know what will happen to those who choose to stay unaware.

the Group:

Those who choose to stay unaware will stay unaware. It is a very valid question and we tell you something about this because it is very misconstrued. It is very misunderstood for you have an image of a ladder. We call it the ladder of human advancement and it is your perception that in order to get to Heaven you must climb this ladder. Each rung of the ladder is a different vibration and you believe that you must go up to the top of the ladder to ascend. That is not what is happening. For it is only when every person takes their entire spot on each rung of the ladder, including those holding the feet, that the entire ladder will then ascend.

Please do not think that because someone does not appear to be as vibrationally in tune as you are, they cannot be as advanced. They are simply holding a different section of the ladder in place. Please do not think that the third grade is better than the second, for it is not. They are only different.

When you see those who are not enlightened, when you see those who do not have the same understanding that you do, open your heart to them and thank them for the role they are playing. That is the new energy. That is the connection of Unity consciousness.

What would it be like for you to be nine hundred years old? What would it be like to be three hundred years old? Can you imagine all the wonderful knowledge you could amass, the level of mastery you could attain in one lifetime, if you did not have to deal with diapers? You will have that choice, dear ones. Yet, to make your choice you will need to have a true understanding of Unity consciousness and re-member the misdirections of Atlantis. Even though you will have that choice, many of you still will not choose to stay. Why? Because the pull of Home is very strong, and there will come a time when many of you will realize that you have done your work. Whether you live to be nine hundred years old or whether you live to be one hundred years old or whether you live to be seventy, you will all be welcomed Home with the greatest of honors. And we will celebrate your re-union Home.

The Nature of Duality

Barcelona, Spain - April 2nd, 2000

Question:

I am a person who can see but can't feel. I have always felt a deep emptiness in my life. Now I feel very full, especially with the Love that I am feeling so much of here during these two days. I always used to ask myself why I was here. What was my purpose? My heart was saying one thing, but my body didn't accompany me. I feel privileged because I had three mothers: my biological mother, the mother who raised me, and the mother of my husband. I learned a lot and I don't want to go Home yet. My question is: If I follow my heart and my path will my body support me?

the Group:

There once was this great stream of water, and in the energy of the water there lived these wonderful fish. The water was constantly moving downstream. The fish lived all their lives with one singular purpose, to stay in the same spot in their stream. Here they were familiar with life and they were comfortable. They learned to swim in such a way that they never had to go anywhere. There were stories about what was downstream, and they were taught when they were young that if they wandered too far away they would be pulled over the great waterfall into the abyss and cease to exist. Throughout all of the fish there was great fear about what was downstream.

One day a very special fish said to a friend, "I'm tired of swimming in the same spot, my body does not support me the way I need to stay here. I wonder what would happen if I simply let go?" Hearing this, her friend said: "Don't let the others hear you talk that way". Still the first fish wondered what it would be like to just let go. One day she was so tired of fighting to stay in the same place that she simply let go. To her surprise, she found that with very little effort the motion of the water guided her down to the most comfortable spots in the river. The river had a natural ability to guide her that she had not been expecting. Life suddenly took on new meaning as she released all fear and just let the river take her.

Downstream she saw many wonderful sights and had grand experiences. She met new species of fish and creatures that she never knew existed. One day she came to the edge of the waterfall and she paused. She felt the old fear overtake her as she sat motionless in the still waters near the banks. She knew that if she continued her journey she must go over the waterfall and her life would then cease to exist. To her surprise, as she sat there thinking, a fish came up the waterfall against the current, and greeted her with a smile. In that moment she knew that she had choices and so she swam directly into the strongest current of the river and was quickly swept over the waterfall. To her amazement, she made the journey easily.

As she continued further downstream, she found herself thinking of her original family. She missed them. If only they knew the truth, she thought. Finally, she decided to swim all the way back upstream to tell her brother and sister that it was okay to let go. After a year of effort to get back upstream, she eventually made it back home. She looked around and said, "I'm so glad to see you! Let me tell you what's downstream. There's nothing to fear. It's beautiful down there. There are many wonderful species to interact with. There's great opportunity down there. Come, swim with me and I will show you".

To her surprise her brother and sister said, "No. You are now an outcast. You have been tainted, and we do not wish to have you around us". Even though it had been offered in love and with the highest intent, they were not ready for the truth. Eventually, the fish understood that she was, in fact, tainted and could stay there no longer. With that, she said her goodbyes. Sad that she had wasted so much time and effort, and heartbroken that her brother and sister did not get her message, she swam back downstream again. Ah, but that is not the end of this story. For even though the fish left, the seeds that she had planted with her brother and sister lived on for years. And every time someone told them a story about the horrible things that were downstream they re-membered their sister, and they said, "I wonder if that's really true?"

One day, many years later, both the sister and brother decided that they too would just let go. To their amazement, they floated effortlessly down the stream and began new and very enjoyable lives. Although they never again saw their sister, their journey had only been possible because of the seeds that she had planted.

Such were your own contracts. You came in to plant seeds of Light long before they were popular. But it was your jobs to plant such seeds early. Now you too have choices. If the choice has purpose and passion, as it did with the fish when she decided to swim back upstream, then you will be supported. Please understand that the lives you have touched go far beyond your understanding. We tell you that there have been opportunities for you to leave which you did not take. You had an opportunity to leave six months ago, but you chose to stay. You chose to stay because the seeds you have planted are now beginning to sprout. We tell you that you have done well. We are honored to be in your presence. And, when you do finally decide to come Home, there will be a celebration that will last for eons. The colors that you will carry for the work you have done already, will be available for all to see throughout the Universe. It is time to let go, dear one, and just enjoy the ride.

This question was asked by Nomi, our Host in Barcelona, Spain. After struggling with leukemia, in late 2001 Nomi let go and returned Home. I have always known that she was called Home to take place in some very important contracts that will help us all move into Higher vibrations. Now, there are some contracts that can be better fulfilled from the other side. Nomi planted many seeds as a master healer and teacher while she was here on the Gameboard and I have no doubt that the reason she was called Home early was to enable her to make even more of a difference. I always told Nomi that she was my sister and she loved hearing that. I also know that the celebration of her return Home continues to this day on the other side, just as the Group promised.

Las Vegas, Nevada - January 20th, 2000

Question:

I have a question about a paradox that I seem to be presented with every day. We talk so much and we hear so much about creating our own reality and yet we are counseled to let go and let God, to let spirit put our choices in front of us, to let spirit open a door for us to go through. Who is it that is opening the door if we are creating all of our own reality? Is it our Higher Self? Or is there actually a force beyond us? Is there an overall plan? Or is it truly all of our own creation coming from an unconscious part of ourselves?

the Group:

Such a wonderful question, we are impressed with the layers you present in a single sentence. The finite expression of the infinite creator known as Human is so uniquely complex. We, on the other hand, are divinely simple. There are many questions here that you have disguised within this single opportunity. We will address them one at a time.

First, "Is there a Grand Plan?" No, not in the way that you think. We will tell you that there is a Grand Potential, but there is only choice and your choices have already led you to a potential much higher than you could have possibly planned for yourselves. When the Game was first set into motion there was Hope but never a schematic to follow. You are much more in control of your own reality than you could possibly know. For that reason there is not a Grand Plan. This is the Grand Game that you have devised. The Grand hope was to be able to re-member your own power and to hold it as a finite expression of the infinite energy. You are wearing the veils and therefore you cannot see yourself as the infinite. For that reason you devised a Grand Game and entered a field of polarity so that you could play in the ultimate hope of seeing and defining yourself.

There is still unbelievable potential for your choices to manifest in ways to help you realize who you are and help you create your own environment. Many of you come here, only to wake up in a physical body saying: "What on Earth have I gotten myself into this time?" Many of you have never felt comfortable in physical form. Believe us when we say that it is no wonder. This is not your natural form. It is not who you really are. This is not Home. It is a Game you are playing to facilitate higher knowledge. We tell you that you deserve to feel good while you are in physical form. You have that right. We have told you time and again that you are not parts of God, you are each *the whole of God*. Dare to give yourself all that you would give to the highest and the mightiest, for that is who you are. Judge yourself not for what you create, for there are no wrong choices. If you are not happy with your reality have the courage to choose again.

Your judgment often keeps you tied very closely to the reality in which you live. Your guilt keeps you tied to realities that do not serve your highest potential. Place yourself first in the energy cycle. This is not being selfish, this is allowing yourself to fill your cup first so that you have more to give others. Accept what you receive as a natural flow of energy and please do not negate it by judging your choices.

The next segment of your question was, "When is it appropriate to let go and let God?" If you are the creator of your own reality where does that creation end and where does Spirit take over? That is the illusion of duality within a field of polarity. You do not fit within the confines of your bubble of biology. Your spirit and your direct connection to all, is what you call the Higher Self. Much as the vast being is too large to see itself, we also tell you that your own Higher Self is not visible to you. Therefore, to work together with that higher part of yourself it is helpful to adopt a life-style of synchronicity. Watch for the cosmic winks, for this is the best indicator that your Higher Self is in accord with your direction.

The final question is: "Where is the line between choice and synchronicity?" We adore your questions. You are wishing to define a line that demarcates you from spirit. We are intentionally blurring that same line, for we wish to reflect that you are one with spirit and not separate. Please understand that even your choice to adopt synchronicity in your life is an act of creation. Reality is not as defined as you would like to think. The problem with reality is that it is only a theory. As the theory of reality evolves, so does the reality itself. Your reality is determined by the point of view from which you perceive it. To shift your point of view even slightly will change your reality drastically. These are the alternate realities that you have been dealing with. In one reality you are God, in another you are a human who feels as though they are without power. Shift your perception to a reality that makes you feel good, for you deserve that. Dare to treat yourself as the God that you are.

Nijmegen, Holland - April 16ᵗʰ, 2000

Question:

If I am to enjoy my life to the fullest, how can I do more to love myself?

the Group:

If you wish to pay the highest homage to the Creator, if you wish to be the most help to your fellow man, if you wish to be everything that you can be to help the Earth, there is one thing that you can do above all else. That is to place yourself first in the energy flow, for you are the center of your own Universe. If you treat yourself as the God that you truly are, you will honor all things that you touch and which touch you. You deserve the highest and the best, although you rarely treat yourself accordingly. You wonder why others do not value your services and we tell you they can only value you as much as you value yourself. The words, "I AM" bring about the presence. The I AM presence is the connection between Higher Self, the physical body and the Earth presence.

When your vibration is clarified, and you are speaking, acting, thinking and believing in accord with the singular vibration of I AM, then you will have centered your energy. That is when you walk fully into your own energy and your own power, leaning on no one and no thing. Then you have become all that you can be. That is also the time when you shall have the most to offer those who cross your path. Fill your cup first, then turn around and help others to fill theirs. For that is the Magic of giving. That is who you are.

Phantom Death

San Diego, California - June 3rd, 2001

Question:

I have felt very strongly for a long time that I was supposed to die in the early 90s. I came close a couple of times and although the veil has thinned out a lot for me, I still have trouble separating what is coming from me and what is coming from the other side. I'd like to know if I was right, that I was supposed to cash it in at that time?

the Group:

Yes. Your Phantom Death, your life experience and all of your contracts with the exception of a very few, were complete. You were complete in your role, as are many here in this room today. In the last year, eight of you here in this room had the opportunity to leave. With the exception of long term and recently scripted ones, your contracts are complete. Yet, you chose to stay. Why? We are sure that some of you are asking yourselves that same question.

The answer is, because you had something to do. What? You may never know the full contract for it is not possible for you to see. We tell you literally there are times you may pass someone in the grocery store and without uttering a word you may actually look into their eyes and change their life. That may be part of the reason that you are here, to fulfill some of these contracts. And you, dear one, have touched many with your work. You have touched many with your love. You are a different person entirely than the person you were prior to that period. All of the fears are gone. All of the expectation is gone. You are here to touch others and you are doing that work very well. Thank you for staying. The Phantom Death experience is confusing to many. Simply regard it as the reset button. Push it and then be ready for what comes up next on the screen.

You also stated that you are having difficulty separating what is coming from you and what is coming from spirit. It is amusing to us that the veil is so thick that you cannot see who you are. We ask that you concentrate on the blending with spirit and not the separation. We would re-mind you here that the act of separation is against the flow of Universal Energy. When the Keeper first began this work he too asked how he could separate our channeled information from his own imagination. He wanted a demarcation line so that he could be sure the information was pure and not coming from him. We told him that he misunderstood our work with him. We consider him to be an important member of the Group, and in fact, he has this contract because of his past experiences and his wonderful imagination. He often blends with us so that he can carry this message into words easily understood. We encourage him to be a part of the work and the message and we do not wish him to be separate from us in any way. As we have spoken before, there will come a time when full integration with spirit is possible for you while you are still in physical form. These are the times we will ask the Keeper to write under his own given name, even though we will still call him the Keeper. You are closer than you think to experiencing this integration in your lives. Trust yourself, dear one, as much as spirit does.

San Diego, California - June 3rd, 2001

Question:

I had a reading with Steve and the Group a couple of months ago following my Phantom Death experience. I am experiencing some dizziness after this event. It feels like a pull slightly behind me to my right. I do not know if that is still something lingering, pulling me. There seems like there is a slight temptation that maybe I still want to go. Although I want to stay, it seems to be a hesitation or something somehow affecting my equilibrium. Can you help me understand this?

the Group:

When you experience the Phantom Death, it is as if there is a reset button right in front of you. All that you have to do is push that button and say, "I wish to stay". From that point on you will start scripting new contracts from your side of the veil. Many of you have pushed this button and said, "I will make my choice later". Let us stress that there is no right or wrong about these choices. As in all things, you have total free choice. When the Phantom Death experience presents itself you may choose to go Home or you may choose to stay. Also you may simply say, I will postpone my decision. When one decides to stay and does not fully commit to the passion of a new life, the physical body can easily become confused.

Even when you do commit and start scripting your new plan, your physical body needs time to adjust. Quite often you will find interesting things happening to your biology that you have not experienced prior. Maintaining your physical balance is only one of the difficulties that may arise as your biology adjusts. A ringing in the ears is also a common symptom. Some of you may experience a flashing of Light at the third eye area, or pulses of light flashing in your head. You may find yourself lying on your bed at night vibrating. You will probably find your own heart skipping a beat every once in a while. Heart palpitations, and/or irregular heartbeat are very common. Most of these experiences are your own biology catching up to the higher vibrational, ethereal body that you have stepped into. The physical body is the highest density of all of your bodies and, therefore, is the last to move. These are typical symptoms that surround rapid growth experiences such as the Phantom Death experience brings. Do not fear it. Seek the advice of healers, for they can facilitate your shift. Your equilibrium will return. You are simply in a slightly different dimension than your body and that will soon change.

Plants and Animals

Richmond, Virginia - June 10th, 2001

Question:

Is there anything we can do to help the animals to form their new relationships with humans?

the Group:

Your connections to animals will change drastically in the times ahead. Life in all forms has been a part of the food chain. Please understand that energy never dies, and, therefore, for it to transfer from one form to another may seem harsh to some, and yet it is the way of nature. Now we ask you to see that some animals enter with the important contract of being in service as food. The challenge has been a lack of honor. Rarely do you honor the *spirit* of the animal that has freely given its energy to you. To take their energy without honoring its spirit is to strip them of their identity. Take what is offered freely while learning to incorporate all of its energy through honor. Diseases such as 'foot and mouth,' and others yet to come, will bring these animals to the forefront of your consciousness and allow you to rethink this process. Even those of you who do not eat the animals should honor them for their work.

In most cases, your relationship with your domestic animals will not change at all. Your relationship to what you have called horses has been all about movement. Their highest intent is to be in movement. It is through combining movement with human connection that they connect to their own higher selves. If you stop one of these animals from moving, they will die. Spend time with them in movement, walking and riding with them and you will strengthen your bond.

There are other relationships that will not change. Your relationships with dogs will grow stronger over time, for they are the teachers of unconditional love. They are here to teach humans what true unconditional love is. You speak now of being able to incorporate unconditional love into your lives, and yet you do not do this. You are not able, at this point, to move fully into unconditional love, yet, every time you express a little more unconditional love you literally pull yourself into a higher vibrational status. As you do this the dogs on your planet are in ecstasy because they have done their job well.

There are many domestic animals that are here for specific reasons. Some of them you know, some of them you do not. We tell you that those in the cat world are here for a purpose that many of you are not aware of. Yes, they teach you much about yourself and yes, they are a reflection of you, but they also balance your energy and that is their primary purpose with you. A human being is a being that breathes in oxygen and breathes out carbon dioxide. A tree is a being that breathes in carbon dioxide and breathes out oxygen, so the two, the human being and the tree being, balance each other out. Cats act as a similar balancing mechanism. A human being is a being that thrives on positive energy and loves to throw off negative energy. A cat is a being that thrives on negative energy and loves to throw off positive. In many instances when you are feeling so loving that you go over to reach for your cat, they feel the positive energy and run away. Actually, they would rather approach you when their supply of positive energy is at its peak and they can download their excess on you. These expressions of you are very patient.

Watch for the new relationships that you will be forming with plants, for that level of life will be the next to change its relationship to humans. It all begins with an honoring process. Honor them for the work they do. Make space for them in your lives, for you all share this world equally. Do that and Heaven will be a very abundant place, in accord with all levels of life.

Atlantic Highlands, New Jersey - September 14th, 2000

Question:

I think you have spoken before about the cetaceans holding power and energy on our behalf and that this is now passing back to us. What is to become of them? Where does their path lie now?

the Group:

We honor you for such a question. The cetaceans are part of your parental races. They are not separate from you, nor will they ever be. In the same way that when you segregate a mother from her son, the separation between you and cetaceans will never be complete. There will be many who choose to leave because their job is now done. This has been happening already. For as their numbers diminish, more of the power is turned over to you. The passing of the torch has been happening for several years.

What is to happen to them? Anything they want. Many will choose to stay and play, for they do love to play. They are far more playful than you. If humans could play as much as they do, your energy would always be balanced. Follow their guide in this, and also take from them their unconditional love, for it will serve you well. They love you no matter what. They have been holding the energy of the planet in their hands. They have been taking care of the Mother by balancing the energy. Now humanity is of a high enough vibration to hold that energy for itself. As it stands at this moment, many of the cetaceans will choose to leave. Bid them farewell and let them go with love. Do not mourn them, for it is their choice. In actuality, there is another place their gifts are needed, for you are no longer the only planet of Free Choice. There will be more about this in the future. For now, we ask you simply to play with those that wish to stay. And if you do not actually go out and touch them in the ocean, then send them your playful thoughts and adopt their playfulness. That is what they are here to do now. Thank you for asking.

Attleboro, Massachusetts - May 20th, 2001

Question:

You briefly addressed the issue of animals and our chang-ing relationship with them. Could you also talk about the changes in our relationship with devas?

the Group:

You know that you are beings of great magnitude and you know that your beings do not fit within these little bubbles of biology that you inhabit. You are well aware that you have bodies outside of your own. You are well aware that you have a Higher Self that is not contained within your own physical body. The bubble of biology is only meant to carry the dense physical portion of your being. Yet you are great in size. Even as you attempt to stretch your own bodies to hold all of your spirit it will not fit. At the very center of your being is the point where you connect to the Universal Energy. The Universal Energy is the greatness of all that you are, and your own connection to God.

Quite often, you ask about alternate realities and other dimensions. We ask you to see plant and animal life as another dimension, for that is what it is. It, too, does not fit within the physical realms of the bodies that it has chosen. The planets and the different levels of animals also have higher selves that connect them to the same central point as your own Higher Self. This is the part of them that you call Devas. Sometimes it is the little playful spirits that are in the forest when you walk around, and you turn to look and they are not there, but you feel them and you hear them chattering and playing all around you. Some of you are aware of them and some will learn to become aware of them. We tell you these are the plant's higher selves. These are the connection points to the Universal Energy that is in relationship to your own Higher Self. That is why you feel this on a higher level, but cannot see them with your physical eyes. The interesting thing is that because most of you cannot see them, you do not even know they exist.

Those that are in tune with this level are often known as an animal psychic. These gifted people often perform great healing work through animals. Most often they heal humans by talking to their 'domesticated' animals. These are people who have the ability to know what an animal is thinking. All humans have the ability to talk to the animals and the plants. Learning to listen will serve you well in the times ahead.

Powell River, Canada - November 15th, 2001

Question:

This is an age-old question about meat. With the way that we keep animals in captivity, and the trauma they go through, is it necessary to eat meat?

the Group:

Such an excellent question, for it is on the minds of many. We will take it a further step. We would never tell you that this is necessary or this is not. The word "should" does not exist in our vocabulary, for we prefer not to use that word. It is not up to us to take your power in any fashion nor to tell you that this or that would lead you Home, therefore, nothing is necessary for your advancement. We ask you to find what is right for *you*. We will illustrate this with reference to the Keeper, for we are familiar with his patterns and he is one of this Group. The Keeper eats meat, and only in the last few years has he learned to honor the animals which supply that meat. The Keeper pays attention to the energy of food as it enters his body. This in itself is an honoring process. Yet there also comes a time when the Keeper is finished with his meal and then sits back, fully satisfied and nourished. In that peaceful feeling within his body he pauses to honor the plants and animals that gave of themselves so that he could be nourished and satisfied. That is a wonderful time to honor the animals and the plants that have given their energy to be part of your energy. For we tell you that they know something that you have forgotten. Energy never dies. It can only change from one form to another. One way for a plant or animal to shift into higher vibrational status is by allowing its energy to be assimilated by higher vibrational beings. From their point of view this is not a sacrifice, but rather, is part of an ascension process. This is the reason that plants and the animals willingly give themselves to be part of your energy, for that allows them to achieve expression in human form. In turn, this allows them to raise their vibration and become part of the higher vibrational energy. On a higher level they know that all are actually one and, therefore, not separate from each other. Thus, the food chain, as you call it, functions perfectly, even though from your perspective it appears to be barbaric. What *is* barbaric is the way that you treat animals when they are being raised for food. This is the reason you are now seeing a re-evaluation in their relationship to humans. Honoring the animals and the plants that you ingest is simply honoring all that is. It is also very good for your own digestion.

The concern you expressed was about animals. Please understand that if you pull an apple from a tree, that tree feels pain. However, it, too, experiences that pain willingly, in order to find expression in a higher vibrational form. So honor the tree as you take its apples. Honor the animals as you take their meat to the table. When you chop down a tree to use its wood to warm your house that tree is killed. If you honor the tree and Earth by planting a seedling in its place, your house is twice warmed. Honor the plants and animals for their part in providing the energy that you are. In honoring the animals, plants, fish, and insects you will be helping them to achieve higher vibrational status through you.

Your moments of gratitude before you eat work well to help your body assimilate the energy of food. When you are sitting back, as the Keeper does, feeling nurtured and satisfied, take a moment and understand that the energy your body is now assimilating was given unconditionally by plants, fish and animals in the hope that you would use their energy to its highest potential. Accept the responsibility for carrying that energy for the best use, and the plants, fish and animals that gave themselves for this cause will be honored most highly indeed.

Attleboro, Massachusetts - May 20th, 2001

Question:

I am very blessed to have a kindergarten school next to my home, and I am also very blessed to have a beautiful golden retriever. This dog has made a strong connection with the children next door. I feel she is a real love emissary come to the planet, and I would like to know what you have to say about that.

the Group:

There are many of you who have contracts with your animals. In your lower vibrations you did not think this was possible, yet now that you have evolved it comes as less of a surprise. There are many of you who have cats or dogs or even horses that help you heal. In fact, there are two of you here today who have cats that insist on being present when you are doing your healing work. You did not think we knew that, did you?

Some animals contract simply to be your friend. That is why it is so difficult sometimes when they transition, for you feel they are such a part of your family. And so they are. There are some on your planet who say that animals go to a lower level when they transition, and thus can never interact with humans. We think this is quite amusing. Animals or plants are not less than you are simply because they exist at a different level. You do not normally mourn a tree when it dies because it is further from your own vibration. Still, we tell you that it is also possible to have a contract with a tree. For example, if you had a favorite tree that you climbed as a child that tree would have become a part of you and you it. In this case you may very well mourn if that tree were to die. The closer the vibrational level, the stronger the connection between the life forms that exist at those levels. There are many of you who do not believe in eating meat because you do not wish animals to suffer. Yet, you do not think twice about killing a tomato. Ah-ha! They are the same, only different vibrational levels. Because one is a little bit further removed from you vibrationally than the other, you do not think of it in the same way. We tell you that being on your plate may be the tomato's highest purpose. In offering itself in this manner the tomato is not only being of service to you, it also ensures its own evolution to a higher vibrational status by assimilating its energy with your own. You think of humanity as separate from all other life forms, yet it is not. When humanity evolves, so does the tomato, and so does every other life form.

And, yes, to answer your question, your dog does hold the energy for these children. That is a contract it made before being born. Your dogs, your cats, and other animals have abilities which you are beginning to recognize and harness in the treatment of diseases such as dementia and Alzheimer's, as well as in maintaining your overall health. They can communicate with people who have lost the ability to communicate with other humans. They can quickly connect energetically and ease their pain. Some animals come in with contracts to do exactly this.

The children are another story. Some children have such vivacious energy that even adults will run like crazy to avoid them. Some animals have contracts that will draw these children to them, thereby allowing a calm exchange of energy to occur that will balance them both, even at great distances.

The truth is, the school of which you speak is in an area where there are many pollutants. Your dog and four other animals in your neighborhood are helping to neutralize this energy and make it safe for the children. That is their higher purpose. We thank you and your dog.

Relationships in the 5th Dimension

Barcelona, Spain - April 2nd, 2000

Question:

Of all the problems I encounter as a facilitator, relationships seem to be the most troubling for people. Can you tell us ways to help with this?

the Group:

Now we will speak of relationships. For this is very confusing for some of you. Many have chosen lessons in this area. It is not your normal form to be in one sex or the other. For on this side of the veil we do not split into one sex or the other. Sometimes we take form as a male or female, but that is only to present ourselves to you, for your understanding. In order to play the Game, you passed through the second dimension to come to rest in the 3rd.

In the second dimension you gained polarity and it was necessary for you to split off into one of the sexes. As you did this, there is one-half of you that stayed on the other side. This is the yin to your yang. This is the balance of your energy. And most of the time when you are on the Planet they are holding the energy for you in the place we call Home. If by chance you do both incarnate at the same time and find each other you may be pulled together. In most cases, however, this does not generally make for good relationships as you are really looking at yourself. That can be very frustrating and somewhat aggravating. We tell you that healthy relationships require a heart connection with another being that is just far enough apart vibrationally for you to be supportive of each other.

What you call relationships is only possible within a field of polarity. Here at Home we can always see each other and know that we are never separate from one another. On our side of the veil we are not separate from one another so we do not experience relationships in the same manner as you. We can only imagine the joy of being able to hold someone close enough that you can see yourself from behind the veil. That is a relationship. That is the grand union of two souls that fully support each other. That is only possible by being completely open with your communication, and learning to dismiss the head long enough to speak from the heart. Speak your Truth from the heart. Tell all those around you of your needs, for you deserve to be happy on this Planet. The moment you have what you need, the moment you are supported, is the moment that you have things to give to other people.

That is the very moment that you will attract relationships into your life. Understand that relationships are built through communications. You may be pulled by through sexual attraction or a desire to share your life, yet no matter what pulled you together, a relationship must be built. Learn to love what is before you and not the possibilities of what could be.

There is only one relationship. . . You with You. Get that one right first and you can have all the others you wish. Relationships are similar to your life insurance. You can only get one if you do not need it. *(Laughter)*

San Diego, California - June 3rd, 2001

Question:
 I'm experiencing confusion around a relationship. In this marriage we connect at the soul beautifully. Especially when we go to seminars together or even when I am in a seminar by myself he is just right there. The communication is there and it seems we are in step. But when he returns to normal life he's just not there at all and it is like we are two personalities that are incompatible. I keep having the conflict of just releasing

the relationship and letting us both go our own ways into different energy but it is like playing a slot machine for thirteen years, I keep thinking "Well, maybe this really will work out".

I wish to be enlightened in this lifetime to hold that vibration of unconditional love and it seems he is a perfect way for me to practice. So do I stay there and practice until I finally achieve this unconditional love and I know that only I can make that decision but I just keep bouncing. Once I make a decision I bounce the other way and it is unlike me to be indecisive. So I'm really not sure where the answer lies.

the Group:

As you came through the first dimension you passed through the 2nd dimension in order to land in the 3rd. Now you have even moved through the 4th and stepped into the 5th. As you passed through the 2nd dimension, you split off into parts of yourself that you call the sexes. You chose male or female for each individual incarnation and to facilitate certain lessons. Here is where you began to feel incomplete, as if you were not whole. You feel as though you need to add something to yourself to make you whole. You look at the potential of being whole through a relationship. This thinking is clearly a misdirection of energy. It is an illusion for only when a person is whole unto themselves can they actually have a relationship. You are finding that out. There is only one relationship and that is you with you. The biggest challenge of course is that you often fall in love with what you think a person could be rather than what they are. We ask you instead to focus on that person as they are right now. If you can make it work today you have the magic. If you can look at this person and find the things that drew you together and find the support and find the love and more importantly than all, find the passion then you can make that magic work for you. If you cannot, move on. Have the courage to release in love and center your energy on yourself for only in doing that can you find healthy relationships.

Often you form relationships that you think make you whole. In this instance you have created a leaning relationship where two people lean against each other to create a whole being. The problem here is that two people never grow at the same rate. In this type of relationship when one person grows, the other person falls. Instead, let us suggest that you look for one who can walk along side of you without either of you leaning. When two people can grow individually while still sharing their lives, the magic grows.

Here we will illustrate on the relationship keyboard. As you are all various forms of vibration, we will use a piano keyboard to illustrate this point. You humans are so wonderful for you are always looking for someone playing the same note as you, and when you do find them it is very validating and very boring. So you pull someone next to you who is playing a vibration that is very close to yours and you end up playing chopsticks which is tolerable but aggravating. It is not until you move a comfortable distance apart that you hit a chord. Here two vibrations overlap each other at regular intervals synchronizing and supporting each other. Here they actually create a third vibration which is what you call a relationship. Find the chord where you are now. Identify how it sounds to you and ask how it sounds to him. Then between the two of you find ways to communicate to find that chord. Work with him on the communication for that is what creates the chord. Two humans, once they find the chord, do not stay on the same notes. They are constantly evolving and there will be times you hit very awkward chords. If the communications are in place it will be easily identified and corrected. The whole idea is to make sure you are playing on the same keyboard.

There is another caution that we see so often in your game. Humans are so afraid of change that they would rather live in the shadow of what used to be a relationship, rather than to place themselves first and declare what they need. A comfort zone is a very dangerous place to be. Do not ever think that there are no options. If the passion is gone find ways to rekindle it or have the courage to let it go. Sex is a form of communication that adds to a relationships. If you feel that you have passed the need for sex in relationships we suggest that you check to see if your partner feels the same. Sex is a form of intimate communications that add to a relationship. Sex alone will not sustain a relationship but may help it to grow to new levels. Find ways to rekindle the fire and watch the magic of physical communication.

When to stay and when to leave is also another good question that you have asked. No one can answer that for you. There may come a time when you take an honest inventory and assess that a relationship takes more from you than it gives. If this is continual it will eventually lead to physical ailments. Still many of you are aware that there were contracts to complete in this relationship. So how do you know when they are complete? We tell you that contracts are agreements that are usually fulfilled in a very short time. Relationships that start as contracts are simply two people pulled together with a contract. The contract is usually fulfilled very quickly and two people are then left to build a real relationship.

You have asked a specific question about your husband. As far as where he is going and where you believe his systems are, we tell you he is moving into his own vibrational advancement. This may no longer fit with yours. Communication is the key to relationships in all areas. Start the communications about the problem as you perceive it. If the communications are in place then the relationship can develop to the next level and hit the next set of keys on the keyboard. If the communications are not there then the relationship does not exist and you are living only in the shadow of a relationship. You are on a good path. Speak all of your truth to him and allow him to speak all of his truth to you and you will quickly find whether you are playing the same notes or whether you are playing on different keyboards. You are closer than you think, dear one. Enjoy the ride.

Powell River, Canada - November 15th, 2001

Question:

Just a month ago, a relationship ended for me. One of the problems I faced with my partner was that we had different beliefs about monogamy in relationships. I was threatened by the idea of them having other lovers, even though for her it was a good way of being in a relationship. I want to come to a greater understanding of what relationship really means, and I don't want to enter into another relationship putting rules on my partner like: "You can only be with me if you don't see other people". I wonder, is a healthy way of incorporating that and being in relationship, and still having intimacy with other people?

the Group:

Your question shows honesty to yourself that is to be thunderously applauded. Developing that honesty with yourself is the first and most important part of any relationship. In truth, there is only one relationship, and that is the relationship of you with you. When you get *that* relationship worked out, you may have all the others you choose. It will not be for us to tell you that this is right or wrong, for in truth there is no right or wrong and we will not take your power from you in that manner. Being in a field of polarity makes you see things as male or female, up or down, right or wrong, good or bad and love or fear, and they are not. These are all illusions of polarity on the Gameboard. They are all an integral part of each other.

You will see many changes occurring in the area of relationships as you start incorporating higher vibrational truths. You are beginning to incorporate unconditional love into your experience, and as you do you will find less need for boundaries and rules. At this stage of your development you primarily utilize conditional love. There is nothing wrong with this, yet you must understand that even your own wedding vows are a statement of conditional love. Please do not place yourself in a position of thinking less of yourself because you need such commitments to define yourself at this time. Dear ones, do not find yourself in spiritual competition with yourself for it is a losing proposition. Rather, we suggest you find as many ways as possible to practice unconditional love in your relationships, for that is how you will make space for your relationships to evolve as you move into higher vibrational status of the New Planet Earth.

Please do not rush this process, give yourself time. And if you can find love in a relationship, and if you can hold another close enough to see yourself, then do it, for that is a relationship. We tell you that you are not separate from one another, you are not incomplete. You do not need a relationship to make you whole. Two half humans do not make a whole human. And yet if you choose to walk along side another and share your life it can add to you both.

Understand that your own heart will dictate where your energy is and what feels good to you. Be true to your heart first, not what you think you should feel, but what you *do* feel. Your belief systems are what stand in your way. And be honest with yourself and your partner about what works for you; what you are willing to try and what you are not willing to do. Again, there is no right or wrong about feelings. No one can argue with what you are feeling.

Bless you, dear one, for trying to understand your own reflection in this area. Use as much unconditional love as you can while still feeling good about yourself. And if that means releasing your lover unconditionally, for you can no longer hold onto him or her and still maintain your beliefs, then so be it. Also please do not think that just because a relationship ends it was not successful. Yours was hugely successful even though it ended.

Two people never evolve at the same rate. Even so, you can still keep your connection as long as there is communication between you.

Relationships are about more than love, dear ones; they are about communicating from the heart. And that is where the magic is, for if you can say, "I like the way you make me feel", then and only then will you be able to share relationships with another.

Watch the area of relationships changing in the coming months, dear ones. You will find all sorts of new relationships coming into your field. You will see same sex relationships increasing on your Planet. You will see different types of relationships that you have not seen before. Fear them not, for they are all based in love. Celebrate the love and watch as the miracles unfold. The Keeper feels your pain and wishes he had a little magic wand with which to touch your heart and make everything all right for you. But he has not been able to find that wand for a very long time. *(Laughter)* Trust yourself. Find what resonates with your heart and you will find love again. Do not worry about reaching a level of understanding so perfect that it will make your next relationship a success. That can only be done one day at a time. It comes down to what adds to you and what takes from you. Just understand that this particular relationship had ceased adding to you. We thank you for asking the question, for in a field of polarity the area of relationships is one of the most difficult to see. You have used it in many ways to facilitate many life lessons. Please do not ever think that any relationship is a failure, for it is not. We thank you for having the courage to love.

Religion

Ardeche, France - October 26ᵗʰ, 2001

Question:

I have heard a lot about ascension lately and I have always connected that with Jesus. Can you please enlighten me about what it will mean in our lives now at this time?

the Group:

You have asked about the Master Jesus. He whom you call Jesus was a Crystal Child. There is a correlation between the words Crystal and Christ, for it is the Christed energy that is now returning to your planet. It has been very unfortunate how some of these stories have been manipulated. We simply ask you to re-member the heart of them and not the details, for some of the details have been changed to suit the specific purposes of a very few. Reach for the love in these messages, for that is where the truth lies.

Jesus was one of several aboriginal healers who held the energy in a very dark time. He came to Earth very early to plant the seeds of what you are now experiencing. Understand that He was one of many, for there have been many masters on your Earth and all of them carry the vibrations of Home. They all sit together and laugh hysterically as you say that this one is better than that one, or that this one is the only path to the light. They are all from the same energy as they understand true Unity. The joke is on you, for over here you channel Archangel Michael, and over there you channel Kryon, and over there you channel the Catholic Church, and here you listen to the Group. We tell you the joke truly is on you, dear ones, for when you finally pull aside the veil, you are going to see that you are all channeling the same entities. Yes. Each of you presents a different flavor of Home. You have asked; "To whom am I praying when I pray?" The answer is difficult for you to comprehend, for it is not a singular personality but, rather, Unified energy. Be patient with yourselves for you are doing well at understanding concepts that were far beyond your reach even just a few months ago. Reach for the higher truth as it resonates within your own heart, for that is the key.

Would you like to see the ascension? Close your eyes and squeeze them really tight as you constrict all the muscles in your face. Then release the tension and open your eyes. You have ascended, dear ones. You simply do not understand it fully at this moment. The ascension has already begun on your planet. No, it does not happen in the blink of an eye, from *your* perspective, for each person blinks their eyes at different times. The ascension is a journey into the higher vibrations of the collective of humanity. From *our* perspective this journey takes place in the blink of an eye. From your perspective you often say, "When is something going to happen? Do I actually have to wait until 2012?" Understand that it has already begun. It is now in front of you each time that you see the new light on Planet Earth. These are the activations. These are the processes that are changing your own reality, your own DNA/RNA structure. As you look at the sunsets and the sunrises and you see new, vibrant colors, know that you are in the ascension process now. Will this process connect you to the one you call Jesus? Of course it will. Will it connect you to the one you call Buddha? Yes. Will it connect you to the one you call Mohammed? Of course it will. Find the truth in your heart, dear ones, for that is where we reside. We thank you for asking that question, for there were many here that needed to hear this.

Richmond, Virginia - June 10th, 2001

Question:
    Could you talk to us about the role of religion in creating Heaven on Earth?

the Group:

Certainly we will do so. Religion has played a great role in the advancement of human kind. The Gameboard of Free Choice has offered many opportunities for religion to open the hearts of mankind. One of the greatest of these is a result of what you call the union of fellowship. Bringing like minds together in any form is one of the highest things you can do on Planet Earth. You form the circles of light and you make a difference. With the veils firmly in place, you cannot see who you truly are. This is as it should be for it facilitated the Grand Game of Hide and Seek. Still, you knew in your heart that there was a central connection point where you all originated. This you envisioned as a higher power and you came together often to celebrate and energize this higher power. No, this was not a misdirection of energy as it actually enabled your own empowerment. The misdirections of energy come from giving your full power to that central point, thus avoiding the responsibility of your own power as creators. This generally results in focusing your power so much outside of yourself that there is no room for other truths to exist within your reality.

Have you not thought it strange that most of the wars fought on your planet have been religious in nature? You would naturally think that one religion would fight another, yet most of these wars have taken place between those with only the slightest variations within the same base religion. More wars have been fought in the name of Christianity than any other. Do you honestly think this was what Christ had in mind? Find your central point and focus your energy on it if that helps you to find your power. That is the purpose and intent of all religions. Some of the greatest accomplishments of the wonderful, sacred religions of Planet Earth have been in the area of fellowship.

Here you look into each other's eyes and you feel Home. What you are actually feeling is a reflection of your own energy. Ah, you were not expecting us to say that. What you know to be the great religions of the world were brought to you as channeled information, similar to the information you are listening to now. What did you think was behind the burning bush anyway? Once the information is brought in, it is up to you what you do with it, for this is only a planet of free choice, is it not? It is your choice. Find that which resonates with your heart. Stay out of judgment, please, for it limits you. Find space for all to be in their truth and you will create Heaven on Earth. Will it surprise you to hear that the creation of Heaven on Earth in its first stages will include many religions? Envision a time when all religions focus on their commonalities, instead of their differences. That is the shift in perception that will bring it all together and show you the first true picture of All That Is.

Powell River, Canada - November 15th, 2001

Question:

I have a Christian friend who told me that the only way to heaven is through a personal relationship with Jesus Christ, and I guess I want to know how the Group explains that.

the Group:

That would depend on how you define Jesus Christ. The cosmic joke is, you think you are all separate from each other. You are not. You are actually one and so are we. For even we in the angelic realm are a part of each other and a part of you. In that way we are all one with the entity that you know to be Jesus Christ. The message that the teacher Jesus brought was about understanding the unity of all things and the power within. When the Keeper first took his place as the spokesman for the Group, he asked us: "What is the difference between my message and that of this person over here and of that person over there? How are you and they different? Do you all know each other up there?" *(Laughter)* We love his humanness so. We answered by telling him that we are all connected. Dear ones, there is only one Truth, but there are eight million ways to get to that truth. Do not ever feel that there is only one way to get somewhere, for there is not. There are many paths Home. The moment you place restrictions on any truth is the moment you cut yourself off from your own source.

The one called Jesus Christ is a master teacher, and one of the first Children of Crystal Vibration to ever inhabit Earth. He planted powerful seeds on the planet and left important lessons in place, and he taught those around Him, and touched the hearts of so many that His teachings still reverberate with truth and grandeur, even though many have been twisted to serve man.

Follow your heart, dear ones. Follow your truth and do not ask us to place that judgment for you, for that is taking your power away. Re-member that discernment is the art of making choices without judgment, and is the first tool in the higher vibrations of the New Planet Earth. If you take the highest and best from all things and simply leave the rest, your vibrations will rise. This does not mean that you cannot be a Christian or a follower of Islam. It does not mean that you cannot follow the Kabbalah. Understand that all of these hold valuable keys to truth. And that is what is reflected most often in the teachings of Christ.

We will also re-mind you here that the motion of the Universal Energy is blending, and anything that is in accord with the Universal Energy in the higher vibrations of the New Planet Earth will be supported. Likewise, anything that segregates, or attempts to separate, will be resisted. We ask you to look at your question in that Light. Is Jesus the *only* way to find Home? If Jesus were standing next to you right now, he would tell you what he said so many times: "You are no different than I".

Scripting New Contracts

Nijmegen, Holland - April 22nd, 2001

Question:

I've done a lot of work with all sorts of people over the past twenty years, first as a teacher, then as a therapist, but now I'm at an impasse. Behind it all there is a longing for a new contract. Is there a contract for me? I am somewhat older but I'm longing for that.

the Group:

Listen to our words well, for this is the difficult part that you as humans now face. You have come into this life with the scripts and contracts that you set up before incarnating. You saw the cosmic winks as you looked into the eyes of your partner and you saw something special. You became aware of the faint re-membrances and you knew deep within you that there was a contract there and you chose to follow it. You fell in love, married and created a life together. You had children, and in doing so you honored those contracts. Then, you took your place as a healer and honored further contracts. You became accustomed to looking for the cosmic winks as you went through life, for you knew they would lead you to other contracts.

But now things are different. Now you have reached up and pressed the re-set button. The rules on the Gameboard have changed, and before you lies a blank piece of paper. You feel that something big is right in front of you but when you look for the usual signs; they are not anywhere to be found. Many of you are having the most difficult time reading and finding your contracts and, therefore, seem to be wandering forever lost in time. The paper in front of you holds the key, but as you search for the words to unlock the magic, you see only white paper. Then you ask, "What is wrong? Where is my passion?" You do not see the quill that is sitting right next to you.

Now is the time for you to script your own contracts, to find your passion and move into even the smallest piece of it. Yes, you are a teacher. Yes, you are a healer. You have done much work in many areas and you had the courage to place yourself first in these last couple of years. We tell you, it was only eight months ago that you had originally scripted to leave this planet. Eight months ago all of your contracts were complete. Eight months ago you had the chance to return Home. Instead, you reached up and you pressed that re-set button and you stayed. Now you hold much knowledge of how to help others and we ask you this: What is it that you would like to do?

Contracts are no longer scripted on the other side. It is now up to you to pull the pen from its stand, to dip it into the ink, and to script your next contract. "Oh, but what if I make a mistake?" you ask. The answer is simple: Then you simply tear it up, throw it away and write another, for that power is now yours. There are no mistakes. There is no failure, only feedback. Listen carefully to the feedback and things will change very quickly now. The phantom death that you experienced eight months ago reset your energy and you now sit in a higher vibration. Your passion has always been about being the mirror and holding that mirror up for other people to see themselves. Your passion has always been to be the best mirror that you can be. You have helped people to see the good parts of themselves and the difficult parts of themselves in a new light. You have helped people to move the energy in a lot of different areas. Now we ask you to take the quill in your own hand and script the highest for yourself.

The paper in front of you is blank. That is why you feel lost as you search for your contracts. Dip the quill in the ink and script that which is in your heart. Move forward into the passion of those things that you love to do and you will make a difference. You have been collecting knowledge for such a long time. You have such gifts of being able to go right to the center of the energy and even though people come in with all the smoke screens and all the illusions and all the drama around their lives, you can go right to the heart and touch people. That is a gift that you have had to work very hard at, but you are very good at it. Find a way to use that gift and you will be in your passion. You will also then be of the greatest use to the Universe and all things around you. That is what you came here to do. And you are not alone.

Welcome Home.

Second Wave

Baltimore, Maryland - March 18th, 2001

Question:

Would you tell us more about the second wave and what this means?

the Group:

The waves of which we speak are waves of collective energy. They reach much farther than the energy waves of which you are aware. The energy is in the ethereal realm and as the energy creates a wave, it also creates a vacuum as the wave is in motion. These are very large waves of energy that span vast periods of time. The first wave was the wave of creation upon this planet. It has been spoken of many times, even in your biblical writings, and as such has often been misinterpreted. But we will state that there was indeed a wave of creation that started the entire Game of Free Choice on Planet Earth. This energy has been kept alive and re-used, re-directed, re-cycled and re-created for a very long time – for much longer than your recorded history. In fact we tell you that *all* creations are simply a continuation of the first wave of creation.

Now you are living in a different time. The energy has shifted and through your choices opportunities have opened up for you to move to the next dimensional level. Do not wait, dear ones, to be plucked off the Earth and taken up in your spaceship to a new land. The ascension is taking place right here, right now. The ascension is changing the vibrational state of Earth so that you can create Home right here, right now. In order to do this, it was necessary to introduce a separate and higher vibrational wave of creation that would complement and support the higher vibrations of the New Planet Earth. This is the Second Wave of Empowerment. In fact, these waves are similar in nature yet the

Second Wave opens many more possibilities for carrying your true power while still playing the Game.

There is a more practical way to watch as the Second Wave of Empowerment shifts the energy of Planet Earth. Humans have always gathered in groups as families and friends. You started this practice with your own spiritual family at the first incarnation. As those families grew, you defined these families within boundaries of space, and in so doing you drew imaginary lines on your planet and said; "This area is 'mine' and that area is 'yours' and when you cross this boundary you are in a different country". Oh, how we love the games you play. You are so imaginative. We never would have thought to draw those lines. Even now, there are still those who try forcibly to move or enlarge their lines. Please be patient, dear ones. It does not mean that you are in a state of turmoil when that happens. When there is global aggression on a planet that is moving to higher vibrational levels, it simply means that the final vestiges of the old energy are leaving. As they attempt to do things the old way they will find that their old ways are no longer valid.

Stand firm in your truth, for those of the old energy are still trying to create using the old energy of the first wave of empowerment, and you are already waiting patiently in the second. Oh, dear one, we would love to answer your question in three little words and we cannot yet, but the time will soon come. Instead, we will simply say that the first wave of empowerment, during which you built your clans and your cities and drew your little imaginary lines, was all about creating leaders for yourself. As such, the first wave of empowerment had a paradigm of follow the leader. Now you are into the Second Wave of empowerment. Now you are learning to follow yourself. It is no longer necessary to give your power away to the leaders of your planet, for in the Second Wave your leaders will become the trusted servants they were always meant to be.

The developments of technology and its blending with your own biology, is giving you new senses. Since the introduction of radio, television and the internet you are no longer in the lower vibrations. You have advanced even with the limited technology you have experienced. Even now with this blend you have reached a stage where there will be NO MORE SECRETS on the New Planet Earth. If there can be no more secrets, there will be no more clandestine governments. You have already seen things changing. We tell you that it was the Second Wave of empowerment that brought down the great wall of Germany.

When there are no more secrets, things that have been kept from you time and time again in your governments will no longer be tolerated. Your leaders are asking, "Why has this happened to me?" We answer that question with the statement: "There will be NO MORE SECRETS on Planet Earth.

As the Second Wave of empowerment flows over the Earth, the imaginary lines of division that you created will begin to disappear. Even now you are seeing economies blending together as the lines of what you call Europe are becoming less defined. This emulates the flow of the Universal Energy. Watch as the power of the Second Wave now takes form. Watch for the magic that the Second Wave will bring.

When I first created the Lightworker.com site the Group asked me to place the words Second Wave somewhere on the front page. At times it has been rather faint but it is still there to this day.

Baltimore, Maryland - March 18th, 2001

Question:
Ernest Holmes said that more light would be given to us as we use that which we have. Is that what the second wave is about? More light?

the Group:

There is a candle in this room. What happens when one uses that candle to light another? The light doubles. We have spoken about the new light that is now apparent on Earth. [See the chapter "Seven Seconds to the New Light" in this book.] You are already in the new energy. You have already created the new Planet Earth. This is a powerful time. You have more personal power than you ever thought it was possible to carry in human form. You are in a time where you will create your thoughts just like that. [snap!] The time lag that was required to create your thoughts in the 3rd dimension is growing shorter. That time lag was necessary as a safeguard so that you would not hurt yourself with your own thoughts. Now you must learn to become masters of your thoughts, for life will become very confusing for you if you do not. Before, you had the luxury of having all sorts of thoughts that did not manifest, simply because the length of the time lag allowed ample room in which to correct any errors of thought. Now you have little room for error. What you hold in your thoughts will now manifest much quicker than before.

Additionally, there is a new light that will be seen on the Earth. This is the light that was specifically spoken of by the channel known as Ernest Holmes. More will follow on this subject soon. For now we ask you to light your torch and then use it to light others. Then the New Planet Earth will be seen in its New light. That is what you came here to do and that was the contract you made the day that time stood still.

Seed Fear

San Diego, California - June 3rd, 2001

Question:

I have known for some time that my passion is to teach. What I have not known is when or how or where. Now I have come up with a plan, which entails starting a nationwide crusade with the high schools in our country. But I'm afraid. I get so far and then I just get petrified. I have all these excuses why I shouldn't step forth. I do not know whether it's my ego or not. I feel it's something that I should be doing because I feel it so strongly and then sometimes it's just that I get so petrified. And I would like to have your input if I may please.

the Group:

You stood at the edge of the valley. You looked out at the city below and watched in horror the people running up the hill for safety. Everyone was trying to reach higher ground as the waters came in. You looked to the sky and you said, "Why? What have we done that was so horrible?" That energy was permanently stamped in your being that day. That is the seed fear that you have carried ever since in your cellular memory. That day you made a commitment that if humanity ever reached the same level of vibration again, you would do things differently. You found the most ominous, threatening guardian and asked him to stand guard at the gate. If ever you got close to holding the same power that you held during those fateful times, the guardian would step in and re-mind you of your past mistakes. That guardian has remained with you lifetime after lifetime. Ahh, but the day you reclaimed your full power, you activated the guardian and of course you felt the fear. That is simply the guardian doing the job you entrusted him with.

So here you now are, asking yourself: "What if I do it wrong? What if I am not up to it? What if I do not step forward when I am supposed to?" Feel the fear, dear one, for that fear confirms that your guardian is still working well, and that you are getting close to your power. In fact, the closer you get the more vocal your guardian may become, for he is a most important ally. Now, it is time to reassign his duties to utilize that same seed fear to keep your ego in check. Thank you for having the courage to walk past the guardian at the gate.

Sleep

Nijmegen, Holland - April 22nd, 2001

Question:

When I go to sleep every night, there are a lot of angels, entities, souls. And when I wake up, I know I have traveled but I don't know where to or what's happened. Maybe you can tell me.

the Group:

There are many of you who are going through vibrational changes and are waking up at three o'clock in the morning. The Keeper has called this the 3 A.M. Club. Many of you are members. Many of you will join this club. Others will start sleeping through the night and some will start waking at differing times. Many of you will have experiences at night, for that is a special time. It is a time when your own consciousness relaxes and goes into a state of rejuvenation. Up to this point in your evolution, it was necessary to put your entire consciousness to sleep in order to do these things. It is no longer necessary to do this. It is entirely possible for you to walk around in a restful state and be fully functional. As you awaken at 3 A.M. you are actually in a state of enhanced creation known to you as an alpha state.

In this state, many things are possible. What is happening is that you are evolving to a biology that will carry a higher energy. Soon your patterns of sleeping/waking will change to incorporate a triad of sleep in which you will sleep for three hours, wake for two, and then sleep for three more. This will become your norm. In the meantime, however, there are many interim patterns that will come and go.

We have just spoken here of the general, overall energy of what is changing with regard to sleep. Now we will address you specifically for your situation is different, since you have chosen a very special contract. You stitch the time and the dimensional realities together and the truth of the matter is, you do most of this work at night. There are many others like you who work in the inter-dimensional realities at night. There are even some of you here in this room. This can be challenging for some of you, for you may awake up tired.

You and those like you are the stitchers of time. Imagine another dimension, much like your own, in which people are sitting around a table holding a séance. In their reality they contact a strange and discarnate entity that gives them information. In your reality what is occurring is that these other dimensional beings are communicating with *you* as you sleep. In this way the gaps of time between realities are being stitched together. Who is doing the stitching? You both are.

There are many healers who work in other realities. These too are stitchers of time. Even as you sleep, many of you are working diligently in other dimensions, as healers, teachers, communicators and guides. Would it surprise you to know that some of you are even doing this work in your waking hours? This is not as common but it does happen. In those moments when you may find yourself withdrawing to an inner plane, what do you think is happening? Consider for a moment that instead of contemplating, meditating or daydreaming, you are actually communicating with other dimensional realities, other beings, or even other aspects of yourself existing in another time and place. Consider too that many people who spend more time in this inward state, such as those you refer to as autistic, may actually be happily at work.

You and those like you are the weavers of time. You have a very special contract and as before, most of your higher work will be done in the sleeping hours. That is when the other dimensional realities in your field are relaxed enough for you to do your work. Fear it not. We laugh at your thoughts for you are now thinking of how you could get paid for this work. You humans are so imaginative! Do not consider one sleep pattern to be a measure of your advancement. You are no less spiritual if you are not waking up at 3 A.M.

There are many levels that you all will be going through and incorporating into your energy. You happen to have chosen a more challenging one, and despite your lack of sleep you are coping very well.

☉ime

Nijmegen, Holland - April 22nd, 2001

Question:

With time changing, as you say it is, would it be possible to undo the crucifixion and bring about Jesus' ascension without painful death?

the Group:

The first part of your question will be answered differently from the second part of your question. The first part of your question is, "Would it be possible?" Yes. All things are possible. There are no limitations. You will see this soon for as you begin to witness the abilities of the Crystal Children you will understand more of your own power. You will also begin to understand your new relationship to time. And this is at your very doorstep now.

Now as to you the second part of your question about the possibility of a crucifixion without pain: With an event that has made such a difference to so many lives, the interesting thing is that, even though you will have the possibility you will not choose to change this. Rather than changing it, we tell you, carry it high, for it is no longer necessary to carry the portion that is the pain.

In the first paradigm of human life, there was but one motivating factor and that was survival. Your relationship to pain has been your primary motivating factor up to this point, and it has overwhelmed your life. You are now moving beyond that first paradigm and are incorporating a new energy as you re-script the entire Game. Thus your primary motivation is no longer survival. Seeking unity and a higher truth is what is motivating you now.

With a primary motivation of survival, it was not possible to experience real growth without experiencing some pain. The interesting thing is, misery has always been optional, but some of you chose it anyway. Now we ask you to take those lessons, and to take that part of you which has burned itself into your cellular memories lifetime after lifetime, and move to the next evolutionary step. Create the paradigm for yourself that does not include that type of pain, for it is no longer necessary for you to feel it. You do not need to hit the brick wall in order to know that it is time to turn. For a time this was necessary. Now it is not. The most effective way to accomplish this is to release your fear of pain. As you incorporate the new energies and paradigms, you will be able to turn before you hit the brick wall. Is it possible? Yes.

There is one other important thing to consider. The one known as Jesus had an important contract to fulfill. That contract included experiencing the greatest of fears; human pain. If pain had not been a part of that contract, its effectiveness would have been greatly reduced. So before you change an important contract we suggest you check with the owner of that contract.

You are in charge of every moment and we ask you, instead of re-writing the past to re-write the future and to work on learning to flow with the energy. Learn to follow the path of love. Then, when you experience that which you consider to be painful, find a different way to look at it. When you are Home you will re-member physical pain with sweetness consistent with all Human experience. Shift your camera angle to see from the perspective of Home and you will see an entirely different movie. Those are your ultimate realities. Those are your possibilities and your choices. Choose a life that brings joy. Choose the passion and fear not the pain. Feel the energy of all those that have come before you. Choose to learn their lessons and to take the essence of what they were teaching and apply it in your own life, for that will make the pain worthwhile.

Esoteric Society - United Nations - Vienna, Austria - May 3rd, 2001

Question:

There is, I feel a problem with time. People seem to struggle with time schedules, with doing things. Time is getting shorter. What is going on? How should we see this? How should we interpret this? And what is your advice as to how to deal with it in a constructive way?

the Group:

We will start with one simple keyword and then we will expound from there. There is a word that will help you control time, and that word is *breathe.* So many times you forget to breathe. You get so wrapped up in the stack on your desk that you do not take the time to breathe. Breathe in through the nose, out through the mouth. Complete the energy cycle through yourself first.

Your own senses are expanding. The Keeper loves to take the information that we have given on alternate realities and show you this in practical examples of how to warp time. Some of you will see that this weekend, for that is part of the agenda he has planned. For the rest of you who will be reading these words, we will re-mind you very simply that you have been in what you refer to be a linear hallway of time. It is linear in the sense that you see time as past, present, and future. The interesting thing is that you do not walk down this hallway facing forward. You walk down it backwards, thus you can only see clearly your past. If you pay attention you can experience the present, but you cannot see the future. You are so concerned about where you are going and the time it will take to get there that you lose the moment, and that is where time closes in on you.

Find first that very center of each moment that is inexorably yours. Learn to own that moment. Once mastered, you can find that centered energy in any given moment. Here you have nothing to 'do.' Here is where you experience the art of Be-ing. In this sacred space you can interact with the Universal Energy.

In this space of Be-ing, you become the presence of "I AM", rather than "I will", or "I should". Own the moment and you will retain your control over time. If you do not change your relationship to time and take purposeful control, it will take charge of you.

We have said before that your relationship to time has changed. Thus, it will come as no surprise to many of you to hear that there are only twenty and a half hours in what used to be your twenty-four-hour day. Is it getting worse? Yes, but only if you let it. Begin to breathe first. Own the moment and in this manner you will own the time around you.

Begin in the morning. There is one exercise that we have given before that we call twenty-six seconds. Connect the energy cycles in your fingers by placing your thumb to your two middle fingers on both hands. Breathe in through your nose and out through your mouth and do your best to clear your mind of any thoughts of what you are going to do later. It is no longer necessary for you to learn the intricate details of deep meditation to be spiritually advanced. You can do it in twenty-six seconds. Breathe. So, at the beginning of your day take twenty-six seconds for your mind to run through all the events you have planned for the day. Imagine yourself driving to work and all the lights turn green. Imagine yourself walking and being greeted by an abundance of love energy. Imagine yourself sitting down to your desk, and even though you have a huge stack of papers everything falls into place and magically goes exactly where it is meant to go. Imagine that someone comes into your office and gives you just the help you need. Twenty-six seconds, that is all it takes. And if you find your mind wandering into some difficult thing, or if you find yourself driving to work and all the lights turn red, no problem. Simply break the energy, take three deep breaths, and then begin again. Find the center of the moment you are in and just *be*. This completes the energy and sets it into motion.

26 Second rule

Now here is the interesting part. As we told before you have choice, and if at any time during your day things are not going to your liking, find a quiet space, spend twenty-six seconds and re-write your day. Simple tools. We hope this is not too simple for you to understand, for we know humans love to complicate things. Complicate it if you wish. It makes no difference. But use it and you will take control of your perception of time. For even if you are making great strides in your work, even if you are doing great things to change the planet, if you are not in your passion it will all be for naught. Be in the moment, be in your passion and please re-member to breathe.

Transition Teams & Death

Las Vegas, Nevada - January 20th, 2000

Question.

I've had the opportunity in my life to witness many miracles for which I am extremely grateful. There was one episode which has always disturbed me. I had a patient once who had attempted suicide by overdosing on medication. He was on a breathing machine and was declared brain dead. They did all the tests and there was no neurological activity and when we were instructed to remove the breathing apparatus, the man began to rise up and writhe around in what appeared to me to be excruciating pain. I didn't know what to do, I was very scared but I didn't try to hook him back up to the breathing machine and eventually he died from lack of oxygen. I'd like to know what was happening to that man in that process because my other experiences with death have been very peaceful.

the Group:

First let us address the fact that you have been thankful for witnessing many miracles. We wish to thank you for creating those miracles. We enjoyed watching them as well. The gentleman of whom you speak had made a connection with you personally before he left his body. We will tell you that he was grateful for what you did and the role that you played. He was dancing on both sides of the veil unable fully to disconnect. We will tell you what this looked like from his perspective, for he was there, up in the corner of the room, watching the events of his own death unfold. He watched as you took on the pain that you thought he was experiencing. You carry this pain within your own cellular memories to this day. But he did not feel the pain in the way that you imagined. In fact, that which you describe as pain is a human experience that is often re-membered as a sweet human condition with those returning Home. What you witnessed was the death of a physical body and the instinctive process that occurred as the cord was cut. That was all you saw. The soul of this gentleman had already excused himself and was watching from over your shoulder. He was saddened by your stress.

What you witnessed was very similar to what happens with some people who spend time in a coma. In this state, their spirit has left the body without cutting the cord. Some even get to experience Home without fully severing the cord. Some of these experiences have been termed 'near death experiences'. The writhing you saw was merely a physical reaction. In fact, there was a moment when you looked deep into the soul of this man with the compassion of a master healer. Though you did not know it you were the one that gave him permission to leave. In that brief moment you fulfilled a beautiful contract with him.

Your willingness to be a Transition Team member and help people at the most difficult times of their life is honored beyond your imagination. There will come a time when you will see the effect that these beloved 'Transition Team' members have.

We tell you that the work of Transition Team members plant seeds far in the future that will ease your return and raise the collective of humanity. As with sleep, if you go to bed with something bothering you, by law of energy, those same troubled thoughts must visit you first thing in the morning. In the same way, whatever energy imprint that accompanies your transition at death, must be experienced on your return. In other words, if you leave troubled, you will return troubled.

A Transition Team member can make all the difference between a troubled departure and a smooth one. With a simple smile, a squeeze of the hand or a loving embrace, Transition Team members set the energy for an entire lifetime to start out on the right footing.

Those of you who deal with people in comas, those of you who deal with people who have Alzheimer's that their spirit is disconnected from their physical bodies and yet we tell you they are often on both sides of the veil at the same time. It is not as if they do not see you. It is not as if they do not hear you, feel you, they do. But they do not always see you, feel you, hear you from inside their own bodies. We tell you that you personally have made a difference as a Transitions Team specialist. And we also tell you that the gentleman of which you speak, that you so elegantly helped to the other side, will visit you soon to tell you personally how grateful he is.

Baltimore, Maryland - March 18th, 2001

Question:

After my son, David, made his transition, I slipped and hurt myself so badly that I needed an ambulance to take me to the hospital. And that prevented me from connecting with him on the other side. I want to know if that was some kind of angelic intervention protecting me from connecting with him and I also want to know if he completed his contract?

the Group:

Yes and yes. More importantly, he took on a new contract. We tell you that there was much going on here for it is so difficult for us to interact in your world sometimes. There are times when you ask for things and in response, we reach into your world and move the energy around you, directing you to walk this way or that. We are right here. We are whispering right in your ear and sometimes all you feel is the hair raising on your arms as you move in the opposite direction. Yes. David was complete. Furthermore, that time was necessary for he was in assimilation and needed his space. There needed to be a time lag, for there was a major transition taking place. There was a contract being scripted at that very moment that needed time on Planet Earth to finish. There were energies being lined up and when it was absolutely necessary, the slip was created for you.

This also facilitated the separation that you needed to begin your own grief process. As a healer you wanted so much to help that you were neglecting your own grief and your own healing. Would it surprise you to hear that David had a hand in your slip? You were in the perfect spot at the perfect time.

There is much more to this than you will ever know. Even as you had to be taken to the hospital yourself, you touched a person there very deeply with your own inner work. In the midst of your own trauma, in the midst of a larger game, you still reached out and touched another being with your heart. That was wonderful. We tell you that in David's transition a very unusual thing happened. Several souls came together to create the vibrational integrity for this transition to take place. We also tell you that this was done for a very specific reason. David was to be one of the scouts for the Crystal Children and he knew that. What he did not know when he scripted this life for himself was that the Crystal Children would be coming to Planet Earth this soon. It was necessary for David to take his place here at Home for there is much work here to be done. There will be many that will take their place on the other side of the veil in preparation for what is to come. The seeds are being planted and it is necessary to do that.

Ahh, but you asked the most important question. Ahh, "Did he complete his contracts?" No, but the largest one he is completing now. Rarely does anyone complete all of their contracts. He made a difference in many lives for he planted many seeds and touched people in such a way that you would not see the results for several years. Embrace him and embrace the gifts. Welcome the gift that he gave you in his early passing. For it helped to awaken many of you to whole new levels of purpose, action and power. That was the gift. Accept it. Release the guilt and the grief. It is possible to hold souls back through your own denial of the grieving process. Your own Love can prevent you from releasing his spirit. Help others to release in this same situation, for there is a large process of re-cycling underway. And it is important that the energies move forward once they leave here for there is work to do and David is about that work. Thank you for asking your question as that will answer so many.

Question:

My question has to do with my father. He seems to be actively dying, but something seems to be holding him here. He seems to want to die, but he can't. And I really would like to know if I need to go to Phoenix and be with him to help facilitate that.

the Group:

Transition, dear ones, is such a difficult time of life. To move energy from one form to the other means leaving the physical body behind. The physical body resists; the lower self, which you call conscious mind, resists change and instinctively fights for survival. Still, it is the Higher Self that is in charge. And when the energy is complete the release and transition begins.

There will be many of you who feel the draw to be part of the Transition Teams that will be forming here on Planet Earth, for many will be leaving and transitioning is one of the most important parts of life. For as this energy moves from one form to another, certain things can happen. People can be afraid. Trauma can set in and confuse everyone. As with sleep, if you go to sleep with very great difficulties on your mind, it is law of energy that those same difficulties will be the first energy that you must experience when you awaken the next morning. The same is true with death. The same is true when transitioning from one form of energy into another. If you are afraid or troubled when you leave, by law of energy you must experience those same situations on your return. Therefore, members of Transition Teams are some of the greatest healers on your planet. Holding someone's hand, giving them permission to leave, is one of the greatest gifts that you can give to someone. Allowing them to pass in dignity and understanding can be a gift that will span the ages of known time. Letting them know that it is okay; letting them know that you are with them and that they will retain their spirit forever is the highest work a healer can perform. In this way Transition Teams help raise the collective vibration of humanity. At this time on your planet you do not support Transition Team members, nor do you even refer to them as healers. It is easy to see why. After all, most of their patients die. Still, we tell you that these special healers *will* play an important part in the New Planet Earth.

There are three separate parts to Transition Team work. Some of you will find one or two areas that will attract you and some will be attracted to all three. This is the reason we refer to people working in this area as teams. The three roles of Transition Team members are:

1. To work with a patient until they either have made their transition or have returned to health. This is where you will play an active role in holding the person's hand and helping them to know it is okay to heal or to let go. This area also includes education so that when people leave suddenly they have an idea of what to expect and are not traumatized. This work also includes helping souls entering as babies. The first look into their eyes and a "Welcome to Earth" from a caring soul in the delivery room will be more helpful than you understand. This is the front line work of Transition Teams.

2. To work with the soul after it has left the body. This is particularly true in the case of sudden death. Here you will actually help the soul transition, to find the light of Home on the other side, and to start the process of this cycle anew. When one leaves the physical body suddenly or traumatically, it is easy to become confused and feel lost. Upon arriving on the other side one is in an enhanced state of creation. In this state a soul could mistakenly create a reality that supports their belief that

they are still alive. [A good example of this is what happened on September 11th 2001. Many Lightworkers had wonderful experiences of helping others to find their way Home. The Group says that this also opened a doorway for countless others who had been stuck for eons, to also find their way Home.]

3. And the third, which is very important, is to help ease the grieving of the family and those left behind. For it is entirely possible to hold a spirit in an inter-dimensional realm and keep that spirit from advancing by not dealing with and letting go of your own grief, guilt or pain. Helping others to learn that the highest expression of their love is to let go is an art practiced by these wonderful healers.

In the times ahead you will see the Transition Teams take their place as important healers once again. Welcome them and support them. They will raise the collective very rapidly with their love and their work. Transition Team members will be those that lovingly step forward to be a part of this important work.

Now for the rest of your question: Is it necessary for you to go to Phoenix? No. However, if you chose to do this, you will find that your father is actually hoping to establish a different relationship with you in the last days of his life. He is stuck in a pattern that is difficult for him to break. If he does he will attempt to connect on a higher level with you in his remaining time. This would benefit you both greatly. Is it important that you be there at the last moment? No. Is it imperative that you be there in person? No. But he is waiting for permission. He is waiting for the opportunity to complete the energy cycle with you. For that, we would strongly suggest that you make space for that to happen. For you will be the big winner.

Questioner:
Thank you.

the Group
You are most welcome.

Columbus, Ohio - June 9th, 2001

Question:

My question also involves Transition Teams. I have a friend who has begun seeing spirits, and she is in fear about that. I think she's been selected to be a part of the Transition Teams. Is there any information we could give her that would help her overcome the fear of dealing with spirits?

the Group:

There are many seeds being planted in your field of Earthly vision. As humans, you watch the movies and we love to plant seeds in movies. Watch the *Sixth Sense*. It is very close to the reality that exists. And yes, anything outside of the ordinary, anything outside of the explainable, often causes the vacuum of fear. Fear is a lack of information. It is simply something that is missing. It is the unknown and the lack of light called darkness.

Your friend has a gift. Many people that have seen beings in this vibrational range shut it off because of this overwhelming fear. Please understand…spirits can be scary. The truth is that this is only one of the inter-dimensional realities in which you exist. We tell you it is very common, especially in the case of a sudden death, for a soul to get up out of physical body and walk away, thinking they are still alive. The moment they leave the physical realm they are in a state of enhanced creation. In essence, they are Home pretending they are still on Earth. So they walk around, instantly creating that which they are accustomed to experiencing. They find themselves attracted to physical things and they get caught up in the cycle of re-living their attachment to those physical things. Sometimes you see these spirits attempting to interact as if they were still alive. These you have often called hauntings. Some carry the emotion of anger and reflect back that same anger as a human emotion.

The frustration of being caught up in this cycle only adds to that anger. These can be very scary to someone who already has a fear of the unknown in the area of spirits.

Most of what you see in this other realm is simply people who have left who do not know they are gone. They do not know where to go. They do not know what to do. They think they are still in charge, and they think they are still on the Gameboard of Planet Earth. Sometimes it is simply a question of people letting them know that they are gone. Sometimes it is only a question of giving them permission to go Home. Your friend has a gift. She will see it in time. She also has the choice, for it is entirely possible for her to shut it down and look the other way. She has chosen, at this point in her life, to not do that. We thank her for that for she has an important job to do with her abilities. Help her to see the lighter side of this work. As in all of life, this does not need to be serious. Humans take life way too seriously.

You will find many in the days to come that have these abilities, for as your extension of perceptions is increasing, you will be able to see some of these other realms that you did not know existed within your own time and space. Sometimes they try very, very hard and expend a lot of energy to come in and do some simple little thing in your world. They can see you even though you rarely see them. Sometimes they believe they are still here, but they are once removed. Much more of this will become known in the times ahead for as you go through your own human evolution. Welcome it.

Walk - Ins

Red Boiling Springs, Tennessee - February 19th, 2001

Question:
Thank you for being with us. Would you care to comment on the possibility of a walk-in president within the next decade?

the Group:
No.

Questioner:
Thank you. (Laughter)

the Group:
We love the humor. Please feel our energy and let us explain. We do not involve ourselves in your human Games. It is your free choice that is so terribly important to be honored here, and that is the reason we will not get involved. We interact with you in a vague manner, and that is a source of great frustration for some of you. The days of 'cast in stone' predictions are no longer. It is now this vagueness, sometimes seen as Cosmic Winks that allow us to interact with you without taking your power from you.

We will elaborate on the possibilities. There are some wonderful seeds that have been planted. The challenge is that sometime you feel that a 'walk-in' is carrying a very special energy from Home. 'Walk-ins' are here with primary life lesson, just as you are. In fact, they *are* you. They are not more advanced than you, only less removed from the memories of Home. Most of them incarnate in order to complete energy cycles and they make agreements with the soul to complete contracts and commitments made by the original host. Most of them are not public people and they go out of their way to blend in quietly. There are fewer 'walk-ins' on this planet than you imagine. Many of those you regard as 'walk-ins' are in altered states of original ego. Pushing the re-set button itself is a huge shift of energy within a single personality. Even in the Phantom Death you may seem like an entirely different person afterward, yet it is different than a walk-in.

A 'walk-in' is a very challenging situation, for they come in without a history or the connections that one would normally build during the course of a life. Their main focus is simply to honor all the connections and commitments made by the person who originally inhabited the body. It is rarely an easy job. Most of the 'walk-ins' that you will find are recluses. Most would never place themselves under public scrutiny, for they have a blank spot in their history. It is a very difficult job to take on the task of a 'walk-in'. And you are making it easier through your techniques, through your healing modalities, through your love, for people to stay. That is the greatest gift you have given to all of humanity. In the days ahead there will be new types of walk-ins that will accomplish a specific purpose.

Is it possible for a 'walk-in' to be a president? Yes, of course it is. And would that person make a fine president? Yes, she would. If you are asking is there a divine plan for a 'walk-in' to take power and save planet Earth, the answer is no. There *is* no divine plan, for you have not written it yet. Chances are very slim at this point that a 'walk-in' would ever take such a role. However, we cannot wait to see what you will do next!

We tell you it does not make any difference *who* is president. It is *you* that hold the power, and we do not just mean the power to vote. We mean if you do not give the president your power to make your life choices it will not be that important. In the times directly ahead such a role will be only that of a trusted servant. That is the way you scripted the Game. Play the Game so that *you* hold the power, for if you continue to give away your power to such people, their egos cannot help but get in the way. You have already found that happening, since war once again inhabits planet Earth. It has happened in only the last few days and there is more yet to come.

Questioner:

Hopefully next time you'll be able to comment. (Laughter)

the Group:

Perhaps, we will see. *(Laughter)*

ᏯWhen to create, when to allow

Syracuse, New York - March 11th, 2001

Question:

I have a question. When we put intention out, when we've asked for the highest good to be served in what we choose to co-create, how do we know when we need to let go? How do we know when it is not correct?

the Group:

Oh, dear ones, if we could only move aside the veil, as we often do during your sleep time, and show you the secrets of the Universe you would understand how simple it all is. Ahh, some of you have had that experience, have you not? And you wake up with the understanding of how simple it is. That is the veil. That is how you have agreed to play the Game so your first question is: "How do we know if it is for the highest good?" and we tell you that you cannot. There are circumstances that you do not see in play, for there are many co-creations going on simultaneously and it is up to us to direct the traffic. Trust in spirit and make room for synchronicity and we will direct the traffic to the highest good for all.

So, how do you know when to stop the action? How do you know when to take charge and when to let go? You are responsible for all action on your side of the veil. Do not sit in your chair and say, "If Spirit wants me to do it, they will send a limousine to my door to pick me up". You need to call the taxi yourself. You need to set things into motion and do the mundane tasks, for that is your job and we do not intervene as much as you would like to think we do. Do what you can and step into the action fearlessly. Follow synchronicity to help you understand when your actions are complete. When all is done on your side of the veil then let go.

Some of you have grabbed hold of synchronicity as your primary guide. We ask you to hold your own power. Give it to no-thing - even that which you call synchronicity. Living your life, waiting for spirit to lead you in every move, is not taking responsibility for your own reality. Without responsibility there is no power. Sometimes you take everything with deep meaning. "Where is the meaning in this? Where is the meaning in that?" Sometimes, dear ones, a cup of coffee is just a cup of coffee. Watch the synchronicities as indicators, and then make your choices. And re-member to be careful what you search for, as you will create it. And sometimes when you feel resistance it does not mean that it is wrong, it just means that you have done your work and now it is time to stand back and let spirit do its work. Sometimes when you feel that things are not going quite right and yet they are not being completely blocked, but you are starting to find resistance to your actions, it simply means that spirit has a better idea. Take a step back and look at it again. Trust that the highest and best will be sent to you in some form and watch the magic.

Play the Game. And above all, do not take it too seriously, for it is just a Game. There are no more wrong moves on the Gameboard, dear ones. Praying to a cup of coffee for your answers is simply a misdirection of energy in the higher vibrations. Right and wrong are simply an illusion of polarity. Enjoy the Game. Have fun.

Where is my passion?

Sydney, Australia - August 26th, 2001

Question:

Some of us are having trouble finding our passion. Is there any guidance you can offer us on this?

the Group:

You may find yourself doing something that others would consider to be very mundane and yet still be fully in your passion. You may be experiencing little sparks of passion in your daily life, yet your brain often tells you, "Oh yes, but I cannot make a living at this". So therefore you separate the two.

We will tell you of a young man who enjoyed eating lollipops. As a youth he thought it to be a delightful sin. As he got older he spoke to himself; "Oh, this is wonderful, but I cannot be a lollipop taster". That is more humorous than you know, for there is a lollipop taster here in this very room.

Find the things you truly love to do, and that is where you will find your passion. Stop thinking long enough to *enjoy* and your passion will appear in front of you. You believe that when you find your passion you must experience it fully in every single moment, but for most of you moving fully into your passion will be a slow progression. Find the small pieces. Do what you need to do to first ignite those small sparks of light. Find the crystals that you placed upon your own paths. Do not worry about translating your passion into making a living. Carry the vibration of passion first and then watch as the energy lines up for you to start experiencing it more and more. For those of you who are working in jobs that do not fully feed you, start by finding areas of your passion in the evenings and weekends. Connect with others of similar passion and see the osmosis effect in your life. Do you think that this young man of which we spoke went to his parents one day and told them that he wanted to be a lollipop taster? If he had there would have been trouble in that household, we can tell you. In fact, it was not the lollipop that he was passionate about, it was what the lollipops represented: the act of being childlike.

"But what if I cannot find my passion?" you ask. Here we will speak of perspective, for if you are using the perspective of the angelic realm, you will have no difficulty finding your passion. "Ahh, what is the perspective of the angelic realm?" you ask as the pens come out. Humor. You humans take yourselves far too seriously. We often tickle your funny bone to re-mind you that it is just a Game and still you hold a serious demeanor. Find ways of shifting your perception. Find ways to laugh about every difficulty and challenge that enters your field. If you allow yourself to enjoy the Game you will quickly find your passion. Choose your realities by choosing your point of perception. Choose humor and you life cannot fail to be filled with passion. Watch the magic. And do not forget to laugh.

The lollipop-lover the Group referred to in this channel was sitting in the back of the room and he later told us his story. There was a time in his life when he had actually owned a lollipop factory that made really large, giant-sized lollipops. Today he and his wife own the largest party and catering supplies company in Australia. The "Kid" in him is still going strong! Thanks for sharing your passion with us, Geoff and Beryl!

Las Vegas, Nevada - January 20th 2000

Question:

We are working in jobs to support ourselves financially yet we know that our spiritual work is much more important,

How do we make that transition so that we can support ourselves doing our spiritual work?

the Group:

We will tell you quite often people see what they *think* to
be their spiritual work and they feel drawn toward moving to a
place or into a specific area, only to find they are not supported.
Then there are those of you who have been here holding the
door open, planting seeds in the ground of the collective of all of
humanity. Many of you feel the resistance and lack of support
around you even as you do your spiritual work. What we tell you
is to experience the joy within you first. It is your own belief
systems that have caused you difficulty. Most of you hearing or
reading these words feel so drawn toward spiritual work that you
feel your real usefulness on the planet will be as a facilitator. To
address this further we must first define the word "spiritual".
From our perspective spiritual is everything that is not physical.
Therefore, emotions, ideas, feelings, and everything else
outside of the physical world are spiritual. With that definition in
mind you can now see that many of you will indeed be
facilitators of spirituality. Even those of you who work with the
physical body in many cases actually work more with the
nonphysical aspects of the body than you do with its physicality.

Look for the joy in your life. This is not something that you are
used to doing, yet it is what holds the key to your success in the
higher vibrations. The more you can experience this during your
off hours the more doors will eventually open for you to
experience this in your work. What happens here is that as you
resonate with your joy and your passion, as you begin to work,
even in small ways, with what you came here to do, so
eventually will it gradually change your vibration, which in turn
will help you attract new opportunities and affect changes in the
environment around you. So do not hesitate to reach for as
much joy and passion as you can hold in a day, for we tell you
this: Your success in the higher vibrations of the New Planet
Earth is directly proportional to the amount of joy and passion
that you can experience on a daily basis. If you are not finding

sufficient joy and passion in your job then find it where you can and then watch as your job starts to get better.

In times past, you have walked down the linear hallway of time and you have chosen doors which you thought you wished to go through. Sometimes you chose by the look of the door itself. Sometimes you chose by the label that is hanging on the door. Sometimes it was because you believed there was great abundance on the other side of the door. Then you commenced to work very hard to get through that door. You bought the key, you picked the lock, or your kicked the door down in order to gain entrance. You called it determination and hard work. Most often when you gained entrance to a room, you discovered it was not where you wanted to go in the first place. Or you found yourself sitting behind a desk and wondering what happened to your life. We tell you the paradigm has now changed. You are now walking down the corridor, pushing ever so slightly at the doors. Those that open just before you get there are the ones that spirit is helping you to open. You are learning that spirit is playing a part in your life through synchronicity, and this is the part that you are now getting quite good at. However, quite often a door opens ahead of you, and you take a peek and see what is in the room, and you say, "That is not where I wish to go". But if only you would take a step further into the room, you would see that there are side doors that were not visible from the entrance. We tell you that you are not far from your path. In fact, you are *on* it. All it takes is a very slight shift in your perception for you to see doors that are standing right in front, waiting to open. Your heart's desire is much closer than you think.

Section IV

Where do We Go from Here?

Points to re-member when

creating a New Reality.

Chapter 12

New Realities

A glimpse of Home

A live channel presented
November 15th, 2001
Powell River, Canada

This chapter is somewhat different from the rest of this book. So often we hear from people who cannot make it to one of our seminars or live channels. Barbara and I have always wished that we could give everyone a chance to experience the incredible energy and vibrations that fill the room when the Group begins to speak. When we finished editing this book this direct experience was the only thing we felt was missing. So, we decided to include the following live channel in which the Group did something unusual.

Just prior to the channel Barbara led a special meditation where she had everyone hold hands and run energy in a circular motion to create a vortex. That night, we left a break in the circle for those family members who were not there with us. As you read this, we invite you to travel in your mind and place yourself right in the room taking the hand of the person next to you. Now the family is complete.

The Group always says that when they speak they shift the energy in the room to accommodate the actual vibrations of Home. In effect, for that time during which the Group is speaking, everyone in the room is Home. Even as you read this, the Group is extending those same vibrations of Home to include you.

We now invite you to find your center, breathe deeply and join us as, together, for a few brief moments we return Home.

Greetings from Home

Here you sit in a circle, holding hands, passing energy from one to the other. Do you know what you have done? Do you know the joy we experience on this side of the veil when you do that, connecting one to one, heart to heart, creating energy that is moving in an endless circle? When you do that you are creating the greatest expression of God within your own bubbles of biology. Well done, dear ones, well done.

This is a very special time, for humanity is stepping into a very important role. You, the Human Angels, have come together this evening to look into each other's eyes and to re-member who you are. Ahh, some of you do not think you belong here, but you do. We tell you that you have come a very long way to be in this energy - and we are not just talking about the physical distance you have traveled to be here tonight. Many of you have re-turned from the days of Atlantis and the days of Mu. You have asked to be here at exactly this moment. After the waters came in and claimed all the land, and took all the lives, you came together in spirit, and vowed: "If ever the collective vibration of humanity becomes high enough, we will return in force and next time we will do it differently".

And here you are.

You returned en masse and you began to reclaim your power. You began to hold the energy for one another. You came at the perfect juncture of time and space. Oh, and when you hold hands as you just did, and when you focus your intent, the miracles begin, for you are the magic ones. You are the ones who will first see that you hold the power of God within your own biology. You have a responsibility to find that power within you and use it.

And we tell you, use that power first to create your own reality.

Many of you are concerned about being selfish. You wish to create realities for everyone else in your field first, thinking that by arranging *their* lives, your own will become better.
You say; "If only my daughter would do this or do that, then I would be happy". We tell you it is only possible to help another when you create your reality first. You have been told so often that you are *not* the center of the Universe and we are here to

tell you that, in fact, *you are* the center of your own Universe, and treating yourself differently does *nothing* to serve the whole. It does not mean that you are the *only* center of the universe. What it means is that you must treat yourself *first,* before all else, in order to line up the energy.

There are four of you here in the room tonight who have silently requested healing. We stop this message for just a moment to accommodate this. [pause]

Oh, dear ones, we have no conception of what it is like to not be able to re-member who you are. You have asked to play the Game behind the veil of forgetfulness, and you do not re-member that you are heirs to the throne of forever. You do not re-member that you are sons and daughters of the King. You do not re-member that you rule the royal house. It is our job to help you re-member. If nothing more, all we wish to do in these brief times together is to reflect your magnificence, for if you can experience the joy of yourselves, you will reclaim the power of who you are. Then you will serve the higher good of the whole. This act will create the miracle of bringing Home to your side of the veil. This is in process, even as we speak.

Let the magic begin, dear ones. We will share with you this evening an experience which will allow each and every one of you to really feel the energy of Home. In a moment we will ask the Keeper to raise his hands, and as he does so, he will pull aside the veil for you to receive our energy directly. Ahh. . . but there are conditions. You did not think it was going to be that easy, did you? First, all healing must be personally requested in the higher vibrations of the New Planet Earth. It is no longer possible for you to heal another person. It is only possible to create a space in which another can become sufficiently empowered to heal themselves. And that is what we wish to do for you this evening. So first of all, we ask that if you do not wish to receive this energy when it comes your way, simply keep your hands at your sides and this energy will pass you by. Secondly, there is a vital new paradigm that will apply now that you are in

the New Planet Earth. This is the first attribute of the Human
Angels. It is illustrated by the call of the Human Angel, which is:
"There Before the Grace of You Go I". Therefore, if you accept
this gift from us this night, it is a secondary condition that you
find a way to pass it on.

The energy that we are about to send you is the pure energy of
Home. In the days ahead, you will be carrying more of this
energy in your everyday lives, but especially for the next few
days you must understand that you will remain highly charged
with this energy. We ask you to be conscious that you are
carrying the energy of Home as a Human Angel and spread it to
all who are ready to receive it. Do so quietly and unassumingly.
Please also understand that you are not responsible for how or
whether another accepts it, you are only responsible for giving it
when you have an opportunity to do so. Ask, and when you are
given an opportunity, take it. With the touch of an Angel, reach
out and touch another's heart chakra. Touch them on the back
of the heart chakra, or on their shoulder. Touch them on their
feet, or on their hands. It makes no difference where you touch
them, just so long as when you have their permission, you pass
this energy on. Hug them if you dare, if they will let you. Look
beyond their eyes and deep into their soul, for this is an
important new way for you to activate dormant seeds of light.
As you are looking into their soul, feel the love, feel the power of
the energy, and in that way you will be raising the level of the
vibration of your own energy and passing it on.

We have adjusted the energy in the room twice since we have
been talking. Have you felt the shift in temperature? It has to do
with your relationship to space and time. The reason we make
these adjustments is to create space for all the visitors that are
here now to lend their energy to what is about to happen. It is
magical, dear ones, for each one of you has no less that 77
entities watching your every move in support. Yes, it is getting
quite crowded in here, but we are very good at parking, so fear
not. *(Laughter)*

And now on to the magic. If you wish to receive it, simply hold up your hands. It is yours for the asking. In fact, it has been yours all along.

[Steve holds up his hands with his palms facing outward toward the audience, and silently and slowly sweeps them from side to side. Suddenly the room is filled with the soft sounds of sighing and gentle moaning as everyone experiences the love wash of the vibrations of Home.]

You have just spent a few moments in Heaven. You have been charged with a powerful healing energy unlike anything most of you have experienced while in human form.   It is only recently that your biology has been able to carry this energy.   As we passed by just then, you felt the energy flowing directly from us into your own hands. Now we will tell you a secret: That was not *our* energy you just felt. . . it was your own. It was yours all along. It is because of your new higher vibrational status that you can now begin to see and feel your own power.

It is our highest honor to reflect your magnificence and your energy back to you for you to experience. As promised, this was truly the vibration of Home. Please do not negate the powerful energy you have just been charged with simply because it originated from you. Watch the magic in the way people react to you over the next several days. We challenge you to find at least one person to pass this onto within the next seven days. And we tell you that if each one of you here in this room does exactly that, the vibration of Planet Earth will increase by no less than sixteen times beyond what it is today.

Dear ones, we know the Game has been difficult for many of you. You had no idea when you were scripting these plans that the veil would be so completely thick. Of course, you do not re-member. As you scripted the roles you now play, your best hope was to wake up on Earth and be confused. You are more successful than you know. *(Laughter)* Many of you arrived on Planet Earth and said, "Oh my God. What have I done? What have I got myself into? Next time I will read the small print".

During the time we have been together many of you have been worked on by your own guides. As you came into our energy this night, you opened yourself for healing. That healing was yours the moment you asked for it. Walk from here and carry it proudly and re-member to pass it on. Walk from here, dear ones, in the confusion of not being able to re-member who you truly are. Reach out and take the hands of those next to you, for that is where the magic will begin, the circle starts from there. And the next time you look in the mirror, squint your eyes ever so slightly and you will start to get glimpses of who you are. For we tell you, the beauty reflected in your mirror is so grand that the veil could not let you see it fully. Dare to own the fact that you are heir to the throne of forever. Dare to own that you are the Human Angels. Dare to own your own power. Let the magic begin on Planet Earth and let it begin right here and right now. For it is time, dear ones. Welcome to the 5th dimension. Welcome Home. We thank you for having the courage to be here.

Use your own abilities of healing, for every single one of you hearing or reading these words has these abilities. You have earned the right to carry this power, not because you are the heirs to the throne, not because you are the sons and daughters of the King, but because of what you are doing every single day. This is the role of the Human Angel and although you may recognize this is who you are, and though you may never hear any words of thanks until you return Home, still you bravely step forward and do the work of your heart. For this we thank you and we love you always. You are the masters of the Gameboard, and *we* are so honored to be in *your* presence. It is with the greatest of honor that we ask you to treat each other with respect, nurture one another, and play well together. And so it is. . .

the Group

Chapter 13

What's Ahead?

A View from the Top of the Bus

The Group is very quick to point out that they do not tell the future. They say it's not possible to foretell the future because we have yet to write it. They can, however, clearly see the direction we are heading. They say we are in for some exciting times. This chapter will discuss some of the important changes that lie directly in our path.

Greetings from Home

Your evolution has placed you at a most exciting place. You have spent much time living in the dark recesses of the tunnel. Within that tunnel it was necessary to pass through the darkest of passages. You have just passed through a particularly dark passage. As a result of that journey you are now beginning to see the flickering of light at the end of the tunnel. You are closer than you think. In fact you have just turned an important corner and will soon be standing at the end of the tunnel facing out to a bright new day. Welcome Home.

Decreasing Magnetism

If you look toward the many animals that inhabit your world you will see many of them with an acute sense of direction. You have called this a sixth sense or a built in homing device. We call it simple magnetics. Your own biology had this same sensitive relationship to magnetics. Some of you are seeing it in the healing devices that you now use. Deep in your being you know there to be a connection even though your science has yet to find it. What you are seeing here is a changing connection. As you continue to evolve your need for the energy of magnetics will lessen. Even within your own biology at its early stages you had your own magnetic homing devices. Your biology was extremely sensitive to magnetic waves and the grid lines that the Earth are built on always gave you a sense of guidance. As you move back into higher vibrations your relationship to the magnetics of the Earth will change. In fact your entire relationship to magnetics is changing even now. Quite some time ago you have lost your own magnetic homing device. Your own biology no longer has the same needs. Your biology is changing as the magnetic strands of the DNA now begin holding the imprints within. As your own DNA reconnects the magnetic strands and you continue to move back into Lightbody, your biology no longer needs the magnetic fields that it once did. In reaction to this change you will see the Earth continue to decrease her magnetic field over the next 182 years. The magnets that you use as healing devices give you the feeling of stability as the larger magnetic field of the Earth continues to decrease. This is the reason that so many of you are finding comfort using magnetic fields.

Time ~ Space ~ Magnetics

Magnetics have been the glue that holds together the Game you have so successfully built. Magnetics are what keep the spirit contained within the human form. Therefore as the magnetics continue to decrease on Planet Earth you will see the spirit emerge from behind the veil. Simultaneously, you will see increases in other planets in the Universe including your own sun. This has to do with their new relationship to you as evolving beings. The evolution of humanity is aided by the decrease of the magnetic fields of the Earth. As your spirit moves back into Lightbody, your existence on New Planet Earth will be less dependent on the magnetics of the Earth. You will always have the magnetic connection yet it will have less of an effect as your vibration increase.

The Earth has cycles very similar to your own biological cycles. You have not always been aware of these cycles. Your study of geology will verify that there are large blank spots of hundreds of years in what you know to be the history of the Earth. Here it would seem that time stood still. These blank spots are times when the magnetics of the planet have gone through cycles that have changed the relationship of the Earth to time and space.

Here your entire planet slipped into other dimensions. The specialist known as Kryon is responsible for the magnetics of your planet and has carefully monitored and adjusted the grids as needed. The magnetic grids have been adjusted three times including the original set thus far and the third adjustment completed in December 2002. These adjustments have been necessary for your own connection to the planet and the evolution of Planet Earth.

The cycle of magnetic fields is well documented in your own study of geology. Many times have the magnetic fields altered. There are regular cycles that have taken place in relationship to the magnetics. About every 500,000 years the magnetics of Earth go through a complete cycle and are reset. These are quite different than the Grid adjustments made by Kryon. This is a natural life cycle of Planet Earth herself. These cycles begin as a decreasing of the magnetic fields which leads to a reset of the entire magnetic field. As magnetic fields increased on your planet, Humanity fell into lower vibration and denser physical form. Then, as the magnetics decrease on the planet, the corresponding collective vibration of humanity rises.

Because of the interconnection of magnetics and the collective vibration of humanity, your rise in vibration has generally been accompanied by cataclysmic events that balanced and reset the magnetic energy fields. Five times prior this was known to you as a magnetic pole shift. That cycle is now changing. Due to your evolution the cycle has been interrupted in the hopes that you would awaken from the dream in time to take your power. Imagine our excitement as we watch your eyes begin to open. At this time you are currently about 700,000 years overdue for a reset. You are the ones who set this extension into motion, yet the actual adjustment has been accomplished by Kryon.

Your DNA has ten magnetic strands that have been disconnected since the early times that you have called the fall from grace. We have spoken of these events and see them quite differently. [See the chapter: "Sex ~ Understanding the seeds of your past" in the first book "Re-member ~ a Handbook for Human Evolution".] Your evolution is now reconnecting those strands to restore the original configuration of twelve. The re-connection of these strands will set into motion the eventual move into Lightbody. As the magnetic fields in the ten hidden strands start activating, your biology will become less dependent on the magnetic fields of Earth. This will change your relationship to the Earth and allow you to cross lines that now separate inter-dimensional realities. That is when you will find the blank spots in your own history. Then you will stop searching for the missing links. This also means that as the Earth completes her next cycle that you will no longer be forced into lower vibrations as the magnetic fields increase. Humanity has changed the Game. Your relationship to magnetics will always remain yet you will hold much more of that connection within.

The Grid of Light

You have seen intentional grids forming on your planet for some time now. Even your telephone and power cables have formed an intentional grid that has enabled you to reach new levels of connection with each other and therefore take steps toward Unity consciousness. We can tell you that this is only the beginning of the intentional grids on the New Earth. As you continue to evolve you will see the grid of communication move into the field of Light. It is not hard for you to imagine an intentional grid of light instead of cables that will carry power and communications in many forms to each and every one of you. This grid is now being built.

In the days ahead watch for breakthroughs in the understanding of Light. The speed of light, which you thought to be a Universal constant, can be controlled. Imagine a time when you will be able to control the speed of light. Here it will be possible to freeze it in mid flight, program it and then send it on its way again. You are much closer to this than you know. The returning interest in your toys of war will actually bring about an understanding of coherent light and how it can be harnessed to connect you all very easily. Your first uses of this 'new' discovery will be power transmission. Then communications will find applications. That which has started as the internet will expand very quickly onto this new grid of light. In place of wires imagine a network of fiber optics without the transmission wires. Beams of coherent light that carry information will connect over the globe in a network of Light. This is the next intentional grid placed upon your planet. As it develops you will see a geometric form that illustrates the 3rd dimension moving into the 5th dimension.

Technology

Advances in technology have been on a temporary hold as the planet regroups. Technology on Planet Earth has always been in direct proportion to your spiritual advancement. Technology has been dropped on your planet by 'advanced' races many times. On Planet Earth the technology will only hold if the collective vibration of humanity is high enough to support it. That which you call the Philadelphia experiment and the Montauk project are examples of technology that was dropped and did not hold. The technology simply did not work in the same way as it did for its originators. There have also been times where technology has held for hundreds or thousands of years only to be suddenly lost when the collective vibration of a civilization lowered. Technologically advanced civilizations such as the Mayans and the Atlanteans have disappeared suddenly from Earth because of choices that reduced the collective vibration below a point which would support the technology already in place. In your Game you have seen a steady rise in vibration. You have become accustomed to a continual advancement as time moves forward, and may not be aware of the larger picture as we see it. Let us simply say that there have been many advances and many recessions. Your events of September 11th 2001 were an example of the latter. If the collective vibration is high enough to support an understanding that you are all one and not separate from one another, then your technology will make huge strides in the times directly ahead.

Biology + Technology = Triology

Like a magician who attracts your attention to one hand while he performs 'magic' with the other, the focus of humanity has been misdirected. As you have been off playing war some very important advances are being made in the area of biology. Cures for diseases that have eluded you for some time will soon be in place. If your collective vibration remains high enough, they will emerge. You have been aware for some time that the human body was originally designed to live very long life spans. This will *soon* become a reality.

You now hold an understanding of human biology that will allow the blending of biology and technology into Triology. This is progressing nicely. Understand that any resistance to human empowerment is simply a direct result of the veil. This explains why you have a great resistance to taking your power. You do not wish to play God. We are not asking you to play God either, but simply understand that you *are* God, and as such you have a responsibility to create.

There are those who are so attached to the human experience that they are afraid of pain in any form. They believe that the slightest infliction of pain on another being is wrong, and because of their own sensitivity to pain they overreact in an attempt to eliminate all physical pain. Dear ones, please do not think that you are your physical bodies. That which you experience as pain is only a very effective illusion of the Gameboard. Understand that even as you partake of the fruit of a tree to sustain your life, the tree feels pain as the fruit is harvested. Upon returning Home the pain that you avoided will be remembered with a sweetness that you cannot at the moment imagine. Pain is a unique part of the *human* experience and you will always re-member it with love. Those who strongly oppose the advancements in biology do so either because they fear their own power as creators, or because they fear pain. We tell you that their voices will be loud indeed as their fear is very strong. Even so, they play an important role here. Though their voices will be 'loud' they will enable you to keep a balance. The advances will go forward in any event, as long as they are supported by the vibrational rise of humanity as a whole. If you take a restrictive position and enact laws that prohibit the advancements that are directly in front of you, these innovations will go underground and become available only to a select few. If you trust yourselves as creators and embrace that which now lies before you, these innovations will become available to all. Either way the debate has now begun. If you do not settle this yourselves, the Indigo children will, for they have little fear. One hand of the magician is 'loudly' attracting attention while the other is 'quietly' ushering these advances in. If you want to see the true magic, keep your eye on the 'quiet' hand.

Life-spans will increase dramatically over the next thirty years. Within the next ten years the average life-span on Earth will increase to over 120. The vast majority now on Earth will have the opportunity to live for up to 300 years. Depending upon your collective choice, your life-span could increase to 900 years or beyond within as little as 70 years.

The point to re-member here is that at this juncture in your evolution you are seeing through eyes that had an original primary motivation of survival. Humans' greatest desire has always been to live a long life. We tell you now that there will be many of you who choose to leave after only 100 years or so. Because the process of rejuvenation needed to extend life will itself require take energy, some of you will simply make the choice to leave and then return in one of the sleek new bodies of the Crystal Children.

The blending of technology with biology will continue at a rapid pace. Do not fear your own creations, dear ones. We find it very humorous when you hide from your own shadow. The astounding advances that lie ahead with the blending of technology and biology will lead you all to a more balanced existence on the New Planet Earth. Computers will not only blend with biology but even be made of biological material. The possibilities that lay directly in front of you are more than your minds can fathom.

The key to the medical advances that are now at your doorstep lies in the blending of the physical and the metaphysical sciences. The seeds have already been planted in fertile ground. Watch as the magical and the mundane blend to create real magic.

Not only will advances be seen in the human form but also in the other direction. Have you ever heard a computer that says "I AM?" No, they will not take over your planet, exterminating the "inferior" human life forms. We so love your imagination. What you call artificial intelligence is already a part of you and that connection will always remain. In the past you have envisioned yourself as the offspring of God with different qualities and attributes than your Father/Mother in heaven. So too will this next evolution of 'artificial' intelligence look toward you.

Ahhh. . . now we see the wheels spinning.

Communications

Advances in communication have activated your evolution in a big way. The last fifty years has activated the global connection and emulated the Universal Energy as a blending of all humanity is underway. The introduction of radio, telephone, television and the internet have all helped you to understand that you are actually one and not separate from one another. These advances have mostly been a result of advances in technology. These will continue, even to the point where technology will blend with biology in a spiritual being capable of communication on many levels, and into other inter-dimensional realities. Even your own intuition has expanded tremendously in the last fifty years. Watch now as the study of what you have called your sixth sense is moving out of the mysterious and into practical applications.

As mentioned above the internet has created a communications grid that will move out into the creation of the Grid of Light. As the blending of the technology with biology continues the grid will become a form of Light such that you have yet to witness with your eyes. Imagine that there is a net, much like a loosely woven fishing net, hanging just above your head. Everywhere you go on Earth this invisible net is within reach. To connect to anyone anywhere all you need to do is reach up and grab the net. The next incarnation of this net will be the intentional creation of the Grid of Light. Again, that which you thought to exist only in the spiritual realm will have very practical applications. This grid has already evolved from physical phone lines to fiber optics (a crude form of light) and is moving toward radio wave and laser technology. The Light Grid in its final form will reach all areas of the planet equally. Your study of the attributes that exist outside your own atmosphere will make possible the first incarnation of this grid very soon. The first truly light grid may be created for use as a protective shield, but eventually it will find use as a Grid of Light that will provide communication on many levels. In the future you will not even need a physical grid to make these same connections.

The Mineral Kingdom

The Crystal Energy, which originates from the Central Sun, has been entering through the energy ejections of your own Sun to be stored in the tectonic plates of the Earth. As this energy is being released into your atmosphere it passes through much of the inter-dimensional reality of life known as the mineral kingdom, changing the energetic structure of the minerals. Once a critical proportion of the mineral kingdom has been affected, it triggers change in all minerals everywhere. This change is now underway. That part of yourself known as the mineral kingdom is about to shift, and as a result, the mineral kingdom will redefine its relationship to humanity. Those of you who are empathically sensitive to Earth energy may find this quite confusing. Your inner sense of balance or feeling of belonging may suddenly shift. Places that have supported you may no longer feel comfortable.

You have always been aware of the existence of magical 'hot spots' on your planet, many of which you have come to regard as sacred sites. Over the past fifty years these energy spots have begun to shift their energy in preparation for this event. Some energy 'hot spots' have cooled, while new ones have heated up and emerged. This shifting will continue.

Have you ever wondered why, of all the minerals at your disposal, it should be crystals that you have always considered to possess spiritual properties? The Earth is largely crystalline in nature. Even the energy form you know to be water is actually crystalline in structure. Crystals have the closest of all vibrational ranges to humans. Watch as the properties of crystals begin to change now. Some that are opaque will suddenly start to become clear, while those that are clear will become cloudy. Inclusions may appear within the crystals themselves, and some may even break in half as they complete their tasks.

You are aware that crystals store vibration. You have discovered that by applying a small amount of electric energy to quartz crystals they release a vibration so precise that they are used to keep your watches in perfect time. You will now begin to see vibrations released from the crystals themselves. Crystals retain vibration and therefore hold specific properties. You have learned to use some of these properties in the crystal you call semiconductors. These are the switches that make up the heart of your computers. The changes now in motion may cause stress on your computer systems. We tell you that now that you are at the brink of making computers that will have the capabilities to reason. The shifting of the crystals is simply an awakening as they prepare for their next role.

The true nature of crystals, as an energy source and as reflectors of energy, was deliberately hidden from you. It was your choice to play the Game in this fashion. You wanted to see if you could overcome the temptations that you experienced in the days of Atlantis. In the days ahead you will start to re-discover more about the two primary uses of crystals.

Gemma with Atlantean Crystal.
ESPAVO Conference Mt Shasta Ca. 2001

The Plant Kingdom

In all the areas of great change you have seen relatively little alteration in the plant kingdom. The plant kingdom has been very happy to hold the vibration of the Earth up to this point. That will begin to change over the next twenty years. Those that some of you have come to know as the devas of the plant world are actually the higher selves of the plants themselves. As you raise your own vibrational level you will become able to connect your own consciousness with the higher selves of plants. Then you will begin to understand that plants have feelings too. We also tell you that much like some members of the animal kingdom, the greatest purpose of plants is to provide a transfer of energy as part of the food chain. Honoring that intent, and honoring plants themselves as living sentient beings will make the adjustment to the higher vibrations much easier.

The Animal Kingdom

You have already seen the animal kingdom begin to redefine its role on the New Planet Earth. That which you know as mad cow disease and foot and mouth dis-ease are precursors to this change. There are many levels of existence referenced as kingdoms, yet very few that have experienced as much disrespect as the animal kingdom. Part of this disrespect emanates from the fact that the animals are very close to your own vibration in biology. Your origins are of an animal nature, but for this discussion we will separate mankind from the animal kingdom. You cannot see yourselves with the veil firmly in place, therefore you cannot see the role of animals either. Energy by nature is in motion. To change forms and shift into higher vibrational levels is the specific intent of some energy forms. While humans are aspiring to reach ethereal levels of existence known as Lightbody, the energy form known as animal, aspires to reach their next level known as human. In this process the animals may take on human traits often that are not indigenous to the animal kingdom to prepare for that transition.

Animals hold the balance of energy for humans on the Earth. They are one of the connecting links between Humans and the Earth. Honoring these pure beings for their work is something that you often neglect to consider. The key to the changes in the animals as a whole will hinge on your abilities to help them move to the next level of their existence. Begin with honor. If you eat meat, honor them for their role as an energy exchange. If they are companions honor them for their role as reflections. More and more humans will begin talking to animals in the days ahead. You will be very interested in what they have to say.

The Feminine Energy Returns

The Crystal Energy that is entering your reality is a blend of the male and female energy. Planet Earth has been dominated by male energy for a very long time. You will now see the feminine energy returning to the planet. Some will resist this energy as you have already seen. Those very stuck in the male energy alone may still continue to overreact to what they perceive to be a threat. This you have seen in the events of your Game in recent days. [September 11th 2001] What you have seen is only the beginning. There are many now who will reach out and grasp desperately at the old ways in a desperate attempt to return them to what they think is their power. In time the beliefs they cling so desperately to will change. The feminine energy is quiet yet powerful. Now is a time to find peace in the hearts of Lightworkers everywhere and watch as it spreads outward to the New Planet Earth.

The feminization of the planet has also been underway on many levels. Your own use of hormones has led to a feminization of planet Earth that now reaches to the mineral level itself. This is not a problem as this had to shift very far to achieve the intended swing back into balance. The stage is set for the balanced energy to enter the New Planet Earth. The Crystal Energy filtering in from the Central Sun is bringing back the balanced energy.

You have seen drastic reactions to the feminine energy from the 'Old Guard' that live solely in the male energy. But even on a more personal level you will note that there are very few female world leaders. The feminine energy has a strong connection to emotions. In the lower vibrations of who you once were this was perceived as a weakness. In the higher vibrations of the New Planet Earth this will be seen as strength. The conversion will take time but it is well underway. In the interim, you will soon see female leaders taking their place in high levels of government and business.

Barbara next to the sculpture 'Woman Free'
United Nations Vienna Austria

Vortexes & Portals

As the Crystal Energy enters into your reality it is shifting the very fabric upon which your Game is being played. One of the most effective ways to ground this energy is to intentionally connect to the Earth with an Energy Vortex. An Energy Vortex is simply energy moving in a circular motion. This can be accomplished on an individual basis by turning in a circle. As children you often did this with no idea of what you were accomplishing energetically. By creating your own personal vortex, you were in fact grounding your own energy and blending it with that of the Earth. Creating a personal vortex is a form of moving meditation that can help you feel better and more grounded in yourself.

Collective vortices are a very effective way of grounding the Crystal Energy into the Earth. In a gathering of any size you can easily create a vortex of energy by moving together in a circle. You can work with the Earth to make a vortex by connecting with her energy and allowing her to guide you as to the appropriate direction in which to move your energy. Decide which direction to make these as a collective connection to the Earth and work with her to create a vortex. Unlike personal vortices, once a collective vortex is placed into motion it remains in that spot. These funnels will be used by the Earth to anchor and distribute the Crystal Energy onto the planet. Later, some of these same energy fields will turn into portals that will be used to travel between dimensional realities. That is when things will start to get very interesting on the New Planet Earth. Questions you have been asking for eons will then be revealed to you.

New Energy Sources

Water is a form of energy that you have not understood. Directly ahead of you is an opportunity to uncover the 'secret' of what you call water. Water itself is a crystalline form and as the Crystal Energy enters your field you will create a new relationship to water. If you utilize its energy, one cubic centimeter of this substance could light even your largest cities for more than a year. Watch for the magic to unfold here.

The use of Crystals as an energy source in the days of Atlantis is still very fresh in your cellular memories and you therefore placed a blind spot in your own vision to keep you from seeing the two attributes of Crystal Energy.
Now as the Crystal Energy emanates in from the Central Sun you will see re-minders and evidence of the times you have used this energy.

Spiritual Evolution

You are already in the process of establishing a new relationship to your own guides, since it is no longer appropriate for you to receive guidance in the manner you once did. Your thinking has always been that as you progress spiritually your connection to your guides would increase. In fact, the opposite is unfolding. Your guides have taken a step back in order to help you to learn to walk fully into your own power. For a limited period, specialist guides will be available to you for specific guidance.

To some of you this may feel like a carrot is being held just out of reach. In fact, this is the way that YOU yourselves designed it. Just as your parents did when you were first learning to ride a bicycle, your guides have been running alongside, holding you up and giving you the confidence to take off on your own. Now they have stepped back and released you to steer your own bicycle. Can you understand the pride they felt as they released you to chart your own path? The only time they step in now is when your bicycle is wavering, and even then only when absolutely necessary. You are now in control of your own bicycle and you are now in control of your own life.

You are so fascinated with the mysterious. It is easier for you to believe in magic than it is for you to believe in your own power. Your guides have not left you alone. They are simply standing further back, allowing for your full integration with spirit. This is

of your Higher Self with spirit while you still walk
biology. If you listen carefully you will still hear
nly now they sound much more like your own

That which you know to be channeling will become
commonplace. It is for this very reason that we do not care for
the word 'channeling' itself, as it implies a mysticism that is not
needed, and can often get in the way. Understand that it is your
connection to source through your own Higher Self that is the
source of all inspiration. Thus the days of following spiritual
leaders will soon be gone. Now it is up to you to learn to step
into your own power and follow *yourself*. Teachers, facilitators
and channels that can help you attain this level of connection
will become very valuable. We will take this opportunity to tell
the Keeper something that we have mentioned a long time ago.
The concept of channeling and the word itself will fall away as
you begin to make more direct connections yourself. As you
become accustomed to holding your power within, the mystery
and mystique of chan-neling as being something external will no
longer be required.

Many forms of ritual will fall away as you move forward. When
we started communicating these messages only six years ago,
they began as the Beacons of Light Meditations. Now, even
meditation is no longer needed for spiritual contact. Times
change quickly. The energy is now more direct and the need for
ritual is diminishing. Please understand that there is no right or
wrong way to find spirituality. Tradition is a wonderful expression
of humanity for it preserves your rich history in an expression of
spirit. However, practicing a ritual will NOT advance your spirit.
If you choose to enjoy tradition or ritual in any form, please
understand that the tradition or ritual holds no power of its own.
You are the power and if tradition or ritual can help you hold that
power then enjoy them to their fullest. Rituals and traditions
hold no harm and can be very enjoyable, as long as you do not
give your power to the ritual.

Even the practice of prayer that has been so important to your development will evolve. Prayer is a reflection of your own energy out into the Universe. This has been a way for you to look in the mirror. The veil is thick and you cannot see yourselves as the creators that you truly are. Prayer has been a wonderful way for you to place your love energy out into the Universe to be amplified as it is reflected back to you. Quite simply, *prayer works.* It has always worked. What is changing is the manner in which you create. Praying to an imagined entity or something outside of you is no longer as effective. As infants, you looked to the very large beings, (parents) upon which you relied for all of your needs. Even as adults you search for that large omnipresent higher source to take care of needs you cannot. This has worked quite well for you even though it is your own creative energy being reflected back to you. You are now beginning to understand that *you* are that higher source.

If you are looking to be ahead of everyone else and dedicated to finding the fastest way to spiritual evolvement, then you have missed the meaning of spiritual evolution. Watch carefully the temptation to fall into spiritual competition, as it carries great opportunity to misdirect your energy. Re-member, that was one of the two primary misdirections of energy that caused the fall of Atlantis.

[See the final chapter 'The Altantis Connection']

Know that even by reading and entertaining new thoughts you are changing the world. Be patient with yourselves and allow the shift to higher vibration to be comfortable and joyous. Please re-member that this is not a race. The one who gets there first wins nothing. Those who enjoy the ride win it all.

One promise we make to you: What lies ahead will be interesting, for you do live in interesting times! In fact, from a cosmic perspective, these are the most interesting times thus far! It is our joy to reflect your magnificence for you as you awaken from the dream. Please re-member to treat each other with respect, nurture one another and play well together.

Welcome Home

the Group

Chapter 14

The Crystal Walk-Ins

Enter the Crystal Vibration

Presented Live
San Diego, California
May 8th 2002

This book was two weeks away from going to press when we presented the live channel you are about to read. Barbara and I thought it was too important to omit, so we literally stopped the presses to include it here:

Greetings from Home.

Ah, do you hear the vibrations of those words? Do you feel the energy that now surrounds you? Have you felt the changes in the temperature in the room? All day we have been here waiting to talk. The Keeper takes so long with his words at times, *(laughter)* and we are behind him nudging him along saying, come let us speak.

Dear ones, you came in carrying the vibrations of Home. Now we share with you those same vibrations, for they are an integral part of who you are. You have worked very hard to raise the vibration of your world and to change some of the things that have made up your reality. As you evolve into higher vibrations, that which once served you as truth in the lower vibrations no longer applies. Now, you are beginning to see truth as an evolution and not the fixed standard that you once thought it to be. For that *we* are eternally grateful.

You have no idea what you have already done. You reach for our words because you want to experience and re-member the vibrations of Home. You feel incomplete because you cannot be Home, and we tell you that we also feel incomplete. Home has not been the same since you left. This is the reason we so love sharing our time with you. What you have yet to understand is that we miss you as much as you miss Home. Each and every one of you has a space in *our* hearts, for *you* are part of *us* as *we* are part of *you*. This connection is growing stronger every day, not because of anything we are doing, but because of the advances you have made. You are literally moving closer to Heaven, and now you are creating Heaven on your side of the veil. This we call the New Planet Earth.

Enter the Children of Crystal Vibration

Dear ones, we have much to discuss this day, for we have told the Keeper that we will be speaking of the Children of Crystal Vibration, and indeed even more than that. There is much that you need to know as the process of evolution unfolds.

The children of Indigo hue have been working very hard to change the existing paradigms and beliefs about raising and educating children. The Indigos are doing what we have asked all of you to do - make space for empowered humans in all areas of your lives. Some of the Indigo children have run directly into a brick wall. It is so difficult for them, for they have felt as though they are the only ones working to bring about change. They feel as though no one understands them, and we tell you that actually very few of you do. Yours has been a very cruel world. Recently, some have even reverted to the brutality of the middle ages on Earth. Those were harsh times indeed. Hold the highest vibration that each one of you can. Open the door to your future by helping the new children to take responsibility for themselves. Work with them the best you can and at the same time work on your own fears, dear ones, for if you fail to do so you will encounter even greater difficulties with the Children of Crystal Vibration as they enter.

The Indigos have come in with several important purposes. One is to show you through experience that many of your current systems will not fully support empowered humans. In order to help humans re-evaluate long held beliefs, the Indigos have taken contracts that sometimes include going head to head with all your systems relating to children. Now things are starting to get exciting, as some of the early Indigos are beginning to move into positions of influence within your businesses and governments. Soon they will be graduating to senior management positions and senior levels of government. Here, the effect they will have on your entire Game will make it easier for humans to assume both their true power as well as take their rightful place in the Universe.

Crystal Attributes

The Keeper has asked many times; "Exactly when *are* these Crystal Children going to be born, what do they look like and what signs will mark their entrance?"

The Children of Crystal Vibration have a much greater potential to hold their full power while still in their bubbles of biology. From time to time throughout your history Crystal Scouts have incarnated to test your vibrational level and also to plant important seeds of Light. Many of these scouts you know today as ascended masters and teachers. Many more you have never heard of, as they were protected and kept hidden from public eye. This secrecy was necessary to give them the space to complete their work.

Crystal Children are quite different than those of Indigo vibration. As we have indicated prior, these are the children who will be born into your Game carrying enormous power, while at the same time being extremely vulnerable. They are balanced in a way that you have yet to understand, as it is their vulnerability that enhances their strength. They will be born into a higher vibrational energy matrix, and they will enter with all twelve strands of their DNA fully operational. Even as very young children they will display great powers beyond your current scope of understanding. It will be nothing for a Crystal child to know, not only what you are feeling, but also what you are thinking. We cannot wait to watch what havoc this will wreak on your planet. As this unfolds you will understand why we keep saying that on the New Planet Earth THERE WILL BE NO MORE SECRETS. We are telling you this now so that you may prepare for what is ahead.

We must warn you, however, that there will be much fear when their powers first become apparent. This will present an immediate problem, for it is not possible to bring these gentle beings into a fearful and warring world. Because of their sensitivity, their powers can be influenced by the emotional energy that surrounds them. It will be important to know that the Crystal Children have an extreme vulnerability to an emotion for which they have no reference, and therefore no understanding. The human emotion of fear exists only in the lower vibrational stages of human development. In the higher vibrations of the New Planet Earth it will not exist. In much the same way that Indigo children have no reference for the human emotion of guilt, Crystal Children have no reference for fear. It is very difficult for you to eradicate fear from your world. Your primary motivation up to this point has been survival, and fear has played a very important part in accomplishing that goal. To erase fear from your reality would cause problems, and is simply not possible. Yet, to bring the Children of Crystal Vibration into an environment that is riddled with fear is also not possible, as they would reflect it back at you, and amplify it in the process. This is the reason why you are facing so many issues at this time that deal specifically with terror and fear. We tell you here that if each person on planet Earth were able to reduce their own personal 'fear factor' by a mere ten percent, what you call terrorism would simply cease to exist.

Please be aware that we label them Crystal Children, not solely because of their aura, but because they carry the Crystal Energy into biological form through the birthing process. In reality, the Children of Crystal Vibration are simply reincarnations of yourselves in a higher vibrational form. Please understand that the worst possible situation would be for parents to fall prey to spiritual competition. This is important to know, for it will not help to segregate your children by labels or titles; a Crystal Child is not better than an Indigo or any other child. To place them in that position would only hinder their work.

The Crystal Scouts

The forerunners, or scouts, of the Crystal children will now be seen with increasing regularity. Small pockets of these children have already formed on your planet. Some have already been discovered. Many of these scouts will bond together as groups in order to support and protect each other energetically. Some of these groups will not necessarily form in the same geographic locations, but rather will bond in energetic groupings.

Crystal scouts carry only a small portion of the true power potential of the Crystal Children that will follow. The fully attributed Children of Crystal Vibration will not actually begin to incarnate for another four to five years. This time period is necessary to create a safe environment for them to enter. Even then it will be your choices that will determine the exact timetable.

We are not telling you that you must eradicate *all fear* on the planet before they come. We are not even telling you that you must eradicate all war on your planet, for it is your children, Indigos and Crystals alike, who will do that for you. As the Indigos now start moving into higher positions, they will begin to make a huge difference, as they refuse to tolerate what you have allowed up to now. Make no mistake, they *will* take charge and they *will* change planet Earth in order to make space for the Children of Crystal Vibration and *all* empowered humans. Those carrying that form of energy must be in an environment where they can feel free to utilize that empowerment. Finding places on your planet, in your businesses, in your governments, in your organizations, that makes space for the empowered human is the greatest gift that you can give. This you can do now to prepare for the what is to come. Know that you are not alone in your efforts.

The Crystal Walk-Ins

We speak now of something that has not been spoken of before. It is time to reveal to you an area where you will receive help in changing your world. This will not be from the Spirit world alone, although that help has always been in place. This will not be from the aliens as you call them, and not from the children themselves. We tell you that you have help from within, help directly from Home. For something that you have not seen for a very long time will be happening more frequently. Although it has not been appropriate to speak of it up to this point, it is now appropriate for you to know. We tell you now that the Children of Crystal Vibration will not all come in as children. There will be some that will enter into physical form as what you call Walk-ins. They will be holding themselves several steps removed. The Crystal Walk-Ins that will be here soon will be stepping back. They will be in hiding. They will be taking over contracts of some of those who intentionally choose to leave. Like all Walk-Ins, they will choose roles and life lessons. They will take the contracts of the departing souls that have retreated from their human form. When a soul wishes to leave the Game it is possible to call in a substitute. There is no penalty for leaving the Game early. Please understand that this is not a way to avoid life lesson, it is simply a postponement to be continued in a later incarnation. There may be a situation where this can be quite helpful as a soul may have problems fulfilling their life lessons due to unforeseen circumstances. This is simply a way for them to try again at a later date without setting back their own soul progress. After full examination of the circumstances, a soul can simply ask to be replaced. This request will then be followed by a period of not less than forty days where all life circumstance will be evaluated by the higher self in relationship to the primary life lessons. If this is in accord with the higher self, the soul will retreat and the Crystal walk-in will take over from that point in the life line. They will be much like the original soul with the exception of the core personality. After the exchange, the core personality will be that of the entering soul. The line up of souls waiting for an experience in human form, numbers far beyond your comprehension. The first planet of free choice is a very sought after soul destination. Because of the difficulties experienced as a walk in, only very high vibrational souls will take that position.

In reality, at this time there are far less Walk-Ins than you thought. A Walk-In is most often an extreme reclusive. They will not gravitate toward the public life. It is difficult for them to interact without the social learning process you gain as children. For the Walk-In, this process is skipped. Imagine all the difficulties of taking over an adult body, often misused, and attempting to have a life experience with it. Now imagine the added difficulties of extreme sensitivity and vulnerability of a Crystal and you will see the tremendous challenge that these beings will take on. They will be, however, working often behind the scenes to touch lives, hearts and souls as powerful Human Angels. They will most often do this from behind closed doors. An extremely small number will venture out as teachers and healers. This requires a mastery process that is most difficult to obtain. Now that you know what to look for, they will become more evident in your own reality for there are even some on Earth as we speak. As this becomes more prevalent you will see adults walking quietly with very magical abilities. No, they will not be evangelical. They will not stand on a street corner and say "I am here to save your planet". We see that some of you are disappointed. (Laugher.) They will be here very quietly to plant seeds as the Human Angels. They will work most often behind the scenes, and when they see a perfect opportunity to work with another, they will connect and plant seeds very deeply in the collective consciousness of human kind. Then and only then will they use what you will see as "magical abilities". Some will eventually evolve into teachers. But they will be teachers with no ego, dear ones, as they are not plagued with a primary motivation of survival and therefore do not need the ego to balance. They come in with an understanding of unity. They come in with a different motivation, a motivation of the heart, not of the head. They will teach you now, if you will only open your eyes and your hearts.

The Opposite of Love is Fear

All healing must be requested in higher vibrations of the New Planet Earth. Therefore, all teaching must also be requested. Make your intent known that if you wish to have contact from one of these dear souls, that they have your permission to do so. Shortly after you give intent, you will feel a peace that will tell you that you have been heard. Then we will ask you to do something that is very difficult for humans; be patient. Contact may come through many ways including ethereal, dreamtime and even physical meeting. These are teachers in higher vibration and will not teach you in the same way you have become accustomed. Some will only brush your arm to help you see your lesson circumstance. Some may enter your life only to give two words of encouragement at exactly the right time. Some will trigger events in your life that will set you into passion. Please do not give your power to them, for this will only retard their work and their teachings. Do not worship them or strive to be them, for this too is against the Universal Energy. They, as are we, are attempting to give you information that will help you hold your own power as the creators that you are.

These Crystal Walk-Ins are now starting to come in. They will very quietly plant seeds in very important places to make a difference on your planet. The one thing that they cannot do is to eradicate your fear. Fear is nothing more than a lack of information. It is a vacuum that is created where nothing stands. Sometimes all things around that vacuum are sucked into it, taking all your dramas, taking all your attention, and all of your energy. The funniest part for us to watch is that you always create your greatest fears. Dear ones, you are in a state of enhanced creation even as we speak. You are living and breathing in the fifth dimension now. Learning to use that

of rejection in business

power intentionally as you eradicate your own fears, is what this is all about. First identify these fears. Truthfully examine their attributes and the power they have over you. Find ways of using those same attributes in a positive manner, and this will fill the void of the vacuum. Look for opportunities and other people to reflect your own fears back to you, so that you can begin this process of transmuting your energy. If you will only take that part, we will show you ways of eradicating your own fears. That is underway as we speak.

Take the responsibility of holding your own heart and looking for the purity and the fear within your own heart. You have always thought that hate was the opposite of love. We tell you no, *fear* is the opposite of love. Fill in the missing information for that is what will open the door for not only the Children of Crystal Vibration, not only the Indigos, but for you to evolve to *your* next level. As you see these magical beings appearing on your planet you will have the inclination to be in awe of them and to say "Look, here is a master. Let's follow him". Please refrain from doing so. *(Laughter.)* Instead as you see the magic that will now begin, look at them as your equal with a quiet knowing that they are simply where you are going. They are coming to help you hold your power. These are the true Human Angels that are now stepping into adult bodies on planet Earth.

Can you love me when I'm up?

To learn how to enable another person without taking their power from them, is where the magic is dear ones. Find ways of doing that now. Do that with your children, do that with your husband, do that with your wife, do that with your boss at work, do that with problem people and friends alike. Make space in your life for the empowered human in all areas. Oh, it is so easy to help one another when you get the call when someone is down. When you see someone fall it is easy for you to reach out and say " Here I am. I will give you a hand. I will love you unconditionally". But can you love that same person when they are on top of the ladder, dear ones? That is true unconditional love. Can you say "You are doing so well in your life. You have done so well in such a short amount of time. I am so happy for you." Can you love those who are doing well as easily as you love those on the ground? That is the true test of the Human Angel. For now the ego must go out of it as you begin applying the higher truth of loving unconditionally.

This you will see clearly as the Crystal Walk-Ins start to show. Over the next four to five years, dear ones,, you will see an increase in the Crystal scout population, but also, if you look very closely, you may also see Crystal Walk-Ins. It will be very rare, and yet it will be enough for you to see if you are looking. Make space in your own life for empowered humans, and you will experience that of which we speak.

Our time today is at an end. We tell you from the time that you entered this sacred space you have been in the vibrations of Home. Those of you reading these words now, have also entered this sacred space and experienced these same vibrations. We have created an opportunity for you in this space to be re-freshed and re-minded of Home. You are the ones who are building Home on your side of the veil. You are the ones who will go from here today, back to your jobs, back to your homes, back to your relationships and will begin creating Home in all that you do. For that reason *we* are truly honored to share this experience with you. Take these vibrations of pure love, and carry them with you. Claim *your* right as a Human Angel. Fear not stepping into your power. No longer look outside of yourselves, for the God that you seek to understand is within your own heart. You are God . Take the responsibility of being the creators that you are. Use it with your own heart. Dare to create an energy that is abundant for you. Dare to create what you desire in your life first. Love your family when they are on the ground and you are helping them up. Love them when they are standing next to you as equals and love them when they are on the top of the ladder. As each one of you climbs higher, all of you move higher.

It is with the very greatest of honor that we share with you, through the Keeper, the memories of Home. Know that you are a part of our hearts and we miss you. We will welcome you with open arms and the greatest of joy when you finally decide to come Home. But also know we are applauding your every step as you choose to stay and create Home on your side of the veil. It is with the greatest of honor that we ask you to treat each other with respect. Nurture one another, and play well together. Espavo.

the Group

Chapter 15

The Atlantis Connection

Two Misdirections that Sank Atlantis

Greetings from Home.

It is our greatest honor to be in the presence of you, the "Chosen Ones". You are the ones who have changed the direction of the big game. You are now in a new reality and a new game. Like the first one, this too is a reality of your own creation. Living with the responsibility of holding your own power is changing even the smallest aspects of your daily life. We tell you that you are the ones who are making this change possible. It is your willingness to walk blindly, with the veils firmly in place that gives you the greatest possibility to set into motion your own evolutionary process. Even with all the might in Heaven, it was not possible for us to do what you have done. The love we have for you stretches beyond the distances that you believe separate Heaven and Earth. All of the beings that helped start your Game now watch expectantly to see what you will do next. We are truly honored to be in your presence. You are the expression of God known as human. You are only now coming to understand your true origins and your true power. You are the Chosen Ones who are writing the scripts for the New Planet Earth.

Collective Vibration

Our time together in this session will be focused on the changes that are now in motion and your possible reactions to that change. As you now move quickly into the New light, we tell you that you do not move alone. It is the collective vibration of humanity as a whole that has enabled the advances you are now experiencing. You are not separate from one another, you are one. The New Game will allow you to find expressions and an understanding of that oneness.

With the higher vibrations the intensity of the Game you are playing has increased in the last few months to make possible the changes that now lie directly in your path. The time you are experiencing at the moment is a resting time and a time for assimilation of the new energy. This will not continue so we ask you to enjoy your rest period. There is work to do and you are feeling the strong push to get into action and on with your real purpose. You know you came in with a specific purpose although it eludes you consciously. We tell you that you will soon see more of your true purpose. You often feel that you must step into your work in a very public manner to make your mark and be in your passion. Some of you will certainly do that but we tell you that all of you can make a big difference by becoming accustomed to using your own power in your daily life. This is what most effectively raises the collective vibration of humanity.

You are at a crossroads. You have been here before yet this time it looks like you will take a new road. You are in very interesting times on the New Planet Earth. There is a lot being asked of humans right now. You are faced with restrictions. You feel these restrictions and think you are stuck. Yet, these restrictions are necessary to prevent you from moving more quickly than you can assimilate. In the field of polarity in which you live, you can only see the past with clarity. The present is fuzzy at best and the future is concealed from you completely. Because of this view, even though you are moving at the speed of Love, you feel like you are stuck and not moving at all. From your perspective nothing is happening, from the cosmic perspective you are evolving in the blink of an eye.

The Atlantis Connection

In working with this wonderful family of Lightworkers the Keeper is very much aware that the people that are reading this communication are those who chose to move at the fastest possible rate. You are so anxious to get into the next stage that you do not see that you create many of your own restrictions. Many of you are here from the days of Atlantis. You have waited eleven thousand years for the chance to be here at exactly this juncture in time, space and alternate realities. Most of you reading this material were in Atlantis for at least one life time and some of you had decisive roles that you played during these special times. You are seeing that Atlantis is now in your collective consciousness. You are seeing movies, stories and discoveries about Atlantis on a daily basis. This is because you are at the same vibrational level as you were back then. After the fall, each of you made a commitment to return and make different choices if the collective vibrations of humanity ever reached that level again. Guess what. . . you have made it. Atlantis has returned.

Two Problems that Sank Atlantis

Your goal is the creation of Home on your side of the veil. We tell you that at this stage of your development there are two potential restrictions that can derail your advances and allow you to fall into the same problems that led to the eventual destruction of Atlantis. Please re-member that Atlantis was a technological wonder blended with a spiritual base that opened the possibilities of being in true power No one set out purposely to misdirect the energy in such a way as to cause the destruction of this great land. Much like today, your personal power was radically increased in those times. It was your reluctance to take responsibility for using that power to create your world that caused the problem. This can be seen in your lives today in two areas:

1. Fear of Power.

This is a basic fear that causes people to move into a back lash of old energy. It is caused by the fear of moving forward. This is the fear that causes people to give their power to others. The responsibility of using your power to create your reality rests only within you. You cannot give it to another, be they spiritual or governmental leaders. Signs of this can now be seen on your news everyday. This is also the backlash that has caused some of your world leaders to desperately attempt to revert to the old energy ways. [Kosovo, Afghanistan and the Twin Towers] As your collective vibration rises your knowledge will advance in all areas from science, to humanistic studies to medicine. These advances will be resisted by most humans as a natural resistance to taking your power. You cannot see that you are the creators due to the veils that you wear. Even as your power surfaces, you have a tendency to surround it in mystique giving the power to the mystique rather than see that it is you who are creating. This has served only to disguise your own power from yourself.

The properties of the veil you are wearing effectively keep you from seeing your true power. This does not mean that you do not have power. . . only that you cannot see it. You can see great power in others yet you cannot see it in yourself. The cosmic joke is that you are the 'God' that you seek so desperately. Use your power to create your own reality and watch as the magic begins. Humans have an ingrained fear of taking that power. Instead of taking your power you would rather give it to others. You are still fighting wars over your choices of who to give your power to. Now you have a recent increase in power. Add to this mix an increase in pressure as the Crystal Energy enters, and you have the perfect medium for this fear to take root. In your history these were similar conditions where Hitler and those like him found opportunities to take your power from you in the name of leadership. In giving them responsibility for your reality you gave them your power.

2. Spiritual Competition.

The second is even more dangerous and will most likely be seen among those who "sit in the front of the class". To describe spiritual competition it is first necessary to define the word "spiritual". Contrary to popular belief we define spirituality as everything that is not physical. These include belief systems, ideas and that part of yourself [Higher Self] that does not fit into your physical bubble of biology. Spiritual competition pervaded many areas, including your honest attempts to reach into higher vibrations. This has often retarded your progress. Your humanness would tell you that higher vibrations are better than lower vibrations. We re-mind you that one is not better than another, they are only different.

To illustrate this point let us use our own vibrational status. The Angelic realm which we inhabit is of a much higher vibrational level than that in which you reside. However, if you re-member our opening statements we told you that even with all the might in Heaven we could not accomplish what you have done. We tell you often that it is we who are deeply honored to be in the presence of the masters of the Gameboard. The truth is that we, Angels and Humans, are both different expressions of the energy which you call God. One is not better than the other. We are simply different and have different purposes.

In the days of Atlantis you found yourselves in a situation where you felt you needed to create classes of citizens. This is a direct form of governmentally enforced spiritual competition and was a main contributing factor to the fall of a great land. Even larger was a related belief that some of you could move into higher vibrations while leaving others behind. Even today some of you believe that you will ascend leaving others behind. We tell you that this is reminiscent of the same spiritual competition that sank Atlantis. Use your powers of discernment in all that enters your field. Be cautious of anything that designates classes or holds one vibration to be better than another. We ask you to be extremely cautious of anyone or anything that claims to have the only way. There are many paths to the truth. Each one is a different flavor of the truth. None of them are the singular truth. Take responsibility for finding your own flavor and take only that which resonates with you. This is where your true power lies.

We have spoken many times of the Universal Energy. This is the base energy that permeates *all* things and from which all things are created. The increase in power will bring a clearer understanding of this basic truth and all of its applications. The motion of this energy is blending and self regulating. All things that are in accord with this energy will find support and all things that resist it will meet with resistance and eventually fade away. Look back to your own history to see the events that have shaped your Game and how they aligned to the Universal Energy. When checking for spiritual competition it is helpful to check the alignment to the Universal Energy. Is what you are doing encouraging the blending and self regulation of energy or is it promoting segregation and separateness?

Recap

The times ahead are full of possibilities. You are creating the New Game. The Love we have for you is not describable. This is the most exciting time ever on the Gameboard of Free Choice. Human evolution is at hand and with that evolution the entire Universe moves forward. Re-member Atlantis proudly. You are here to make a difference both individually and collectively and this you will accomplish. The days ahead will give you ample opportunity to get comfortable with your power. In the interim we ask you to re-member two simple points:

1. **You are God, and you have a responsibility to use your powers of creation.**

2. **You are not the only God.**

We hear your laughter and we hope you hear ours. It is with our honor and deepest love that we ask you to treat each other with respect, nurture one another and play well together...

We have touched your heart with the vibrations of Home during the time we have spent together as you received our love through these words. Now it is upon you to carry these same vibrations into your daily life to awaken this love in the rest of the Human Angels on the New Planet Earth. We leave you with a tool for awakening, which was an ancient greeting used for this same purpose in the ancient days of Mu. It is a greeting of Lightworkers that spans all the ages. The word is ESPAVO. Literally translated it means 'Thank you for taking your power'.

ESPAVO dear ones. . .and Re-member. . .

You are never alone.

the Group

About the Author

Steve Rother was comfortably settled into life as a General Building Contractor in the San Diego area when, through a synchronistic series of events, he was placed firmly in the middle of his contract. Steve and his wife Barbara began shifting their focus on life and living on New Year's morning, 1995, when they found themselves unexpectedly expressing their intent for the coming year during a ceremony that took place as the sun rose over a California beach. From that day forward, their lives were never to be the same.

Soon after, Steve began receiving divinely inspired messages from 'the Group' which he published monthly as the 'Beacons of Light.'. These monthly writings from 'the Group' are about re-membering and accepting our own power, and living comfortably in the higher vibrations now on planet Earth. The Group calls Steve the 'Keeper of the Flame' or just 'Keeper' for short.

Steve never returned to his contracting business. Today, he and Barbara, his wife of 30+ years present empowerment seminars to Lightworkers throughout the globe. They have presented these in many countries, and have three times presented to the Eso-

Barbara & Steve Rother

teric Society at the United Nations in Vienna, Austria and twice to the Enlightenment Society United Nations Staff Recreation Council at the United Nations headquarters in New York. In April of 2000 in Vienna, Steve and Barbara presented a class on channeling, believed to be the first such class ever presented at a U.N. facility.

Steve and Barbara make their base in San Diego, California, where they work together in Love and Lightwork. They have formed the nonprofit corporation of Lightworker and, together with the volunteers and staff, plant seeds of Light through personal empowerment on a global basis. More information about Steve, Barbara and the Group, including their seminar schedule, can be found at the web site: http://www.lightworker.com

Connect with spiritual family:

http:// www.Lightworker.com

'*The Beacons of Light Re-minders from Home*' monthly messages from the Group, are available online or as a free e-mail service by request.
http://www.Lightworker.com/beacons/snailmailjoin.shtml

Connect with original spiritual family on the message boards and in the chat rooms. Set your creations into motion in the 8 Sacred Rooms. Lightworker is a large site where the Groups information is translated into 13 languages. Come spend time creating Home.

Re-member. . . You are not alone. . . Welcome Home

Also see the magazine for discerning Lightworkers

connecting lightworkers all over the planet

PlanetLightworker.com is a free monthly online magazine that provides information from the cutting edge of the higher vibration.   http://www.PLANETLightworker.com

Regular sections include:
Children of the New Earth – Indigos and Crystal Children.
Vibrational Healing – New thought, new modalities and new paradigms in healing
Meta-Physical Snippets From the Far Side of Science
Notes From an Animal Psychic's Casebook - Heart warming, true life stories plus online lessons in Animal Communication & Healing
Exclusive Chapter-length Book Extracts from the very latest works of some of the leading names in the New Age/New Thought movement

Plus... ***Featured Articles***, ***Series*** and ***Regular Monthly Columns*** **written by leading authors and inspirational writers in the meta-physical/spiritual arena**

Paths to Empowerment Seminars
from Lightworker

Paths to Empowerment Seminars provide practical applications of the information for living in the higher vibrations of the new planet Earth, based on information from the Group. All gatherings include practical techniques for utilizing this information in daily life. All seminars include a Live channel from the Group through Steve Rother. The following Seminars present and implement information in this book.

Mastery of Self – A two day experience in the art of Mastery.

The Wings Experience – Two days on Becoming a Human Angel

OVERLIGHT – Two and Three Days of activating the Light within.

Re-membering Home – One day Re-membering Home (Lecture type)

Life in the 5th Dimension – A day discovering 5th dimensional tools.

ESPAVO Conference – A week long life changing experience.

Check the schedule on the web site and watch for new seminars and special gatherings. The Paths to Empowerment Seminars from Lightworker are listed at:

http://www.Lightworker.com/schedule.shtml

You will receive notification of events in your area by adding your name to our mailing list at:

http://www.Lightworker.com/beacons/snailmailjoin.shtml

Circles of Light

Want to know what gatherings are in your area?

Looking to connect with like minded people?

Have a gathering already going?

Wish to start one?

See the Circles of Light at Lightworker.com

http://www.lightworker.com/CirclesOfLight/

This global database lists regular meetings where you can find and connect with other Lightworkers.

See the Circles of Light,

a free service from Lightworker.

Lightworker
a non-profit corporation dedicated to spreading Light through Empowerment.

Lightworker Library

ORDER FORM

1. Online with your Credit Card via a secure server at: ·
   http://www.Lightworker.com/bookstore/
2. Fax your orders to Lightworker (858) 748 7640
3. Telephone orders Toll Free at (877) 248 5837
   Outside the US and Canada call 01 858 748 5837
4. Order by Mail by sending this order form with check payable
   to Lightworker or Credit Card info to:

Lightworker   PO Box 1496 Poway Ca. 92074-1496

Please send
_____ copies of **Re-member @ $14.95**   **(Book 1)**
_____ copies of **Welcome Home @ $14.95**   **(Book 2)**

Name _____

Address _____

Address 2 _____

City_____State_____ZIP_____

Telephone _____

E-mail _____

Please add sales tax of 7.75% if delivered inside Ca.
   Shipping: US: $4 first book, $2 each additional book
   International: $6 first book and $3 each additional copy

CCard # _____ Exp_____

Name on Card _____

Signature _____
                   All Prices in US Funds